IN PLAIN SITE

A BIOGRAPHY OF THE RAF AIRBASE AT CARON, SASKATCHEWAN

JOEL L. FROM

Joel L. From

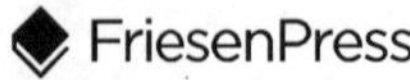

Suite 300 - 990 Fort St
Victoria, BC, V8V 3K2
Canada

www.friesenpress.com

First Edition — 2019

Library and Archives Canada Cataloguing in Publication

Title: In Plain Site: A Biography of the RAF Airbase at Caron, Saskatchewan / Joel L. From

Names: From, Joel L., 1960- author.

Description: Includes bibliographical references and index.

Identifiers:
ISBN 978-1-5255-4055-4 (paperback)
ISBN 978-1-5255-4054-7 (hardback)
ISBN 978-1-5255-4056-1 (ebook)

Subjects: LCSH: Air bases, Canadian–Social life and customs–Canada. | LCSH: Air pilots, Military–Training of–Canada–History. | LCSH: British Commonwealth Air Training Plan–History. | LCSH: Canada. Canadian Forces Base (Caron, Sask.)–History | LCSH: Canada. R.C.A.F. Station (Caron, Sask.)–History. | LCSH: Canada. Royal Canadian Air Force. Elementary Flying Training School, No. 33. | LCSH: Flight training–Saskatchewan–Caron–History. | LCSH: World War, 1939–1945–Saskatchewan–Caron.

Classification: LCC UG639 C2 F76 2019 | DDC 355.70971244

TABLE OF CONTENTS

for Beckie

ACKNOWLEDGEMENTS

It is my pleasure to acknowledge the persons and institutions who assisted me with this project. In May 2011, I spent an enjoyable month at Library and Archives Canada in Ottawa where Marie-Josée Neron and Martin Lanthier put a veritable train-load of archival files at my disposal. The following May, the staff at the National Archives (UK) in Kew, Richmond, Surrey promptly and courteously executed my numerous requests. The efficiency of both national archives amazes me still. The research staffs at two other fine British institutions also served me well. Lauren Woodard, Mary Jane Millare-Adolfo, and Peter Elliott of the RAF Museum made the journey north on the underground worthwhile. Mariusz Gasior, access team librarian at the Imperial War Museum in South London, helped me locate an obscure audio file.

Persons in Saskatchewan also afforded kind assistance. The staff at the Provincial Archives in Regina, particularly Tim Novak and Paula Rein, were unstinting in their help. Ken Dalgarno of the Moose Jaw Public Library Archives located several photographs. And the staff at the Western Development Museum Curatorial Centre in Saskatoon, particularly Kirk Wallace, Warren Clubb, and Ruth Bitner, aptly assisted me on several occasions.

Persons in British Columbia aided me during my visit in May 2012. Grant and Kathleen McMillan of Trinity Western University graciously hosted me in their home. Lea Edgar and Catharine McPherson of the Delta Museum and Archives helped me locate newspaper articles and photographs. Sarah Romkey, University of British Columbia archivist, and Jill Teasley, City of Vancouver digital archivist, arranged for me to view several files in their respective collections. I am particularly indebted to Irvin Johanson, past president of the Aero Club of British Columbia, who put the club's archival material at my disposal.

During a fall 2010 research trip to the province of Manitoba, Pam McKenzie of the Western Canadian Aviation Museum in Winnipeg made my brief stay enjoyable. David Cuthbert ably assisted me during my visit to Library and Archives Canada's Regional Centre in Winnipeg. In fall 2013, Jude Romualdo and Erin Acland of the University of Winnipeg archives generously furnished scans from the Western Canadian Pictorial Index.

I profited from the work of several independent researchers including Arnold Kay of Ottawa, Michael Desmazes, an expert in the history of the air training and operational bases in British Columbia, and Al Kennerley, who graciously loaned me his unpublished work on the Caron airbase. Captain Robert Jones, history officer at No. 15 Wing in Moose Jaw, Saskatchewan kindly directed me to Al Kennerley.

Several persons were helpful with technical matters. Early on, I benefitted from consultations with Huntley O'Connor of Genivar Engineering (now WSP Global). Grant Wilson, of the Canadian Warplane Heritage Museum in Hamilton, Ontario, graciously dispensed his knowledge of air training sites. And Tim Harrington, president of Smith Bros. Wilson (Vancouver) and his assistant, Susan Johansen, searched their corporate archives on my behalf.

It was particularly gratifying to receive assistance from those who had first-hand knowledge of the Caron airbase. Jessie (Reagh) Belcher, Pete Rutherford, Lou Piper, and the late Hank McDowell were outstanding interviewees. Equally gratifying were the conversations I had with family members of those who had served at Caron. Steven and Robert Pape, son and grandson of P/O Robert Pape, DFC, provided me with records from their files. The family of the late Bert Bridgman, the official (civilian) photographer at Caron, generously donated a small collection of original photographs. It is also my distinct pleasure to acknowledge my debt to Sylvia Lindridge, daughter of the late Vernon Peters who figures so prominently in what follows. Sylvia graciously shared her family photographs, documents, and recollections. It was my privilege to introduce Sylvia to her father's war-time letters now held in the Provincial Archives of Saskatchewan.

I am also grateful to my colleagues at Briercrest College. Alan Guenther has been particularly encouraging and helpful. Justin Wolff, now a classics student at Dalhousie University, graciously put his knowledge of 1940s movies at my disposal. Brad Doerksen (now of the University of Regina) and Carla Hoffmann of Archibald Library skillfully processed scores of inter-library loan requests, provided ready access to the college archives, and offered help with the cataloging in publication data for this project. I am also delighted to thank my former dean, Wes Olmstead, PhD, and his senior associates for granting me sabbatical leave so that I could compose an early draft of this study.

And finally, I am pleased to acknowledge the ministrations of the anonymous referees who read early versions of the manuscript, the helpful staff, illustrators, and designers at FriesenPress, and my editor, Mary Metcalfe. Despite their kind interventions, infelicities likely remain. They are mine.

Joel L. From, PhD
June 2019

ABBREVIATIONS

AB	Alberta (Canada)
A/C	Air Commodore
AC2	Aircraftman, second class
A/C/M	Air Chief Marshal
ADC	Aerodrome Development Committee
AFC	Air Force Cross
AFM	Air Force Medal
AFRO	Air Force Roll of Honour
AIR	RFC/RAF archival collection (UKNA)
A/M	Air Marshal
AMP	Air Member for Personnel
AMT	Air Member for Training
ANS	Air Navigation School
AOC	Air Officer Commanding
AOC-in-C	Air Officer Commanding-in-Chief
AOS	Air Observer School
A/V/M	Air Vice-Marshal
B&GS	Bombing & Gunnery School
BBC	British Broadcasting Corporation
BBFTS	Boundary Bay Flying Training School
BBI	Briercrest Bible Institute
BC	British Columbia (Canada)
BCATP	British Commonwealth Air Training Plan

BEM	British Empire Medal
CA	California (USA)
CAAC	Crown Assets Allocation Committee
CAB	War Cabinet papers (UK)
CAS	Chief of Air Staff (UK)
CAS(C)	Chief of Air Staff (Canada)
CFI	Chief Flying Instructor
CFS	Central Flying School
CGI	Chief Ground Instructor
CNR	Canadian National Railway
CO	Commanding Officer
CPL	Corporal
CPR	Canadian Pacific Railway
DC	District of Columbia (USA)
DFC	Distinguished Flying Cross
DFM	Distinguished Flying Medal
DHH	Directorate of History & Heritage
DND	Department of National Defence
DoD	Department of Defense (USA)
DoT	Department of Transport
DW&B	Directorate of Works & Buildings
EFTS	Elementary Flying Training School
ENSA	Entertainments National Services Association
F	Fahrenheit
FIS	Flying Instructor School
F/L	Flight Lieutenant
F/O	Flying Officer
FSGT	Flight Sergeant
G/C	Group Captain
GIS	Ground Instruction School
GRS	General Reconnaissance School
ICRC	International Committee of the Red Cross
ITS	Initial Training School (RCAF)
ITW	Initial Training Wing (RAF)
KC	King's Counsel

LAC	Leading Aircraftman
LAC	Library and Archives Canada
MA	Massachusetts (USA)
MB	Manitoba (Canada)
MG	Private source archive (LAC)
MI	Michigan (USA)
MJ	Moose Jaw (SK)
MT	Mechanical (Motor) Transport
NB	New Brunswick (Canada)
NCO	Non-Commissioned Officer
NGO	Non-Governmental Organization
NS	Nova Scotia (Canada)
NY	New York (USA)
NZ	New Zealand
OBE	Officer of the British Empire
OH	Ohio (USA)
ON	Ontario (Canada)
OTU	Operational Training Unit
PA	Pennsylvania (USA)
PASK	Provincial Archives of Saskatchewan
PC	Privy Council Order-in-Council
P/O	Pilot Officer
R.1	Relief Field (Primary)
R.2	Relief Field (Secondary)
RAAF	Royal Australian Air Force
RAF	Royal Air Force
RCAF	Royal Canadian Air Force
RCMP	Royal Canadian Mounted Police
REMS	Reserve Equipment Maintenance Satellite
REMU	Reserve Equipment Maintenance Unit
RFC	Royal Flying Corps
RG	Record Group (LAC)
RM	Rural municipality (Canada)
RNZAF	Royal New Zealand Air Force
SFTS	Service Flying Training School

SGT	Sergeant
SK	Saskatchewan (Canada)
S/L	Squadron Leader
SRC	Saskatchewan Reconstruction Corporation
SSSSL	Southern Saskatchewan Service Soccer League
TECO	Timber Engineering Company
UK	United Kingdom
UKALM	United Kingdom Air Liaison Ministry
UKNA	United Kingdom National Archives (Kew)
USA	United States of America
VATC	Vancouver Air Training Company
W&B	Works & Buildings
WAAF	Women's Auxiliary Air Force (RAF)
WAC	War Assets Corporation
W/C	Wing Commander
WD	Women's Division (RCAF)
WO	Warrant Officer
WORK	RFC/RAF archival collection (UKNA)
WRNS	Women's Royal Naval Service
WTS	Wireless Training School
YMCA	Young Men's Christian Association
YWCA	Young Women's Christian Association

ROYAL AIR FORCE RANKS, 1940–1944

	RAF Rank	Army Equivalent
ACH	Aircraft Hand	Private
AC2	Aircraftman, 2nd class	Private
AC1	Aircraftman, 1st class	Private
LAC	Leading Aircraftman	Lance Corporal
CPL	Corporal	Corporal
SGT	Sergeant	Sergeant
FSGT	Flight Sergeant	Staff Sergeant
WO	Warrant Officer	Sergeant Major
P/O	Pilot Officer	Second Lieutenant
F/O	Flying Officer	Lieutenant
F/L	Flight Lieutenant	Captain
S/L	Squadron Leader	Major
W/C	Wing Commander	Lieutenant Colonel
G/C	Group Captain	Colonel
A/C	Air Commodore	Brigadier
A/V/M	Air Vice-Marshal	Major General
A/M	Air Marshal	Lieutenant General
A/C/M	Air Chief Marshal	General
M/RAF	Marshal of the RAF	Field Marshal

ILLUSTRATIONS

Figures

Tables

PREFACE

The demolition crew kicked them aside. Yet, the small, steel bracelets that slipped from the fir timbers of the former Royal Air Force hangar at Caronport, Saskatchewan aroused my interest. I would soon learn that these connectors were essential components of the wooden superstructures of Canada's Second World War hangars. Ironically, this simple German invention played a vital role in the spectacular success of the Allies' air training plan.

Further research revealed that over 700 hangars and 7,500 buildings of other types had been erected on military installations across Canada during the war. As I read the literature on the air training plan, I noticed that most accounts offered, at best, only a passing reference to these massive physical assets and the efforts expended in erecting them. It occurred to me that perhaps I could partially rectify this deficiency, at least with respect to the former RAF airbase at Caron(port). Within a month, my colleague, Alan Guenther, drew my attention to a sizeable collection of letters composed by a RAF clerk during his eighteen-month posting at Caron. As it turned out, Vernon Peters' letters to his new bride in Taunton were filled with lucid descriptions, interesting characters, and sparkling anecdotes. With these letters to supplement my initial interest in the physical plant, a biography of the Caron airbase now seemed possible.

We know very little about the processes whereby the air training scheme transitioned from a plan to a dynamic program. As many have done, one could easily assume that its stellar outcomes arose from the straightforward and workmanlike execution of the original 1939 plan. This study will show that this assumption is myopic: it completely overlooks the program's remarkable flexibility as it adapted to novel circumstances impinging from below and from the evolving operational situation in Europe. In truth, it was scarcely the same plan when it reached full capacity in late 1943.

Much of the plan's dynamism arose from the fact that it elicited the cooperation of many agencies operating under extremely fluid conditions. It is nearly impossible to comprehend the acumen needed to carry out a multi-national training scheme, which effectively doubled as it rolled out. By the time that the Caron airbase reached its peak capacity in late 1942, it was five times the size of its sister schools erected just two years prior. Some of this complexity is still inscribed in the soil and the remaining physical plant of what was once a living thing, a mutuality of facilities, open spaces, and personnel carried along by events half a world away.

Reader be forewarned. This is a not a tale of soaring heroes, flying machines, or their dazzling exploits. These have, and should be, sung. Rather, this is a study of the air training plan from the ground up, that is, how it burgeoned forth through the efforts of those who selected its sites, erected its facilities, delivered its training, and disposed of its assets. The detail density, which will be challenging at times, is a mere echo of that which engulfed those charged with executing the plan. Although these thickets can be foreboding, we surely owe those who served us through them our best efforts.

The story of air training at Caron is herein situated in the larger narrative of the Canadian prairies. It is, and must be, a biography of a place. The same climatic conditions that led to the devastating droughts of the preceding decade made the Canadian prairies ideal for flying training. The relative ease with which the weary land and local labour were roused to service had much to do with the recent history of the region and the tenacity acquired in hardscrabble farming. The region's Anglo-Canadian cultural practices, which figure so prominently in the domestic life of the airbase, also aided the RAF airmen who had little trouble fitting in.

The biography of the Caron airbase exhibits the happy confluence of civilian and military contributions. But when these conjoint endeavours are situated within a broader sweep of ideas and practices, there is clearly something else afoot at Caron. As it turns out, Caron's biography bespeaks an ongoing realignment of civilian and military affairs. Its cooperative spirit subverts.

INTRODUCTION

Whatever is worthy of being is worthy also of knowledge . . .
mean things exist as well as elegant things.[1]
— Francis Bacon

Here and there a disheveled shack steels its weathered pate against the gale. Here and there a pocked apron resists the weeds marshalled along its seams. Here and there a runway asserts its crumbling rectitude against the encroaching soil. Here and there an old-timer squints heavenward as antique aircraft drone overhead. And here and there an archivist casts a weary glance at an old air force file. But sadly, little else remains of the air training centres that sprang up across Canada during the Second World War. In their heyday, they had been arrayed along an educational front stretched across the vast Canadian hinterland. They had drawn their youthful vitality not only from the massive natural resources of the dominion and the military spirit of its people but from the unflagging dedication of civil servants, businessmen, and contractors who brandished mighty weapons of policy, procedure, and paperwork.

This study aims to uncover something of the totality of factors that animated one site in this remarkable air training scheme, namely, the RAF airbase at Caron, Saskatchewan.[2] Most accounts of the training plan have underplayed the material circumstances and day-to-day activities of sites like Caron, to say nothing of the critical contributions of civilians and governmental agencies.[3] Most pay scant attention to the internal evolution of the plan and the demands placed on the physical plant and local staff required to make continuous adjustments. These factors shouldn't be overlooked: many of the changes in the Allies' operational policies were only possible because the training infrastructure could be modified quickly and efficiently.

In attempting to capture something of the richness of these conditioning and enabling factors, this study chronicles Caron's earlier history, the site-selection process that led to its discovery, and the process by which the government of Canada came to possess it. It also provides an account of the construction of its aerodrome (airfield) and buildings as well as the modifications imposed on the same by the ongoing expansion of the plan. It completes its biography of Caron's life-cycle with an account of the post-war disposition of its assets.

This study also describes Caron's day-to-day training operations as well as its after-hours social and recreational activities. Caron's so-called civilianization in May 1942 is a central event in a secondary thrust of this study, namely, the relations that arose between the RAF staff and the newly-arrived civilian operators. As the final chapter argues, the cooperative relations between the various parties at Caron reveals something about the conceptual geography traditionally used to distinguish military and civilian affairs. The erosion of these boundaries is apparent at Caron.

The narrative begins with the precipitating events and negotiations that led to the creation of the British Commonwealth Air Training Plan (BCATP), a plan that left the Canadian government and its people with the enormous burden of constructing and staffing some one hundred training centres and other supplemental facilities. By herculean effort, the governmental agencies and private construction firms had the necessary facilities ready six months ahead of schedule, even though the plan effectively doubled along the way.

The second chapter offers a brief history of the land and persons surrounding what would become the Caron airbase. Many of the farmers' struggles in southern Saskatchewan during the Depression era surface in the negotiations surrounding the airbase site. The narrative then turns to the events in Britain that made transplanted RAF airbases like Caron necessary. It became apparent during the Battle of Britain that the UK would soon lose most of its domestic air training capability. By late 1940, the UK War Cabinet agreed to transfer its entire primary air training to Canada. Within months, construction was underway on twenty or more RAF schools in Canada.

The third chapter describes the construction of Caron's aerodrome and buildings. Even as this work proceeded with alacrity, the RAF officers and staff destined for No. 33 EFTS (RAF) at Caron departed from the UK. When they arrived in early December 1941, they found the airbase incomplete and uninhabitable. Nevertheless, after a month of frenetic preparations, the initial cohort of student pilots arrived to begin their training. However, by May—a mere four months into operations—it became apparent that the airbase would be turned over to a civilian operating company.

The civilian company, which took over at Caron, is the focus of the fourth chapter. Many of the leading figures of the Boundary Bay Flying Training School (BBFTS) were successful businessmen from Vancouver who were keen to contribute to the air training plan. After the attack on Pearl Harbor, the Canadian air force urgently needed BBFTS's training facility on the west coast of British Columbia. Suddenly, this displaced operating company became available for a new assignment. With some prodding, the UK Air Ministry invited it to manage Caron.

The fifth chapter describes the tripartite air training curriculum offered at Caron. The first component, the ground school, offered classroom lectures, hands-on exercises, and examinations in accordance with the standard RAF syllabus. The second component centred on the Link Flight Trainer, an early flight simulator, which supposedly developed a student's aerial proficiencies. The final curricular component consisted of airborne instruction in accordance with standard RAF expectations. Notwithstanding the attention given to the formal curriculum, not all learning at Caron was official and prescribed. The chapter concludes with an analysis of the reaction of the RAF personnel to the lessons taught by the Canadian prairie. Not surprisingly, many did not take well to them.

The central air training activities at Caron were supported by the service agencies and other ancillary units discussed in the sixth chapter. The YMCA and later, the Salvation Army, figure prominently. The second section of the chapter considers the supporting roles played by other ancillary units at Caron. The final section highlights several personnel groups that made significant contributions, including the pioneering role of civilian women. An account is also given of the ten airmen and officers who lost their lives in air accidents while attached to the airbase. And finally, those who were decorated for their exemplary service at Caron are given their due.

The seventh chapter considers three important facets of the after-hours activities at Caron. The first section chronicles the many large-scale entertainments on offer. The following section details what we know of several important clubs and committees. The riding club and the station magazine committee figure prominently among these groups. The chapter concludes with a discussion of the sporting life at Caron. RAF personnel were very active in extramural soccer, basketball, and bowling as well as a host of intramural sports.

The eighth chapter narrates the closure of the airbase, its assignment to other duties, and its final disposal. In these processes, the government of Canada's War Assets Corporation and the Saskatchewan Reconstruction Corporation played leading roles. In the end, some ten buildings were purchased and removed from the site; the remainder were sold to the Briercrest Bible Institute when it relocated to what would become Caronport. The chapter concludes with a statistical summation and appraisal of the BCATP's contribution to the war effort.

The final chapter re-visits some of the events surrounding Caron's so-called civilianization. It argues that the cooperation between the civilians and the RAF at Caron demonstrates that the distinction between the two groups is becoming muddied. In fact, these overlapping and interchangeable roles at Caron participate in broader developments, which had the effect of calling the traditional civilian–combatant distinction into question. The chapter argues that there is a way to conceptualize the collapse of this distinction at Caron and elsewhere. This new way of thinking, which is only dimly apparent at Caron, has fully emerged in the decades following the Second World War.

Endnotes

[1]Francis Bacon, *The New Organon*, I.cxx, Lisa Jardine and Michael Silverthorne, eds. (Cambridge: Cambridge University Press, 2000), 92.

[2]The phrase, "totality of factors," is borrowed from Martin van Creveld, *Technology and War: From 2000 B. C. to the Present* (New York: Free Press, 1989), 229.

[3]See, for instance, Allan D. English, *The Cream of the Crop: Canadian Aircrew, 1939–1945* (Montreal: McGill-Queen's University Press, 1996), 41.

CHAPTER 1

A Spirit of Vigorous Enterprise

Providence is always on the side of the last reserve.[1]
— Napoleon Bonaparte

When the First World War began, military aircraft were sent aloft primarily to reconnoitre enemy positions. Unsatisfied with this passive role, enterprising airmen took rifles, pistols, hand grenades, and home-made bombs into the air. Some even fitted their aircraft with trailing cables, hoping to entangle their opponents' airscrews.[2] As the war progressed, task-specific aircraft were developed for bombing and air-to-air combat. Near the end of the war, and in recognition of the increasing importance of air operations, the UK officially established the Royal Air Force as an independent entity.

In the interwar period, it readily became apparent that aircrew training had to be modernized. Whereas previously flying schools were responsible for the entire curriculum, by 1935, separate elementary schools were offering the initial or basic training. The RAF typically delegated this phase of aircrew training to civilian flying companies or avocational clubs so that it could concentrate on the more advanced, or service, training. At the outbreak of the Second World War, the initial stage of pilot training had been wholly delegated to civilian-run elementary flying training schools (EFTSs); advanced training occurred at RAF service flying training schools (SFTSs).[3]

With the success of the RFC/RAF flying training program in Canada during the First World War, it is not surprising that G/C Robert Leckie, a Canadian serving with the RAF, would later itemize the advantages of establishing a RAF school in the empire's largest dominion.[4] Although there is some debate as to the influence of Leckie's memorandum on subsequent proposals, there is little doubt that air training in Canada would be advantaged by the dominion's relative closeness to the UK (compared with Australia, for instance), good flying weather, immunity to enemy intrusion, proximity to the massive industrial resources of the United States, as well as the vigour and hardiness of its people.[5]

In the three and a half years between Leckie's memorandum and the formal adoption of the BCATP, the UK set several flying-training proposals before the Canadian government.[6] Prime Minister Mackenzie King routinely rejected such proposals, believing that they implied either a strategic obligation to British military policy or they would limit Canada's ability to recruit into its own RCAF.[7] To further complicate matters, King typically countered British proposals by interjecting his willingness to welcome RAF recruits to train alongside their Canadian peers in Canada, even though the dominion had no excess training capacity.[8] Many of the parties privy to these matters, to say nothing of the general public, were perplexed by the government's stance.[9]

A joint air training plan took on added urgency after Germany invaded Poland on 1 September 1939. The next day, the UK Air Ministry proposed that four training schools, with an output of just under two thousand pilots per annum, might be needed in Canada.[10] On 6 September, just three days after declaring war on Germany, Neville Chamberlain, the UK prime minister, wrote his Canadian counterpart suggesting that a supply of pilots and aircrew from Canada would be helpful.[11] Four days later, the Air Ministry acknowledged that a great deal of air training would have to occur in the dominions. In a meeting that same day, the RAF's air member for personnel (AMP) indicated that Canada must now be asked to train eight thousand pilots a year.[12] Several weeks later, Chamberlain, in a telegram to his fellow prime ministers in Canada, New Zealand, and Australia, affirmed that "it is now abundantly clear that an overwhelming air force will be needed to counter German air strength."[13]

In mid-September, the high commissioners of Canada and Australia met with officials in the UK Dominions Office to discuss a commonwealth-based-and-operated air training plan. Vincent Massey and Stanley Bruce's proposal called for a joint air training plan based in Canada.[14] To allay chronic Canadian worries, the undertaking would not be a RAF scheme foisted on unwilling colonies but a joint venture among self-governing dominions in support of the RAF. Vincent Massey rightly discerned that a scheme of this sort would be warmly received in Canada since it would be controlled by the commonwealth countries themselves.[15]

Despite his usual apprehension, Mackenzie King accepted the proposal as a basis for negotiations.[16] The agreement would be finalized at a ratification conference in Ottawa the following month.[17] Before the delegations from the UK, Australia, and New Zealand arrived, Mackenzie King delivered a nationally-broadcast speech announcing that an in-principle agreement had been reached on a major commonwealth air training plan. He aptly noted that the scheme would be an undertaking of great magnitude and would "achieve by cooperative effort air forces of overwhelming strength."[18]

The British delegation, led by Sheffield industrialist and diplomat, Lord Riverdale, arrived in Ottawa in mid-October bearing a proposal to train 11,050 pilots, 6,630 air observers (navigators), and 11,310 wireless (radio) operators/air gunners per annum. These twenty-nine thousand aircrew would amount to just over half the estimated fifty thousand per annum believed necessary. New Zealand and Australia would continue to provide their own elementary training. Riverdale's scheme also required the construction of twelve Canadian EFTSs, that is, the facilities necessary for the initial training of the Canadian cohort entering the plan. Since most of the post-EFTS training would occur in Canada, the plan called for a staggering twenty-five SFTSs, fifteen Air Observer Schools (AOS), fifteen Bombing and Gunnery Schools (B&GS), three Air Navigation Schools (ANS), and one Wireless Training School (WTS). In addition, some five thousand aircraft and fifty-four thousand training and maintenance personnel would be needed. In a meeting with the Canadian Emergency Council on the last day of October, Lord Riverdale dropped a bombshell: the proposed plan would cost an estimated $888.5 million over three years.[19] Canada would be expected to cover about forty per cent of the cost.[20]

The expense and scope of the program stunned Canadian officials. A hurried calculation revealed that Canada's projected contribution amounted to $125 million per annum—an amount three times the entire defence budget of the previous year.[21] The cost of the program and the level of British participation were unacceptable to the Canadians, at least on first hearing. Lieutenant-Colonel J. L. Ralston, minister of finance, spoke on behalf of the council when he declaimed that the program would bleed Canada to death.[22]

After six weeks of acrimonious negotiations by the participants pictured in Figure 1.1, the costs were pared down to $607 million. And even though New Zealand and Australia were able to lower their costs by reducing the number of trainees sent to the program, Canada's obligation still stood at $355 million over three years.[23] The UK agreed to help New Zealand and Australia finance their share of the expenses as well as contribute twenty-five per cent of the overall costs, chiefly through the provision of airframes (airplane bodies), aero-engines, and spare parts.[24]

Figure 1.1. Participants in the BCATP ratification conference, Ottawa, 23 November 1939.[25]
Source: LAC/Andrew Audubon Merrilees fonds, PA-195039. Used with permission.

The cooperating parties signed the BCATP agreement just after midnight on Sunday, 17 December 1939. Not coincidentally, Mackenzie King's sixty-fifth birthday fell on the same day.[26] The following evening, the prime minister once again stood before the microphone to announce the details of the plan to a nationwide radio audience. In his address, King emphasized that Canadian concerns were honoured in the agreement: it would be great and decisive; it permitted the signatory countries to repatriate aircrews for home defence; it promised that squadrons would be identified with their home countries when they entered the battle theatre; and, it fell under the administrative control and executive command of the RCAF.[27]

For those unfamiliar with aircrew training, King patiently described the various roles and their associated training centres and curricular processes. Tables 1.1 and 1.2 summarize his account.[28] For security reasons, he did not mention that the BCATP aimed to produce 544 pilots, 350 air observers, and 600 wireless operators/air gunners every four weeks for a total of 19,422 aircrew per annum. (As it turned out, the BCATP produced 131,553 aircrew—an average of 26,310 per annum. Even more remarkably, during its final twelve months, the plan produced an astonishing 38,909 aircrew.)

Table 1.1

Aircrew role descriptions, 1939

Aircrew	Role Description
Pilot	Operates the aircraft
Air Observer	Navigates the flight Operates the reconnaissance camera and bomb sights
Wireless Operator/ Air Gunner	Operates the wireless (radio) Fires the machine gun as needed

Table 1.2

Aircrew training sequence, BCATP, 1939

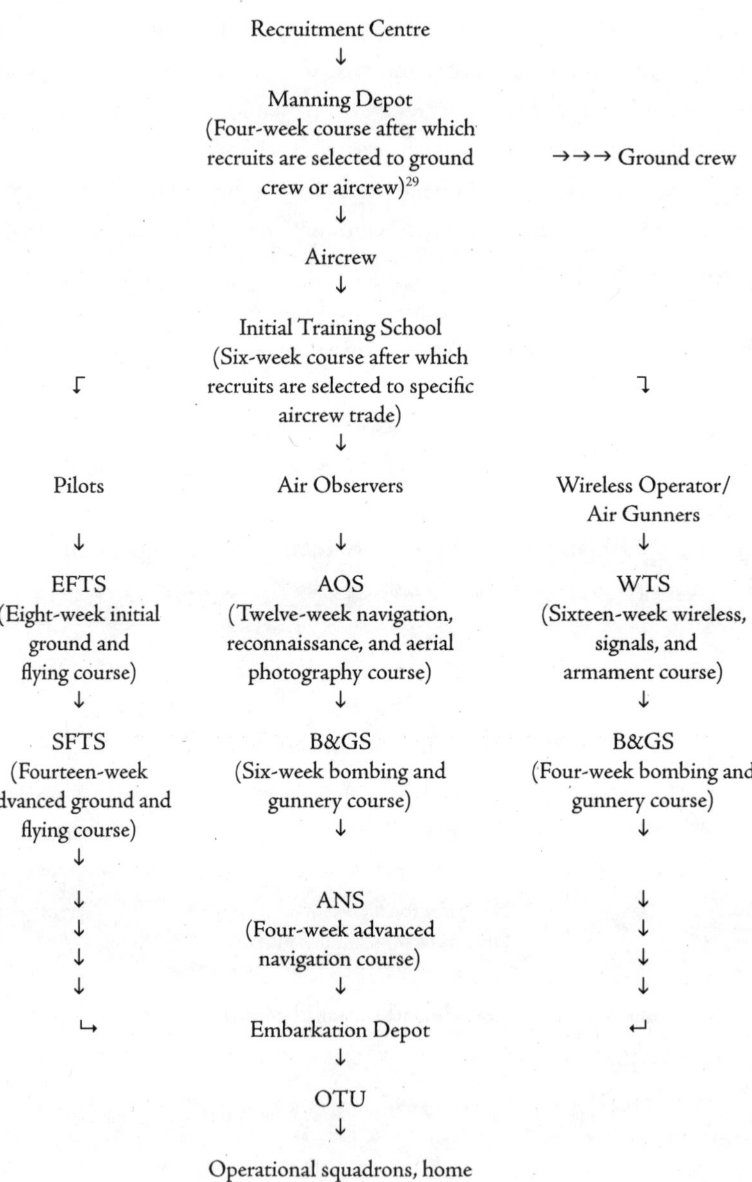

The signatory dominions were expected to provide cohorts of qualified personnel every four weeks as per the quotas listed in Table 1.3. Based on RAF experience, approximately sixteen per cent of student pilots were expected to become "wastage" at each level, that is, they would outright fail, request a transfer, or be reassigned to another trade. Less than seventy per cent of those selected to begin pilot training would earn their pilot's wings after completing their SFTS curriculum.

Table 1.3[30]

Aircrew inputs, outputs, and wastage, BCATP, by nationality and training type

	Australian Input	NZ Input	Canadian Input	Total Input	Total Output	Expected Wastage
EFTS (Canada only)	n/a	n/a	624	624	520	16.6%
SFTS	80	40	520	640	544	15.0%
Air Observers	42	42	336	420	350	16.6%
Wireless Operators/ Air Gunners	72	72	576	720	600	16.6%
Totals (excluding Canadian EFTSs)	**194**	**154**	**1,432**	**1,780**	**1,494**	

Beyond those necessary for aircrew training, the BCATP agreement called for a variety of supplementary schools and facilities. Table 1.4 lists the requisite centres. To staff and maintain BCATP facilities, some 2,686 officers, 30,366 airmen of other ranks, 4,929 civilians, and 1,022 maintenance personnel would be needed by the end of April 1942 when the plan would be fully operational. These forty thousand personnel, although greatly reduced from Lord Riverdale's original proposal, nevertheless amounted to thirteen times the number of personnel attached to the RCAF in March 1939.[31]

Table 1.4

Facilities mandated by BCATP agreement, 1939

Facility Type[32]	Number
Initial Training Schools	3
Elementary Flying Training Schools	13
Service Flying Training Schools	16
Air Observer Schools	10
Bombing & Gunnery Schools	10
Air Navigation Schools	2
Wireless Schools	4
Air Armament School	1
School of Aeronautical Engineering	1
Equipment and Accountant School	1
Flying Instructor School	1
Recruitment Depots	2
Technical Training Schools	2
Repair Depots	3
Equipment Depots	3
Record Office	1

Although the RCAF offered to suspend the BCATP and send all available personnel to help with the Battle of Britain in the summer of 1940, the UK resolved to fight alone in order to sustain a plan aimed at producing "an overwhelming and terrifying strength" by 1942. In response, the RCAF vowed to speed up all outstanding construction projects and have the plan operating at more than full capacity by the end of 1940. Leslie Roberts, a witness to this crisis and response, believed that Britain's early misfortune called forth unprecedented Canadian resolve.[33] Motivated by the steely strength of the old country, Canadians made the air training plan their own. Come what may, they were determined to deliver aircrew ahead of schedule and in greater numbers.

In accordance with the BCATP agreement, thirteen Canadian-based EFTSs were needed by February 1942. Like the RAF, the RCAF planned to deliver its EFTS curriculum through flying clubs, many of which had been teaching the RAF syllabus for some time. Murton A. Seymour, president of the Canadian Flying Clubs Association, prevailed on the RCAF to amend the BCATP agreement to include twenty-six, half-size EFTSs.[34] This seemed the best way to satisfy the twenty-two members of his flying clubs association, each of which was eager to offer elementary training.[35] Since Seymour's clubs were spread across the country, the revised scheme meant that BCATP EFTSs would be small and broadly dispersed.

The physical plant and aerodromes required by the BCATP presented enormous challenges. The RCAF, which had spent less than two million dollars on construction the previous year, did not even have its own engineering and design staff.[36] Further, its modest training capacities were almost entirely confined to bases in Trenton and Camp Borden in Ontario. Despite this woeful incapacity, by the end of 1940, sixteen EFTSs were in operation. As Table 1.5 shows, most were completed between two and six months ahead of schedule. (EFTS nos. 17–22 opened the following year.[37])

Table 1.5
EFTS locations, sponsors, and opening dates[38]

School	EFTS Location	Sponsor	Original Opening Date[39]	Opening Advanced
No. 1	Malton, ON	Toronto Flying Club	24 June 1940	Nil
No. 2	Fort William, ON	Lakehead Flying Club	24 June 1940	Nil
No. 3	London, ON	London Flying Club	19 Aug. 1940	8 weeks
No. 4	Windsor Mills, PQ	Montreal Flying Club	19 Aug. 1940	8 weeks
No. 5	Lethbridge, AB	Calgary Aero Club	14 Oct. 1940	12 weeks
No. 6	Prince Albert, SK	Saskatoon Flying Club	14 Oct. 1940	12 weeks
No. 7	Windsor, ON	Border Cities Aero Club	9 Dec. 1940	20 weeks
No. 8	Vancouver, BC	Aero Club of BC	9 Dec. 1940	20 weeks
No. 9	St. Catharines, ON	St. Catharines Flying Club	17 Feb. 1941	18 weeks
No. 10	Hamilton, ON	Hamilton Aero Club	17 Feb. 1941	18 weeks
No. 11	Cap de la Madeleine, QC	Quebec Airways Ltd.	3 Mar. 1941	20 weeks
No. 12	Goderich, ON	Kitchener-Waterloo Flying Club	3 Mar. 1941	20 weeks
No. 13	St. Eugene, ON	Ottawa Flying Club	31 Mar. 1941	22 weeks
No. 14	Portage La Prairie, MB	Winnipeg Flying Club	28 April 1941	24 weeks
No. 15	Regina, SK	Regina Flying Club	28 Mar. 1941	18 weeks
No. 16	Edmonton, AB	Edmonton & Northern AB Aero Club	7 July 1941	32 weeks
No. 17	Stanley, NS	Halifax Flying Club	7 July 1941	16 weeks
No. 18	Boundary Bay, BC	Aero Club of BC	18 Aug. 1941	13 weeks
No. 19	Virden, MB	Brandon-Virden Flying Club	27 Oct. 1941	21 weeks
No. 20	Oshawa, ON	Oshawa Flying Club	8 Dec. 1941	23 weeks
No. 21	Chatham, NB	Moncton Flying Club	16 Feb. 1942	29 weeks
No. 22	L'Ancienne-Lorette, QC	Quebec City Flying Club	16 Feb. 1942	18 weeks

This herculean effort, and its broader implications, were not lost on LAC Vernon Peters who arrived in Canada from the UK in late 1941. In a letter to his wife, he noted:

> There is a tremendous reserve of energy yet untapped in this great Dominion, such a healthy reminder of the effort which has yet to come. Such a good feeling that we have a long way to go yet before our energy is exhausted, and if only this reserve of power were more widely known in Germany, what a setback it would be to them there, enough to make them wonder if it is worthwhile going on with something that can only end in utter defeat for them.[40]

In the fall of 1939, Dept. of National Defence (DND) undertook the transformation of the RCAF into what would become a complex organization of some two-hundred thousand personnel. Nothing less than a tenfold increase would be needed to achieve the initial mandate of the BCATP, let alone the demands of home defence, overseas operations, and joint projects with the United States. In early 1940, the government of Canada divided the workload of the department by establishing a ministry of national defence for air. Charles Gavan Power, former postmaster general and member of Parliament from Quebec, ascended to the new portfolio in May 1940.[41]

At the outbreak of the war, the RCAF had very little training or operational capacity. It only had 295 pilots and 250 serviceable aircraft; many of the latter were obsolete or only suited for training or aerial surveying.[42] During the lean 1930s, a significant portion of the RCAF's tiny resources had been devoted to "duties that today are often performed by civil agencies: photo-surveying [on behalf of the Dominion Forest Service and the Bureau of Geology and Topography], casualty evacuation, airmail delivery, fisheries and border patrol, [and] utility transport for government officials."[43] These activities were abruptly curtailed just prior to the war.[44]

Appearances to the contrary notwithstanding, the RCAF did not entirely start from scratch. Although it lacked senior administrators, it would soon benefit from the experience of seconded RAF officers. In the first three months of 1940, some 250 RAF personnel were loaned to the BCATP.[45] Further, the

RCAF and the flying clubs had already been following the RAF's flying training syllabus and the division of labour underlying the EFTS–SFTS scheme. However insignificant its training capacity may have been, at least it followed the lead of the RAF and thus kept company with the other commonwealth nations.

Most importantly, the BCATP exploited Canada's civilian know-how and flying experience. By the time the war broke out, the RCAF had already engaged the instructional services of the flying clubs across Canada.[46] Although these joint training schemes produced very few pilots, they did provide the flying clubs with experience in delivering the RAF syllabus.[47] In addition to a standardized ground school curriculum, the clubs' recreational, bush, and commercial pilots, many of whom had flown in the First World War or in northern Canada, were put at the disposal of the BCATP. In the first year of the plan, civilian pilots made up the bulk of the elementary flying instructors.

Perhaps the greatest civilian contribution to the elementary schools came through the professional and managerial skills of flying club members. Since flying is an expensive avocation, its devotees—then and now—were people of means and skill. This talent directly benefitted the BCATP through the companies set up to operate EFTSs. For instance, both Leslie Martin and Stewart McKercher took leave of prominent professional positions to serve as general managers at No. 33 EFTS (RAF) at Caron. It is not likely that the EFTSs and thus, the BCATP, could have operated without the managerial acumen offered by the flying clubs and their operating companies.

The RCAF also drew on the expertise and assets of the Civil Aviation Division of Dept. of Transport (DoT).[48] Many of its senior staff had recent experience in the construction and operation of aerodromes along the Trans-Canada Airway. This coast-to-coast skyway not only furnished the necessary experience and expertise but some of the infrastructure essential to the air training scheme. J. A. Wilson, a high-ranking DoT official during the war, noted that the Trans-Canada Airway offered the BCATP twenty-four aerodromes which required comparatively little work to adapt to air training purposes.[49] The availability of these sites meant that twice as many EFTSs and SFTSs were completed in 1940 as had been originally planned.[50]

To provide the massive physical assets needed by the plan, DND demarcated two broad spheres of responsibility, one of which was delegated to DoT and the other to the RCAF's newly-devised Directorate of Works and Buildings

(DW&B). DoT's chief responsibilities included surveying and recommending sites, purchasing and leasing land, constructing airfields and their runway systems, improving access roads, and providing utilities such as water, telephone, electricity, and sewage disposal.[51] It would work under the authority of the Aerodrome Development Committee (ADC) which, in turn, reported to the minister of national defence for air and, through him, to Privy Council.

For its part, the DW&B designed, constructed, renovated, and maintained BCATP buildings. Over the course of the war, it would situate and erect some 8,300 buildings, most of which served the air training plan. In the fall of 1939, the RCAF recruited R. R. (Dick) Collard, formerly of the Carter-Hall-Aldinger Construction Company of Winnipeg, MB to lead this new unit. Under his watch, the directorate rapidly developed policies governing site design as well as standardized plans for no less than forty building types.

Aerodrome construction began on 24 April 1940. As noted previously, these preparations were greatly aided by the fact that existing airfields and other facilities were taken over by the plan. For instance, the first cohort of trainees to enter the BCATP did so after having spent several weeks at No. 1 Manning Depot located on the grounds of the Canadian National Exhibition in Toronto.[52] Very few, if any, renovations were needed before these facilities could be pressed into service. Existing facilities at Camp Borden, Trenton, and later, St. Thomas, Ontario also gave the RCAF a head start in providing the necessary accommodations.

In the fall of 1939, field parties consisting of a DoT airways inspector, a DoT airways engineer, and a RCAF officer perused topographical maps looking for sites that offered a square mile of suitable land. Promising sites were inspected by air and then on foot. DoT's *Preliminary Investigation Report* appraised all aspects of a potential site, including its soil quality, water sources, the slope of the land, telegraph and telephone facilities, railways, highways, power services, land values, climatic patterns, and availability of gravel. The report also estimated the amount of surface grading necessary and noted any flying hazards in the vicinity.

That fall, DoT field parties inspected some two thousand sites by air, filing preliminary reports on two hundred, and conducting full topographical surveys on 150.[53] Unusually warm weather permitted some eighty per cent of the detailed surveys to be completed before winter.[54] J. A. Wilson argues that this timely work (well in advance of the signing of the BCATP agreement) and good weather accelerated the plan by a full six months. Provincial Dept. of Highways survey parties participated wholeheartedly in this preliminary work. Just as they were about to be laid off for the season, DoT hired many of these crews to survey potential sites. The provincial departments provided contour maps, which served as the basis for the initial identification of possible sites. In its 1940 annual report, the Saskatchewan Dept. of Highways and Transportation noted that "in the fall of 1939 practically the entire staff of field engineers was employed in making surveys of proposed sites for Royal Canadian Air Force Training Schools."[55]

The preliminary reports generated by the survey parties were reviewed by the Aerodrome Development Committee (ADC) in Ottawa. After a careful analysis in terms of the technical criteria itemized in Table 1.6, the ADC typically requested that DoT conduct more detailed studies of the most promising sites. Based on the resultant technical surveys and reports, engineering plans and cost estimates were drawn up. When fully costed, DoT field staff forwarded information on a potential site to DoT's director of air services and then to the deputy minister of transport for their appraisal. With the approval of these officials, the site plans and costs were forwarded back to the ADC where they were carefully considered and compared with competing sites. The ADC routinely requested cost adjustments and rejected sites that were too expensive or not technically viable.

Table 1.6

DoT aerodrome site-selection criteria

Requisite Features

Land—480 to 640 acres with a uniform surface

Slope—slight grade (0.5–1 per cent) for drainage

Soil—suitable for compaction and grass turf

Location—social amenities in the vicinity?

Post-war usefulness—for RCAF or civil aviation

Rapid development—can an existing aerodrome be repurposed?

Services—good road, railway, water, power, telephone

Aggregate (gravel and stone)—available in the vicinity?

Climate—heavy snows or persistent fog?

Proximity to the USA border—too close could disqualify

Immovable obstructions—e.g., major buildings, mountains

Relief fields, ancillary units—can suitable sites be found nearby?

Interference—e.g., too close to other airbases?

Distribution—sites equally dispersed across the country?

Only at this late stage did a site proposal come to the attention of political officials. Final plans and estimates were forwarded to the deputy minister of national defence for air who sought his minister's approval and a financial encumbrance certifying that funds were available should the project be approved. Privy Council gave final approval to recommendations forwarded to it from the minister. This approval process, which entered the political arena only at the last possible moment, effectively shielded site-selection decisions from direct political interference.[56]

At the commencement of the BCATP, EFTSs were equipped with "all-way" grass airfields. As per RAF policy, paved runways were not thought necessary since elementary aircraft were quite light and could safely land on grass. In the summer of 1941, the RCAF began to provide hard-surface runways at EFTSs due to persistent water problems and the mounting pressure to conduct uninterrupted flying operations. This additional work fell to DoT, which now had to provide paved runways, taxiways, and aircraft parking areas as well as their surrounding shoulder ditch systems at each new EFTS.

The Canadian National Railway (CNR) chief land surveyor and property commissioner assisted DoT in acquiring the land needed for its aerodromes and building areas. The CNR had a great deal of experience with property management across the dominion: it had vast land holdings and constantly negotiated right of way claims and railway crossing privileges. Once a detailed survey had been ordered by the ADC, DoT typically informed CNR land officials that they should proceed to purchase options on the specified parcel. Usually an official from the CNR's regional office would contact the landowners and offer an option to purchase their land based on a fair market valuation.

DoT's responsibility also included the provision of power, lighting, and telephone services to dozens of aerodromes across the country. Here again, DoT's experience with the Trans-Canada Airway proved invaluable. In eastern Canada, the well-developed power grid posed no great difficulties. However, in western Canada and particularly in Saskatchewan, power facilities were primitive. Many rural areas did not have electrical power and those that did were often served by unreliable power plants.

Within the first two years of the war, the EFTS syllabus would be modified to require night flying training. This new emphasis reflected the shift in bombing operations away from hazardous daytime missions. For a time, night bombing seemed a likely solution, although it proved to be remarkably inaccurate.[57] In 1941, an official investigation by the UK War Cabinet revealed that only one of four nighttime bombs fell within five miles of its target. In many cases, only one in fifteen or one in twenty bombs came within five miles of their targets.[58] Although later in the war, long-range, daytime sorties would again become prevalent, in 1942, night flying training rose to a place of prominence in the elementary curriculum.

This shift in policy placed a substantial burden on DoT, which now had to retrofit its EFTSs. Contact lights, illuminated wind tees (directional indicators), and rotating beacons were only some of the electrified devices now needed. Coupled with the continuous expansion of many schools, these new requirements placed unanticipated demand on the power supply. In Caron's case, its power supply had to be upgraded even before it opened due to the school's expanding enrolment and the illumination needs of its night flyers. DoT had to provide power to many remote relief fields, sites which heretofore had been little more than grass fields. Since many of these auxiliary operations now required illumination and overnight accommodation for staff, they too needed electricity, which often had to be brought from a considerable distance.

DoT also needed to provide telephone service to its sites. This too proved to be quite complex as communication needs expanded. Since a portion of night flying exercises took place at isolated relief fields, these facilities had to be connected to the main aerodrome's telephone system. This typically involved considerable distance and expense. Here again, DoT found the provincial agencies very cooperative. For instance, the Saskatchewan Dept. of Telephones noted that the demand for BCATP telephone facilities had been a principal concern. It made every effort to complete the private branch exchanges, trunks to nearby town exchanges, and in some cases, additional long-distance lines to meet the need. All telephone installations in Saskatchewan were ready by the required date.[59]

Supplying up to fifty-thousand gallons of potable water per day provided further challenges for DoT, particularly on the prairies. In the haste to construct facilities, water resources were not always fully proven. The water emergencies at Mossbank and Dafoe in Saskatchewan as well as Vulcan in Alberta became well-known to federal parliamentarians.[60] In these three notable cases, initial supplies turned out to be inadequate and water had to be trucked or piped over great distances. Mossbank and Dafoe were eventually fitted with indoor swimming pools that served as reservoirs just in case the water supply system failed during a fire emergency.

Providing all-weather access to BCATP sites also proved problematic for DoT. In many instances, this turned out to be a costly undertaking. The relief field at Boharm, originally attached to No. 32 SFTS (RAF) at Moose Jaw and later transferred to No. 33 EFTS (RAF) at Caron, is a case in point. All-season access to its grass airfield required that the adjacent dirt road be improved at an estimated cost of $10,000. In the end, DoT improved about ten miles of dirt road between Boharm and Caron. But even here, the improvements left much to be desired during the spring thaw or after heavy rains. All-weather access often meant little more than access to the all-weather towing services of a local farmer.

All aerodromes, even those with hard-surface runways, require durable grass turf inside and outside their runway systems. At most early elementary schools and relief fields, these grass turfs served as the primary landing surface. DoT received the assistance of the federal Dept. of Agriculture in these matters. Although primarily focused on sites in central Canada, the department's Division of Forage Plants provided advice on selecting the best seed mixtures and fertilizers as well as watering and cutting schedules.[61] As the building program of the BCATP shifted westward, the department conducted research and offered advice on the best turfs for prairie conditions.[62] In 1941–43, it supervised turfing operations at no less than thirty-four aerodromes and forty-three RCAF building areas. Due to these pressing demands, the division curtailed its own research for much of the war.[63]

Early in 1940, BCATP officials released specifications for the first BCATP schools. Since interest ran high and contractors needed to review a complete set of drawings, an enormous number of blueprints had to be furnished for each major contract. The sheer volume of work overwhelmed DoT and DW&B staffs.[64] In response, on 20 May 1940, Privy Council authorized the minister of transport to override the standard procurement procedure.[65] Since by this time major contracts had been negotiated in the various regions of the country, DoT and the Dept. of Munitions and Supply, which assisted in these matters, knew what to expect in the bidding process. So, instead of issuing public tenders, private invitations were sent to known, capable, and reliable contractors, soliciting bids on specific contracts.[66]

During the first years of the war, Canadian contractors accomplished the impossible. They erected over 8,300 military buildings, including 700 hangars. They laid some 35 million square yards of hard-surface material on runways, hangar floors, and aprons—roughly the equivalent of a twenty-foot-wide highway 3,000 miles in length.[67] During 1942, when construction activity reached its peak, their crews executed some one thousand contracts worth $80 million.[68] Contractors were routinely asked to produce a functioning aerodrome within as little as eight weeks. Contracts were often amended even before they were signed. For example, at Caron, the general contractor had no sooner submitted his bid for erecting the buildings than he learned that major changes would be needed. Midway through the contract, several new buildings were added: these too had to be negotiated and executed in a timely fashion.

Very few accounts of the BCATP foreground the efforts of the contractors, designers, or other officials responsible for this massive undertaking. Leslie Roberts is an exception. His 1941 book devoted an entire chapter to the construction work and went to the trouble of listing the major contractors at most BCATP sites, a list that extends through seven columns and four pages. He singled out Bird Construction (Winnipeg), Dutton Bros. Construction (Calgary), Carter-Hall-Aldinger Construction (Winnipeg), and Tomlinson Construction (Toronto) for the scope of their contribution to the air training effort.[69] The fact that many of the facilities were completed months ahead of schedule even with almost continuous modifications, labour and material shortages, and unpredictable weather is a testament to the world-class efforts of these companies and their employees.

With all due respect to those who flung the Canadian Pacific Railway across the continent and those who dug the St. Lawrence Seaway, the construction of the air training facilities in a few short years surely ranks among the greatest public works in Canadian history. Regrettably, the temporary nature, broad dispersal, rural locales, and sudden disposal of these facilities impedes a proper acknowledgement of the unstinting labour and singular merit of those who designed and erected them.

Endnotes

[1]Napoleon Bonaparte, contradicting the platitude that God is always on the side of the army with the largest battalions. See C. T. Ramage, *Beautiful Thoughts from French and Italian Authors* (Liverpool: Howell, 1866), 346.

[2]See P. G. Hering, *Customs and Traditions of the Royal Air Force* (Aldershot, Hampshire: Gale & Polden, 1961), 9 and Chaz Bowyer, *History of the RAF* (London: Bison, 1977), 19.

[3]Ray Sturtivant, *The History of Britain's Military Training Aircraft* (Newbury Park, CA: Haynes, 1987), 35. See also Air Ministry, *The Royal Airforce Builds for War: A History of Design and Construction in the RAF, 1935–1945* (Norwich: Stationery Office, 1997), 304–05, 312–13.

[4]Robert Leckie's 1936 memorandum, "Notes on the Proposal to Establish a Flying Training School in Canada," is reprinted in his, "A Background to History," *Roundel* 11 (December 1949): 14–15.

[5]Spencer Dunmore argues that Leckie's memorandum is directly responsible for what would become the BCATP. There are several reasons to question this claim. First, the fact that Leckie articulated the advantages of Canadian-based air training in ways that resonated with later proposals does not show that these future proposals depend in any way on Leckie's document or argument. These advantages would have been apparent to anyone who conducted a comparative study of air training locations within the British Empire. Second, High Commissioners Stanley Bruce (Australia) and Vincent Massey (Canada), who first proposed a commonwealth air training plan in September 1939, did not have access to Leckie's memorandum. Dunmore himself notes that Massey "was almost certainly unaware of Leckie's 1936 memorandum" (35). Third, Leckie proposed the establishment of *one* RAF flying training school in Canada and not a comprehensive *plan*, let alone a *commonwealth-based-and-operated plan*. See Spencer Dunmore, *Wings for Victory: The Remarkable Story of the British Commonwealth Air Training Plan in Canada* (Toronto: McClelland & Stewart, 1994), 25–26. See also Norman Hillmer, "Vincent Massey and the Origins of the British Commonwealth Air Training Plan," *Canadian Defence Quarterly* 16, no. 4 (Spring 1987): 52.

[6]Fred Hatch's account of the pre-war flying training proposals and counter-proposals is still worth consulting. See his "The British Commonwealth Air Training Plan 1939 to 1945" (PhD diss., University of Ottawa, 1969), 19–59. See also Dunmore, *Wings for Victory*, 24–37.

[7]For a definitive account of King's fierce rejection of any shared authority with Britain, see Roy MacLaren, *Commissions High: Canada in London, 1870–1971* (Montreal: McGill-Queen's University Press, 2006), 308–96. See also Hillmer, "Vincent Massey," 49–54 and W. A. B. Douglas, *The Creation of a National Air Force*, vol. 2 of *The Official History of the Royal Canadian Air Force*, ed. Norman Hillmer (Toronto: University of Toronto Press, 1986), 193–203.

[8]*Dominion of Canada Official Report of Debates House of Commons*, 1 July 1938, vol. 4 (Ottawa: King's Printer, 1939), 4523–32.

[9]In the summer of 1939, the Canadian government agreed to a small cooperative program in which fifty RAF pilots a year for a period of three years would receive their advanced training in Canada. See "Training of Short Service Officers (General Duties Branch) by the Canadian Government: Memorandum of Agreement," in AIR 2/3408: "Training in Canada of Pilots for the Royal Air Force," UKNA.

[10]Air Ministry, "Memorandum on the Possibility of Increasing Training Capacity in Canada for the Royal Air Force," 2 September 1939, in AIR 2/3206: "Air Training of RAF Pilots in Canada During the War," UKNA.

[11]Hillmer, "Vincent Massey," 52.

[12]"Minutes of a Meeting held in AMP's Room at 1430 hours on September 10th, 1939, to discuss Flying Training Expansion," in AIR 2/3206: "Air Training of RAF Pilots in Canada During the War," UKNA.

[13]Air Ministry, "Air Training of RAF Pilots in Canada During the War."

[14]Vincent Massey apparently operated on his own in this matter. In truth, he had little choice if he wished to get anything done since Mackenzie King was deeply suspicious of any cooperative effort that could possibly impinge on Canadian sovereignty.

[15]Hillmer, "Vincent Massey," 52.

[16]The proposal was perfectly tailored for King's political dilemma since it allowed Canada to make a significant contribution without the enormous casualties associated with trench warfare or the concomitant problem of conscripting young men to fight in those conditions. See Douglas, *The Creation of a National Air Force*, 205.

[17]I. Norman Smith, *The British Commonwealth Air Training Plan* (Toronto: Macmillan, 1941), 3. See also Dunmore, *Wings for Victory*, 35–36.

[18]W. L. M. King, "Text of King Speech Concerning Training Airmen in Canada," *Hamilton Spectator*, 10 October 1939.

[19]In his report to the UK government, Lord Riverdale indicated that the Canadian ministers "were alarmed at the size of the scheme and at its probable cost." See Riverdale, "Mission to Canada in connection with the Dominion Air Training Scheme," in AIR 8/280: "Report of the Riverdale Mission to Canada on Dominion Air Training Scheme: Report and Memoranda, 1939–1940," UKNA.

[20]Fred J. Hatch, *Aerodrome of Democracy: Canada and the British Commonwealth Air Training Plan, 1939–1945* (Ottawa: Canadian Government Publication Centre, 1983), 16. See also Chubby [Charles Gavan] Power, *A Party Politician: The Memoirs of Chubby Power*, ed. Norman Ward (Toronto: Macmillan, 1966), 198–99.

[21]"Defence Expenditures, Canada, 1919–47," in Douglas, *The Creation of a National Air Force*, 629.

[22]United Kingdom Air Mission, "Notes of a Meeting on 31st October with members of the Canadian War Cabinet," file 181.009 (D786), DHH.

[23]Douglas, *The Creation of a National Air Force*, 210. The Canadian contribution to the joint training expenses was pegged at $287 million. Canada's own EFTS expenses were estimated at $68 million. Thus, the total projected expenditure for Canada was $355 million over three years.

[24]*Dominion of Canada Official Report of Debates House of Commons*, 12 May 1942, vol. 3, 2339.

[25]The following appear in Figure 1.1. In the front row (l–r): A/C/M Sir Henry R. Brooke-Popham, RAF; J. L. Ralston, minister of finance, Canada; G/C H. W. L. Saunders, CAS, RNZAF; Raoul

Dandurand, senator, Canada; Lord Riverdale, chief UK negotiator; W. L. M. King, prime minister, Canada; J. V. Fairbairn, minister for air, Australia; Ernest Lapointe, minister of justice and attorney general, Canada; Captain H. H. Balfour, parliamentary under-secretary of state for air (Commons), UK; Norman M. Rogers, minister of national defence, Canada; A/M Sir Christopher Courtney, AOC-in-C, RAF Reserve Command. In the second row (l–r): J. B. Abraham, principal assistant secretary, Air Ministry, UK; Dr. O. D. Skelton, under-secretary of state for external affairs, Canada; T. A. Barrow, air secretary, New Zealand; Sir Gerald Campbell, UK high commissioner to Canada; Ian A. Mackenzie, minister of pensions and national health, Canada; W/C George Jones, assistant chief of air staff, Australia; C. D. Howe, minister of transport, Canada; Dr. W. C. Clark, deputy minister of finance, Canada; A/V/M G. M. Croil, CAS(C), Canada. In the third row (l–r): J. R. Smyth, UK; F. R. Howard, UK; G. V. Kellway, Australia; A/C E. W. Stedman, RCAF Engineering and Supply Branch, Canada; G/C A. Cray, UK; Lieutenant-Colonel K. S. Maclachlan, deputy minister of national defence, Canada; G/C J. M. Robb, UK; A. D. P. Heeney, principal secretary to the prime minister, Canada; G/C L. N. Hollinghurst, UK; R. E. Elford, Australia; W. L. Middlemass, NZ. Source: RAF Museum Images, http://www.rafmuseum.org.uk/images/online_exhibitions/ac71-9-263.jpg.

[26]*Agreement Relating to the Training of Pilots and Aircraft Crews in Canada and Their Subsequent Service between the United Kingdom, Canada, Australia and New Zealand. Signed at Ottawa, December 17, 1939* (Ottawa: King's Printer, 1939).

[27]Leslie Roberts, *Canada's War in the Air*, 3rd ed. (Montreal: Beatty, 1943), 15, 17, 19.

[28]W. L. M. King, radio speech, 17 December 1939, reprinted in Roberts, *Canada's War in the Air*, 15.

[29]From 1941 on, wireless operators/air gunners did not proceed to an ITS but were selected directly into their trade at the manning depot. See W. A. B. Douglas, *The Creation of a National Air Force*, 234.

[30]*Agreement Relating to the Training of Pilots*. A copy of this agreement can be found in the appendix to Roberts, *Canada's War in the Air*.

[31]On 31 March 1939, the RCAF consisted of 357 officers, 1,957 airmen, as well as 96 officers and 868 airmen in its nonpermanent staff, for a total of 3,148. See *Dominion of Canada Official Report of Debates House of Commons*, 1939, vol. 3, 3247. In August 1939, the RCAF only had 295 pilots. See Air Force Headquarters, *Royal Canadian Air Force List, August 1939*, in Hatch, *Aerodrome of Democracy*, 5. The RCAF would reach a peak strength of 206,350 personnel at the end of 1943, an astonishing sixty-five-fold increase in less than five years. See Charles P. Stacey, *Arms, Men and Governments: The War Policies of Canada 1939–1945* (Ottawa: Queen's Printer, 1970), 48.

[32]*See Agreement Relating to the Training of Pilots*. By 31 March 1940, several additions were made to these initial requirements. For instance, twenty RCAF recruitment centres were now needed as well as four training command headquarters, two manning depots, a school of administration, an equipment and accounting training school, an aeronautical engineering school, an aircraft inspection school, and an additional equipment depot and repair depot. See "Royal Canadian Air Force," in *Report of the Dept. of National Defence Canada for the Year Ended March 31, 1940*

(Ottawa: King's Printer, 1940), 94. Canada was also expected to provide its own ITSs, which screened and pre-qualified candidates for its EFTSs and other air trades.

[33]Roberts, *Canada's War in the Air*, 47.

[34]Douglas, *The Creation of a National Air Force*, 223. These twenty-six EFTSs were one half the size of those called for in the original agreement. Whereas the BCATP EFTSs had an expected input of forty-eight students every four weeks, by the time that the EFTS operating companies signed their contracts, they expected an input of only twenty-four every four weeks. Given the eight-week syllabus, only forty-eight student pilots would be in residence at any time. See "Standard Form of Agreement for Operation of an Elementary Flying Training School at an Aerodrome Maintained by the Dept. of Transport," in RG24, vol. 5231: "Supervisory Board—BCATP. Minutes of Meetings," LAC.

[35]Murton Seymour received his pilot's certificate from the Aero Club of British Columbia in 1915. After serving with No. 41 Squadron, RFC, in Belgium and with distinction in several branches of the RFC/RAF (Canada) training program during the First World War, Captain Seymour opened what would become a successful law practice in St. Catharines, ON. In 1928, he incorporated the St. Catharines Flying Club and was one of the founding directors of the Canadian Flying Clubs Association. Later, he would be recognized for these services by DND, the Canadian Flying Clubs Association, and the UK government, which named him an Officer of the British Empire in 1943. In 1967, the Canadian government further honoured his contribution as did the Canadian Aviation Hall of Fame in 1973. See C. W. Hunt, *Dancing in the Sky: The Royal Flying Corps in Canada* (Toronto: Dundurn, 2009), 307. Also see Frank H. Ellis, *Canada's Flying Heritage*, 2nd ed. (Toronto: University of Toronto Press, 1961), 114–17.

[36]*Dominion of Canada Official Report of Debates House of Commons*, 26 April 1939, vol. 3, 3249.

[37]Dunmore, *Wings for Victory*, 350 and "History of Civil Flying Schools," in 180.009 (D3), DHH.

[38]*Dominion of Canada Official Report of Debates House of Commons*, 18 November 1940, vol. 1, 173.

[39]Data in the two right-hand columns are from Hatch, *Aerodrome of Democracy*, 52.

[40]Vernon Peters to Vera, 15 May 1942, in Vernon Peters, Letters to Vera, 1941–1944, in R-1545.1, PASK. Although Peters could not have known it, UK Prime Minister Chamberlain used a similar argument when he suggested that air training in Canada "might well have a psychological effect on the Germans equal to that produced by the intervention of the United States in the last war." See Chamberlain's telegram to Mackenzie King, 26 September 1939, in Hatch, "BCATP," 77.

[41]Power, *A Party Politician*, 186.

[42]*Royal Canadian Air Force List, August 1939*, in Hatch, *Aerodrome of Democracy*, 5 and *Dominion of Canada Official Report of Debates House of Commons*, 26 April 1939, vol. 3, 3248–49.

[43]T. F. J. Leversedge, "History of the Military Air Services in Canada," in *Canadian Combat and Support Aircraft: A Military Compendium* (St. Catharines, ON: Vanwell, 2007), 25.

[44]"Royal Canadian Air Force," in *Dept. of National Defence Canada for the Fiscal Year Ending March 31, 1940* (Ottawa: King's Printer, 1940), 85.

[45]Robert Leckie, *Final Report of the Chief of the Air Staff to the Members of the Advisory Board British Commonwealth Air Training Plan, Monday, April 16, 1945* (Ottawa: DND, 1945), 21.

[46]Ted Barris, *Behind the Glory: Canada's Role in the Allied Air War* (Toronto: Allen, 2005), 69.

[47]Ibid., 11.

[48]Responsibility for the control and supervision of civil aviation passed from DND to the newly-instituted DoT in 1936. See Dominion of Canada, *Air Regulations 1938* (Ottawa: King's Printer, 1938), 4.

[49]In 1944, John Wilson would be awarded the McKee Trophy for his meritorious service in the advancement of aviation in Canada. Although he never flew an airplane, Wilson made major contributions to the Air Board and as the very likeable controller of civil aviation in Canada from 1919–41. See Ellis, *Canada's Flying Heritage*, 218, 366.

[50]J. A. Wilson, "Aerodrome Construction for the British Commonwealth Air Training Plan," *The Engineering Journal* (November 1940): 454.

[51]"PC 3710," issued by Privy Council on 17 November 1939, granted DoT authority to select and develop the aerodromes necessary for the BCATP. See *Dominion of Canada Official Report of Debates House of Commons*, 13 June 1940, vol. 1, 736.

[52]Hatch, *Aerodrome of Democracy*, 47–48.

[53]Wilson, "Aerodrome Construction," 455. Fred Hatch suggests that DoT field parties inspected 1,647 sites by the end of 1939. See Hatch, "BCATP," 150.

[54]In his 17 December 1939 radio speech to the nation, Mackenzie King indicated that due to favourable weather most of the necessary sites had already been surveyed. See Roberts, *Canada's War in the Air*, 19.

[55]*Annual Report of the Dept. of Highways and Transportation of the Province of Saskatchewan for the Fiscal Year Ended April 30, 1940* (Regina: McConica, 1940), 8.

[56]In her study of the BCATP site selection process, Rachel Lea Heide concludes that there is no evidence of any untoward political influence. In fact, neither Minister Power, the federal cabinet, nor Privy Council ever once went against the recommendations of the technical committees. See her "The Politics of British Commonwealth Air Training Plan Base Selection in Saskatchewan," *Saskatchewan History* 53, no. 2 (Fall 2001): 3–15.

[57]Douglas, *The Creation of a National Air Force*, 240.

[58]David L. Bashow, *No Prouder Place: Canadians and the Bomber Command Experience 1939–1945* (St. Catharines, ON: Vanwell, 2005), 65.

[59]*Annual Report of the Dept. of Telephones of the Province of Saskatchewan for the Financial Year Ended April 30, 1941* (Regina: McConica, 1942), [5].

[60]Members of Parliament occasionally directed questions regarding the water supply at BCATP sites to Minister Power. For instance, see the exchange between the minister and Mr. Perley during the War Appropriations Committee meeting on 17 March 1941, in *Dominion of Canada Official Report Debates House of Commons*, 17 March 1941, vol. 2, 1617. See also the exchange in

the House of Commons on 4 June 1943, in *Dominion of Canada Official Report Debates House of Commons*, 4 June 1943, vol. 4, 3355–56.

[61]*Report of the Minister of Agriculture for the Dominion of Canada for the Year Ended March 31, 1940* (Ottawa: King's Printer, 1940), 63.

[62]*Report of the Minister of Agriculture for the Dominion of Canada for the Year Ended March 31, 1941* (Ottawa: King's Printer, 1941), 73.

[63]*Report of the Minister of Agriculture for the Dominion of Canada for the Year Ended March 31, 1943* (Ottawa: King's Printer, 1943), 75.

[64]The DoT and DW&B engineering and drafting staffs toiled arduously in cramped quarters. It is hard to imagine the strain put on these staffs as the BCATP and other defence projects rolled out, ever expanding as they went. Staff had to be continually increased and relocated to larger facilities. Over the course of the air training program, some 30,000 sketch plans and as many as 1.5 million blueprints were issued. See Leckie, *Final Report*, 11.

[65]"Conferences and Committees—Interdepartmental—Aerodrome and Projects Development Committee," in RG12, vol. 368, LAC.

[66]The perils surrounding military procurement were a major concern for the King government. The artillery shell scandal of the First World War and the more recent discovery that a contract for 7,000 Bren guns had been let without competitive bidding greatly agitated the public mind. Only a dire emergency and a pre-determined cost baseline made streamlining BCATP construction politically feasible.

[67]Leckie, *Final Report*, 12.

[68]Leckie, *Final Report*, 10.

[69]Roberts, *Canada's War in the Air*, 99.

CHAPTER 2

The British Are Coming

No plan survives first contact with the enemy.[1]
— Helmuth von Moltke

Persons of British extraction had been settling in south-central Saskatchewan since the late nineteenth century. The 1936 census revealed that almost ninety per cent of Moose Jaw's residents had been born within the empire, making it the most British city on the Canadian prairies.[2] Many of the Anglo-Canadian farmers who settled in the Caron district had migrated from southwestern Ontario. This chapter chronicles the settlement and struggles of those who farmed the land that would one day host the RAF airbase at Caron. Several had already been displaced by drought and economic depression by the time their land came to the attention of BCATP officials. In 1941, a second British incursion would issue from the UK government's decision to transfer its primary flying training to Canada.

In September 1882, James Macmillan surveyed the virgin prairie in the Caron district. His contract stipulated that he lay out ten townships, including the one that would host the Caron airbase some sixty years later.[3] In a report composed later that fall, Macmillan concluded that the parcel surrounding

Caron appeared to be "a moderately good one for Agricultural purposes. The soil changes from clay to sand in many places however."[4] Just months before his arrival, the Canadian Pacific Railway (CPR) drove its ribbons of steel westward through Regina, Moose Jaw, Caron, and Swift Current (see Figure 2.1). This spectacle of relentless forward progress laid as much as four miles of track a day across the land of living skies. In 1882 alone, the CPR stitched some 420 miles of railway to the warm prairie soils.[5] Macmillan's survey was timely: the district was already attracting the interest of settlers streaming into the Canadian northwest.

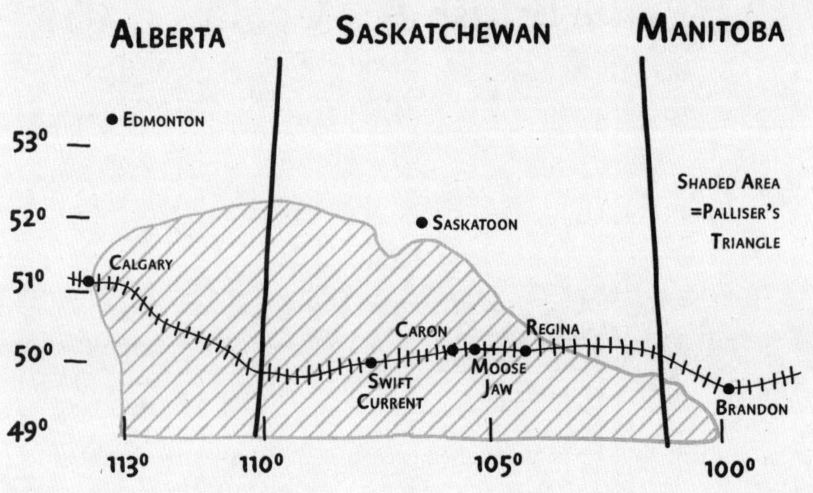

Figure 2.1. Palliser's triangle. Source: *A General Map of the Routes in British North America Explored by the Expedition Under Captain Palliser*. London: Stanford's Geographical, 1865 (redrawn facsimile).

Macmillan may not have realized the controversy that attended his claim that the land surrounding Caron would be moderately good for agricultural purposes. Captain John Palliser had not been impressed with its potential when he passed through the area in 1857. In fact, he famously characterized the surrounding prairie as a desert. This region of "arid plains, devoid of timber or pasture of good quality" would be stuck with this moniker as would the vast prairies of the American Midwest. Professor Henry Youle Hind, who visited the Caron district a year later, reinforced Palliser's bleak appraisal.[6] Consequently, *Palliser's triangle*, a supposed extension of the American desert, dominated the views of those who cared to notice (see Figure 2.1).[7]

John Macoun, a plant geographer attached to various CPR survey parties, challenged the received view.[8] He concluded that the allegedly arid plains could be extremely productive. The lack of timber—typically a sign of soil deficiency in temperate climates—arose from frequent prairie fires and not from the soil per se. He insisted that the region's dry conditions, sunny days, and hard frosts were ideal for wheat and other cereal crops. Although the prairie turf seemed impervious, once turned over, broken up, and its topsoil loosed, it would produce a bounty of crops and vegetables.

It appears that Macoun's optimistic account may have been influenced by several unusually wet years in the region. Under such conditions, the southern prairies do exhibit pluriform bounty. Macoun could not have known what later studies and hard experience have revealed, namely, that years of plenty are often bookended by decades of drought. David Sauchyn, of the University of Regina, reports that tree ring research reveals that prairie droughts can last for a century or more. In other words, the drought that would overwhelm the Canadian prairies in the early twentieth century may have been unusual in that it *only* spanned several decades.[9]

Less than a year after Macmillan's survey, Edward Heath lawfully entered the land that would eventually host the eastern half of the Caron aerodrome. By May 1886, he had only managed to bring seven acres under cultivation and had yet to erect a building. Because he did not meet these conditions of the land grant program, he lost his claim.[10] Shortly thereafter, William Hans occupied Heath's abandoned homestead.[11] Hans had recently come to the Caron area from Wellington County in Ontario (near present-day Guelph). In early spring 1893, he applied for a patent. He clearly met the conditions laid down by the land grants program: he had constructed a small (14' x 16') house, lived continuously on the site, and had 160 acres under cultivation.[12]

Charles McDowell, who also hailed from southwestern Ontario, moved to the Caron district in 1901. When the Hans' land became available in 1925, he purchased it.[13] By 1927, he had possession of 640 acres but his holdings left him with an $8,000 mortgage in favour of the Toronto General Trusts Corporation.[14] McDowell likely did quite well the following year when average farm income in Saskatchewan reached a new high of $1,614.[15] That same year, the province produced a remarkable one third of a billion bushels of wheat.[16] The average yield rose to over twenty-three bushels per acre and, since worldwide demand was strong, farmers were paid more than $1.00 a bushel.[17] But the good times did not last. What happened next is almost unimaginable.

The 1930s buried prairie farmers under an avalanche of calamities including drought, subsistence wheat prices, choking black blizzards (multiple-day dust storms), drifting topsoil, virulent Russian thistles, grasshoppers, saw flies, army worms, and wheat-rust. Due to a worldwide depression, increasingly punitive tariffs, a glut of overproduction spurred on by a massive increase in farmland and the re-emergence of the Soviet Union as a wheat-exporting powerhouse, the price of wheat collapsed to levels not seen in three hundred years![18] Farmers who managed to produce a crop in 1931 or 1932 found that it sold for a paltry $0.35 a bushel, well below the cost of production.[19] Average farm income descended to an appalling $66 per annum. In 1937, average yields dropped to 2.7 bushels per acre and cash receipts fell to less than eight per cent of what they had been in 1928.[20]

The south-central and southwestern areas of the province (which includes Caron) were particularly hard hit. More than forty-five thousand settlers left the area for more northerly and temperate districts.[21] Not surprisingly, Charles McDowell had little success in reducing the principal on his mortgage. Like many farmers who had accumulated large debts in the heady 1920s, he avoided foreclosure only by governmental intervention. For several successive years, the McDowell family received emergency relief. In 1937, the *Drought Area Debt Adjustment Act* relieved them of the burden of re-paying relief loans and most of their municipal tax arrears.[22] By the early 1940s, Charles McDowell had loans totalling $11,000, a sum roughly equivalent to the value of his land.[23]

Russell Little, McDowell's brother-in-law, owned the parcel to the immediate west, land that would eventually situate the western half of the Caron airbase. Like McDowell, Little hailed from southwestern Ontario and borrowed heavily to finance his operation. By the mid-1930s, he could no longer meet his obligations: his major creditor foreclosed in February 1935. Thus, both halves of the property soon to be occupied by the Caron airbase bear witness to the struggles common throughout the region: McDowell was mortgaged to the hilt and Little's farm was in the hands of an insurance company. To round out the bleak picture, a year or so after the airbase opened, DoT purchased 160 acres to the immediate south of Little's former farm. It too was in foreclosure at the time.

No sooner had the 1930s relaxed their grip on the prairies than the Second World War broke out. McDowell still eked out a living. Little had long-since moved on. The war in Europe would soon become a full-on emergency for Britain and drive most of the RAF's flying training to Canada. Thus, another wave of British migration came to Canada and Caron. This time, the newcomers did not intend to settle, but to train for the defence of their nation and, perhaps, the entire free world.

The fall of France in June 1940 shifted hostilities to the skies over the United Kingdom, which had to face the threat alone since the Americans were in no mood to join and the BCATP could not yet offer the services of a single airman. Within the month, Hermann Goering's *Luftwaffe* attacked the UK from purloined bases along the coasts of France, Belgium, and the Netherlands. The Battle of Britain seemed but a prelude to Hitler's intended invasion once the UK's defences and morale were softened by his relentless air strikes.[24]

While the Battle of Britain raged, the UK War Cabinet pondered ways to alleviate its air training crisis. Ongoing enemy interference impeded the training of the twenty-five thousand or more aircrew it would need each year. (These were in addition to the nineteen thousand per annum expected from Canada once the BCATP reached full capacity.) In a series of memoranda on this urgent matter, Sir Archibald Sinclair, the UK secretary of state for air, made a case for transferring most of the RAF training apparatus to the dominions.

In a 1 July 1940 memorandum, Sinclair reported that emergency changes had been made to the domestic air training scheme. EFTS and SFTS courses had been reduced by one week apiece and the number of recruits had been increased by twenty-five per cent. These measures were expected to swell aircrew output by some thirty per cent. Further, steps had been taken to recruit aircrew from among RAF administrators, recently-arrived Polish air force personnel, and British subjects in other countries. However, in Sinclair's studied opinion, all such measures could not make up for the glaring deficiencies. Most critically, British airspace had become dangerously congested. Although more training aerodromes were urgently needed, they would only add to the confusion and peril. What would happen when the push to gain air superiority was fully realized in the coming years? He concluded that the RAF training organization could only be sustained and expanded by finding "sites abroad to which home schools can be moved or where new schools can be established."[25]

The following month, Sinclair again briefed the War Cabinet on the training situation. Over the past five weeks, conditions had worsened: enemy operations now extended across the entire country; trainees had become targets; training aerodromes continued to be transferred to operational squadrons; severe restrictions had been imposed on night flying exercises; and navigational exercises—which require large areas of open sea and land—had been drastically curtailed. Further, he did not have enough aircrew to operate the three thousand aircraft a month that were beginning to arrive from the United States. The current training scheme could not produce enough aircrew for the imported aircraft, to say nothing of those expected from the rise in domestic production. He estimated that he would have to double the number of pilots and aircrew just to exploit these new resources. He concluded that even with all possible domestic adjustments, transferring schools to Canada or South Africa was imperative.[26]

Although the War Cabinet hesitated to transfer instructors and training aircraft during the height of the battle, the Air Ministry pleaded for a change in policy. As early as 5 June, RAF supply and organization officials called for a "definite [new] policy," knowing full well that a wholesale transfer would require months of planning. The RAF's director of plans advised CAS A/C/M Cyril Newall on 9 July that "every training establishment that we can get out to Canada or the U. S. should be got out."[27] The following day, Newall wrote in favour of a proposal to transfer four SFTSs, along with their equipment, pupils, and staff, to Canada.[28]

The threat to air training in the UK had not been lost on Canadian officials. In May 1940, the Canadian government, acting on the advice of the BCATP's Supervisory Board, informed the UK that Canadian aerodromes were available for transferred RAF schools.[29] On 13 July, the British government indicated its keenness to move four existing SFTSs *en bloc* from the UK to Canada.[30] The Canadian cabinet and CAS(C) A/V/M Lloyd Breadner welcomed the request.[31] Speaking on behalf of the government, Minister Power assured the UK high commissioner that space could be found for this and any other forthcoming request.[32]

The British government acted quickly to take the Canadians up on their offer. It immediately requested the transfer of four SFTSs, two AOSs, one

B&GS, one ANS, one general reconnaissance school (GRS)—that is, a school of maritime patrolling tactics—and one torpedo training school.[33] The Canadian government readily accepted. The UK intended to transfer half of these schools to Canada by the end of 1940.[34] With issues of command and control already resolved by the BCATP, these emergency requests were unobjectionable even to the Canadian prime minister since the transferred schools would operate under the authority of the RCAF.[35]

In a meeting of the BCATP Supervisory Board on 16 August, the British representative, Captain H. H. Balfour, noted that although the UK appreciated Canada's offer, there were no plans to move EFTSs to Canada. Despite Balfour's tactful refusal, the board determined to consider every possible means of reducing Britain's air training burden. Even from afar, careful observers ascertained that the UK's "war front in the air" would soon require every available airfield for combat operations. Primary aircrew training would soon become impossible.[36] Coincidentally, the *Luftwaffe* illustrated the BCATP board's concern that very day when two of its Junkers JU 88 bombers attacked No. 2 Flying Training School at Brize Norton in Oxfordshire. They succeeded in destroying forty-six training aircraft as well as eleven operational aircraft stored in a nearby maintenance hangar.[37]

The UK government agreed that the cost of its transferred schools should be charged to its account.[38] The transfer of the first RAF SFTS began almost immediately. Preparations in Canada went ahead with alacrity.[39] The first site to be occupied by the RAF, near Kingston, Ontario, had been hastily readied by the end of September 1940. The transferred staff moved to Canada in four echelons: as a cohort graduated in the UK, its instructional and support staffs relocated to Canada. By February 1941, the entire school—No. 31 SFTS (RAF)—had been reconstituted at Kingston.[40] By the end of 1940, transferred schools had opened in Moose Jaw, SK (No. 32 SFTS), Carberry, MB (No. 33 SFTS), and Port Albert, ON (No. 31 ANS).[41]

Although the political authorization for the transfer program had not yet been granted, RAF officials continued to plan for it. On 21 July, R. E. C. Peirse, vice-CAS, argued:

> [t]he need for dispersing our Flying Training to Canada and South Africa is in my opinion pressing. . . . [I]t is necessary that we should avoid interference with and damage to our training by enemy action in

> this country. Aircraft on the ground in our crowded Flying Training Schools are very vulnerable, and I do not doubt the enemy will attempt to interfere with training aircraft in the air.[42]

The following day, CAS Newall concurred but noted that there were a host of thorny issues that impeded rapid movement. Besides the extensive planning required for the relocation of the schools, Newall had recently become aware of Canadian concerns that RAF schools would be equipped and manned at the expense of BCATP schools, which were in dire need of many essentials.[43]

Figure 2.2. Winston Churchill's coalition government, 11 May 1940. Archibald Sinclair is standing on the far left. Lord Beaverbrook is seated second from the left. Source: © Imperial War Museum (HU 55505). Used with permission.

Beginning on 20 August 1940, Lord Beaverbrook, the Canadian-born newspaper magnate and member of Churchill's War Cabinet, issued a series of memoranda challenging Sinclair's claim that RAF airbases must be transferred out of the UK. As minister of aircraft production, he well knew the disruption these moves would entail. In his view, the shortage of training aircraft and spares in the UK and the need to send trained technicians abroad to service them made transfer unacceptable. Further, technicians and flying instructors were needed domestically in case of a German invasion: even training aircraft could be pressed into last-ditch service.[44] Further yet, ferrying student pilots and schools back and forth across the Atlantic would leave a gap of two months or more in the output of the transferred schools. And finally, Beaverbrook suggested that more EFTS sites could be found in the UK—at race tracks, for instance.[45]

Over the next two days, Sinclair responded to Beaverbrook's counterarguments. He informed the War Cabinet that the shortage of airframes, aero-engines, and spares was not as acute as Beaverbrook suggested. Many of these crucial items were being manufactured in North America and could be easily diverted to the transferred schools. Further, the BCATP had competent technical staff and repair facilities. Very few repair and maintenance technicians would need to accompany the transferred schools. And finally, the rapid adjustment of the Canadians to the abrupt termination of training aircraft shipments from the UK spoke well of their ability to absorb the additional demands of the transferred schools.

Secretary Sinclair's views were in keeping with those of the Air Ministry he represented. As he drafted his response to Lord Beaverbrook, he benefitted from a paper composed on 21 August by the Air Ministry's director of flying training entitled, "Reasons for the Removal of Pilot and Observer Training from the United Kingdom." The paper argued that navigational, air observer, and general reconnaissance schools would soon cease to operate since they required long distances, which were no longer available in the UK due to enemy action. The paper also noted the compounding effect of bad weather, enemy damage, and the pressing need for additional operational aerodromes. The bedrock reason for the transfer, however, arose from the intractable problems associated with night training. Since only a relatively few aircraft could be airborne at one time during the night, disruptions were insurmountable and cumulative.[46]

In further response to Lord Beaverbrook's reservations, Sinclair argued that most EFTS aerodromes could not be upgraded to SFTS or operational specifications. But even if additional sites could be found, the fundamental, irresolvable problem remained: the UK lacked suitable open airspace for night flying and navigational training. Given the growing intensity of enemy activity, operational requirements would not lessen over the next two years. By that time, there would be no airspace available for training.[47]

On 26 August, Winston Churchill, acting in his capacity as minister of defence, formally weighed in on the relocation issue. He recommended a three-month moratorium on transferring schools due to the dangers of the raging air battle; it would be unwise to transfer pilots, technicians, or machines that might be needed in an emergency. In the meantime, everything should be done domestically to mitigate the training shortcomings. Churchill noted that due to the recent completion of major coastal defence projects, many construction machines were now available to help complete the seventy-five aerodromes under construction. He concluded by calling for a review of the situation at the beginning of November. In the meantime, "the utmost effort must be made to get the training establishments in Canada and South Africa ready as far as possible."[48]

After a lengthy discussion, the War Cabinet approved Churchill's proposal that the RAF schools should stay put until further notice. Notwithstanding, it ordered that a few schools should move as soon as possible. It ordered that one GRS and two AOSs should move immediately to South Africa and one AOS and one SFTS to Canada.[49] In October, Sinclair, Beaverbrook, and Churchill once again exchanged memoranda on the issue. Sinclair requested authority to transfer an additional SFTS to Canada.

Since the aircraft for this latest proposal would be diverted from the United States, no airplanes would be shipped from UK stores. Sinclair's modest proposal called for a mere ten pilots to be sent abroad with the school.[50] Lord Beaverbrook replied, pointing out that the aircraft diverted to Canada were previously destined for the UK and thus should be considered a loss to its supply. Exasperated, he queried: "What is the Training Scheme anyway? Its effect is to add two sea voyages to a man's training term. This involves delay, as well as danger, which could only be justified by a breakdown in the training program in Britain."[51]

By the time that the War Cabinet considered Secretary Sinclair's next memorandum on 15 November, the Battle of Britain was essentially over.[52] Six days later, the cabinet approved his plan to transfer and establish new schools in the dominions.[53] Over the next two years, the RAF transferred or established ten SFTSs, three ANSs, one B&GS, one GRS, four OTUs, and one radio direction finding (radar) school in Canada.[54] Additionally, No. 31 Personnel Depot, which could accommodate eight thousand, arose on the outskirts of Moncton, NB.

Beginning in early 1942, RAF personnel entering or leaving North America passed through this massive facility.[55] Although he did not know it at the time, Sinclair's scheme would soon include six, double-size EFTSs.[56]

Even though the possibility that EFTSs would be transferred to Canada had been politely dismissed by Captain Balfour, by the time Sinclair's program had finally been approved, he and the War Cabinet knew that EFTSs would also have to be transferred to provide local input for their transferred SFTSs.[57] Before the end of 1940, the RCAF indicated its willingness to cooperate with a proposal to send two EFTSs to Canada to supply pupils to the RAF SFTSs that had just opened.[58]

In January 1941, the Air Ministry determined that it would be best to staff its transferred EFTSs with RAF officers and airmen. CAS(C) Breadner had indicated in a recent visit to the UK that the Canadian civilian operating companies were "fully employed" with their BCATP commitments. They likely could do little to assist with operating transferred schools. And although the RAF had no qualms about entrusting EFTSs to civilian operators, it appeared unlikely that UK civilian companies could legally operate in Canada nor were they likely to be able to coax their employees to relocate for this purpose.[59] Thus, it seemed best to plan for all-RAF staffs at the transferred EFTSs.

On 12 February 1941, A/V/M L. D. D. McKean, of the UKALM in Ottawa, informed the Canadian government that the UK would like to transfer two EFTSs by April or May. CAS(C) Breadner replied that two EFTSs could move immediately; permanent facilities would be available shortly. Breadner also suggested that the secondary relief fields (R.2s) attached to SFTSs could be rapidly converted into EFTSs if necessary.[60] Proposals to repurpose R.2s as EFTSs had already been bandied about in the UK.

In a meeting eight days later, the RCAF Air Council considered the implications of the RAF's pending request for EFTSs in Canada. The council requested that CAS(C) Breadner once again inquire into the status of the forthcoming proposal. It also thought it wise to query the UKALM as to the expected aircraft requirements, since engines for Canadian-made Tiger Moths were not available domestically. But, if asked, the RCAF could supply the necessary airframes from Canadian sources.[61] By 15 March, the RAF decided (though it did not communicate externally) that it would match its transferred SFTS capacity with a corresponding EFTS capacity.[62]

The UK government did not formally disclose its full EFTS intentions until June 1941.[63] On 11 June, Minister Power informed his cabinet colleagues that the UKALM had finally made a definite request for an additional sixteen schools including six, double-size EFTSs, six SFTSs, three OTUs, and one GRS. He estimated the total charge to the UK account would be $22,865,000.[64] The immense burden placed on Canadian contractors to provide these new schools on top of their own BCATP construction program (some thirty-one BCATP schools opened in 1941[65]) was somewhat lessened by repurposing existing aerodromes, the redeployment of R.2s, and the double-sizing of the latest EFTSs.

The transferred RAF program would become a major presence in Canada. By the end of 1941, virtually all UK EFTS and SFTS training had been transferred to Canada.[66] As the size of the transfer program grew, several problems surfaced. On the one hand, Canadian authorities were concerned that this new program might get too big and overwhelm the BCATP. On the other hand, they worried that British officials, who were quietly looking to expand into the United States, might shift their interest, energies, and resources southward.

On 26 March 1941, the UK high commissioner reported that the Canadian government rejected the assumption that it is "taxed to the full and cannot contribute anything further." Although it understood that the RAF may have to look to the United States for additional training capacity (and the training aircraft and instructors that only the Americans could provide), Canada should not be overlooked on the basis that it had reached its limit.[67] The Canadians worried that the establishment of schools in Canada was now somehow tied to the establishment of competing facilities in the USA.[68]

In early 1942, the high commissioner reported that Canadian officials were not likely to be receptive to further expansion in the transfer program. They were concerned that the scheme might rival the BCATP if it expanded further. And even though the Canadians might resist RAF expansion in the USA by proclaiming their readiness to do more, the high commissioner believed they may have reached their limit. Since the administrative control of both the BCATP and the transferred schools fell to the RCAF, the immense size of the combined training organization and the lack of senior personnel in the RCAF greatly concerned him. And since the Canadians were reluctant to request additional RAF officers—an act that would signal their incapacity—the situation did not favour further expansion.[69]

By early 1942, the RAF had completed the wholesale transfer of its primary training (and much of its advanced training as well) out of the UK. Although a small part of this transfer landed in South Africa and the United States, the bulk of it came to Canada. The prior acceleration of the BCATP in response to the imminent threat to Britain in the summer of 1940 permitted the Canadians to have it *and* the transferred program fully-operational by the date originally intended for the former. The RCAF now oversaw a combined training program approximately twice the size of that projected in the original BCATP agreement.

Meanwhile back in its cramped offices, DoT continued to evaluate sites for future BCATP and RAF expansion. Given CAS(C) Breadner's advanced notification, A. D. McLean of DoT headquarters informed his district staff in mid-March 1941 that the RCAF had decided that R.2s were no longer necessary.[70] Excellent flying conditions had rendered them superfluous. McLean directed that R.2 sites be visited and considered for other purposes.[71] Over the next few months, regional DoT officials visited their local R.2s and filed reports on their potential redevelopment.

The R.2 at Boharm had its grass airfield and environs inspected in early spring 1941. And since the revised RCAF policy called for a relief airfield for each new double-size EFTS, DoT investigators were compelled to locate a new relief field (R.1) just in case Boharm proved suitable.[72] The search led them to a site some ten miles to the northwest and just east of the village of Caron, a site which turned out to be ideally suited for rapid development. Representatives of DoT urged the ADC to obtain the necessary authority to proceed with "the proposed developments . . . if it was hoped to have more than a few aerodromes available this year."[73]

DoT inspectors compared the relative merits of potential EFTS sites at Caron and Boharm. Both were assessed well before the UKALM made its EFTS intentions known. On 4 April, after a thorough inspection of both sites, an inspector composed a formal comparison of their merits.[74] His analysis favoured Caron. Its site sloped gently to the southwest and would only require moderate mechanical shaping and compacting. Gravel could be easily obtained. It also offered easy access to a major water line just a mile and a half south and a power line two miles to the north (see Figure 2.3).

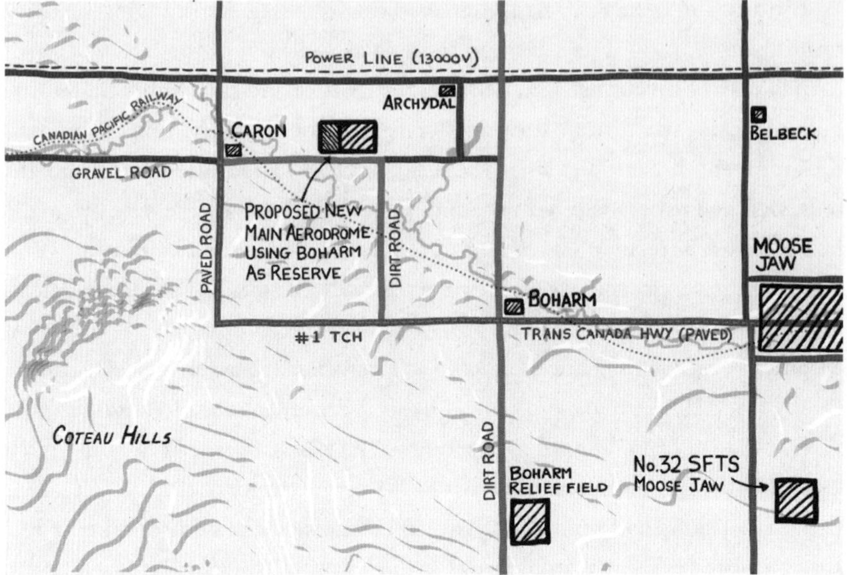

Figure 2.3. DoT sketch of proposed Caron site, 24 April 1941.
Source: DoT, "file 5168-913" (redrawn facsimile).

Based on market prices in the district, the inspector estimated the cost of developing identical EFTS runway systems at both sites. Table 2.1 itemizes his findings. The development costs at Caron were estimated to be about $16,000 less than at Boharm, largely due to the lower cost of transporting gravel. Although these cost comparisons refer to the development of the aerodrome proper, they ignored other major cost differentials. For instance, since Boharm was already owned by the RCAF, there would be no additional cost in acquiring its land. (Early estimates pegged the cost of the land at Caron at $32,000.[75]) On the other hand, the Caron site enjoyed a much better road. The cost to improve Boharm's access road had been previously estimated at $11,870.[76] The cost of supplying water and power were also much lower at Caron than at Boharm. In the end, however, these comparisons were moot since Boharm's poor drainage made its development and future expansion impossible.[77]

Table 2.1

DoT cost estimates for Caron and Boharm, spring 1941

Item	Amount	Unit Cost	Caron Total	Boharm Total
Removing trees, stumps and rocks			Nil	Nil
Shaping & consolidating subgrade	100,000 sq. yards	$0.05 per yard	$5,000	$5,000
6" consolidated gravel base for runways	33,000 tons	Caron: $1.10 ton Boharm: $1.40 ton	$36,300	$46,200
Primer @ 0.5 gallons per sq. yard	50,000 gallons	$0.13 per gallon	$6,500	$6,500
Primer application (labour)	50,000 gallons	$0.02 per gallon	$1,000	$1,000
2" crushed hot top	11,000 tons	Caron: $2.20/ton Boharm: $2.55/ton	$24,200	$28,050
Asphalt @ 4.5%	100,000 gallons	$0.11per gallon	$11,000	$11,000
Hot mixed seal	1,750 tons	Caron: $2.55/ton Boharm: $2.90/ton	$4,500[78]	$5,075
Asphalt for seal @ 7.5%	30,000 gallons	$0.11 per gallon	$3,300	$3,300
Subtotals			**$91,800**	**$106,125**
10% contingency			$9,180	$10,612
Totals			**$100,980**	**$116,737**

DoT regional staff drew up a *Memorandum of Preliminary Investigation for RCAF Airport Sites* on 24 April. In addition to the information contained in the initial field report, the preliminary report added the following. The land at Caron was appraised at $50 per acre. Fifty thousand gallons of water per day could be obtained from the City of Moose Jaw's nearby eighteen-inch water line. The site also had especially favourable drainage due to its uniform but modest slope and preponderance of sandy loam. In the words of the report, it was "naturally suited for rapid development."[79] DoT recommended that the aerodrome and its building area occupy the McDowell and Little farms and straddle the dirt road which ran between them.

By the time that official approval came, site preparations were well under way at six RAF EFTS sites.[80] The time pressures were enormous, especially if these facilities were to be completed before the end of the construction season. In a 30 June (1941) letter to the deputy minister of national defence for air, C. P. Edwards, the deputy minister of transport, assured his colleague that all six EFTSs would be completed by the end of the year. In the case of Caron, he expected that the final approval and awarding of contracts would take about two months. Beyond that, three more months would suffice to complete the project. He inferred, accordingly, that by 15 November the facilities at Caron would be complete.[81]

On 8 July, the ADC officially considered a recommendation from the minister of transport that a RAF EFTS be developed at Caron. It would be double-size and designed to accommodate 180 student pilots. The proposal itemized the estimated costs as per Table 2.2.[82] The aerodrome expenses (which did not include the cost of buildings, equipment, and supplies) were estimated at $393,100 and were to be charged to the RAF as per the recent agreement. The ADC approved the proposal. Three days later, the chair forwarded the committee's decision to the minister of national defence for air for his approval.[83] Construction began within a month.

Table 2.2

DoT cost estimates for Caron aerodrome, July 1941

Item	Cost
Land purchase	$32,000
Grading, smoothing, seeding, etc.	$65,000
Drainage	$55,000
Construction of hard-surfaced runways & taxi strip	$170,000
Construction of taxi strip (alternative plan) & hangar aprons	$38,000
Water supply	$15,000
Revolving beacon	$1,300
Removal of local telephone line crossing airport	$2,000
Removal of Trans-Canada Telephone's lines	$800
Power sub-station (125 kilowatt)	$5,000
Power line, two miles	$3,000
Power distribution system on airbase proper	$6,000
Total	**$393,100**

Endnotes

[1]This saying is attributed to the German statesman, Helmuth von Moltke (1800–91), by the *Little Oxford Dictionary of Proverbs*, ed. Elizabeth Knowles (New York: Oxford University Press, 2009), 284.

[2]See *Henderson's Moose Jaw Directory 1941* (Winnipeg: Henderson's Directories, 1941), 31.

[3]James Macmillan received his surveyor's commission on 19 May 1881. His 1882 contract specified that he survey ten townships, encompassing 360 square miles, roughly centred on present-day Caron. See John S. Dennis, *A Short History of the Surveys Performed Under the Dominion Lands System 1869–1889* (Ottawa, 1892), 96, 65.

[4]J. A. Macmillan, "Letter to E. Deville, Chief Inspector of Surveys, Ottawa," The Dominion Lands Surveyor Series, in R-183, file I. 322, PASK.

[5]See Pierre Berton, *The Last Spike: The Great Railway 1881–1885* (Toronto: McClelland & Stewart, 1971), 112. See also Omer Lavallée, *Van Horne's Road: The Building of the Canadian Pacific Railway*, 2nd ed. (Calgary, AB: Fifth House, 2007), 81–92.

[6]*The Papers of the Palliser Expedition 1857–1860*, ed. Irene Spry (Toronto: Champlain Society, 1968), 9, 18. Professor Hind, who toured the area at approximately the same time, shared Captain Palliser's appraisal. He concluded that the southwestern region of present-day Saskatchewan was unsuited for agriculture. He argued that a fertile crescent at the northern edge of this arid region was eminently suitable for agriculture and best suited as a route for the proposed cross-continental railway. See Henry Youle Hind, *Narrative of the Canadian Red River Exploring Expedition of 1857 and of the Assiniboine and Saskatchewan Exploring Expedition of 1858*, 2 vols. (Edmonton, AB: Hurtig, 1971), 2:234.

[7]Palliser and Hind's characterization of the prairies echoed the judgement of American explorers who visited the Great Plains south of the Canadian border a generation earlier. In 1806, Zebulon Pike influentially dismissed the plains as a great sandy desert comparable to the Sahara. On the map accompanying the official report of his 1819–1820 expedition, Stephen Long labeled the area: "Great American Desert." Although John Frémont and Joseph Nicollet nuanced these dismissive characterizations, the notion that the land west of the Mississippi was virtually uninhabitable (except for buffalo and Indigenous peoples) would exercise a prolonged influence on the general view. See Tom Chaffin, *Pathfinder: John Charles Frémont and the Course of American Empire* (Norman, OK: University of Oklahoma Press, 2014), 65–66.

[8]Irene Spry, introduction to *The Papers of the Palliser Expedition*, cvx.

[9]David Sauchyn's work is described in Curtis R. McManus, *Happyland: A History of the 'Dirty Thirties' in Saskatchewan* (Calgary: University of Calgary Press, 2011), 233–34.

[10]*Township General Registers*, PASK.

[11]Some 4,400 other Saskatchewan settlers entered their homestead during the year ending October 1889. See Dept. of the Interior, *Supplement to Homestead Maps of Manitoba, Saskatchewan and Northern and Southern Alberta* (Ottawa: Dept. of the Interior, 1916), 11.

[12]*Township General Registers,* PASK. A copy of the Dominion of Canada certificate is in the author's possession.

[13]*From Buffalo Trails to Blacktop: A History of the R.M. of Caron #162* (Regina: Print Works, 1982), 276.

[14]*Saskatchewan Certificate of Title,* No. 167TT, 12 December 1927. A copy of the land title is in the author's possession.

[15]N. W. Powell, et al., *The Report of the Royal Commission on Dominion—Provincial Relations: Canada 1867–1939* (Ottawa: Queen's Printer, 1954), 194.

[16]See McManus, *Happyland,* 118.

[17]James H. Gray, *Men Against the Desert* (Saskatoon, SK: Western Producer, 1970), 56.

[18]William A. Mackintosh, *Economic Problems of the Prairie Provinces* (Toronto: Macmillan, 1935), 188, in Blair Neatby, "The Saskatchewan Relief Commission, 1931–34," *Saskatchewan History* 3, no. 2 (Spring 1950): 41n2. See also Timothy Egan, *The Worst Hard Time: The Untold Story of Those Who Survived the Great American Dust Bowl* (Boston: Houghton Mifflin, 2006), 59.

[19]George. E. Britnell, *The Wheat Economy* (Toronto: University of Toronto Press, 1939), 72.

[20]Gray, *Men Against the Desert,* 56.

[21]Donald G. Matheson, "The Saskatchewan Relief Commission 1931–1934: A Study of the Administration of Rural Relief in Saskatchewan During the Early Years of the Depression" (master's thesis, University of Saskatchewan Dept. of History, 1974), 26.

[22]This program also reduced the interest rate on mortgages to six per cent, cancelled all unpaid mortgage interest and penalties through 1934 and translated unpaid mortgage interest from 1935 and 1936 into the principal of the loan. This debt consolidation may well account for why Charles McDowell's mortgage principal was higher in 1941 than in 1927. See George. E. Britnell, "The Saskatchewan Debt Adjustment Programme," *The Canadian Journal of Economics and Political Science* 3, no. 3 (August 1937): 370–71.

[23]McDowell's total indebtedness ($11,000) is mentioned in a letter from CNR land commissioner, G. G. Baird, to Mr. F. Thomas, DoT, on 18 October 1941. Commissioner Baird also indicated in a letter to Mr. Thomas on 5 August 1941 that the total assessed value of Charles McDowell's land was $11,600.00. See DoT, "file 5168-913," vols. 1 & 2, in RG12, file 2345, LAC. A hand-written notation on a site plan prepared for DoT also indicates that McDowell's four quarters of land were assessed at $11,650.00. His total indebtedness as of 31 May 1941 was $10,809.02. "[Caron, Saskatchewan—Dept. of Transportation, RCAF Aerodrome, EFTS]," RG30, box 13808, LAC [Winnipeg, MB].

[24]John Keegan, *The Second World War* (New York: Penguin, 1989), 91, 93.

[25]Archibald Sinclair, "Royal Air Force Training," 1 July 1940, The Cabinet Papers 1915–1982, in CAB 66/9/18, UKNA, http://www.nationalarchives.gov.uk/cabinetpapers.

[26]Archibald Sinclair, "Royal Air Force Training," 7 August 1940, The Cabinet Papers 1915–1982, in CAB 66/10/36, UKNA, http://www.nationalarchives.gov.uk/cabinetpapers.

[27]Air Ministry, "Transfer of RAF Flying Training," in AIR 8/376, UKNA.

[28]Ibid.

[29]Letter dated 20 May 1940, in Hatch, "BCATP," 198.

[30]Secretary of state for dominion affairs to the [Dominion of Canada] high commissioner, 13 July 1940, AIR 46/8, UKNA, in Hatch, *Aerodrome of Democracy*, 61.

[31]The Canadian government accepted this initial request no later than 15 July. See 18 July 1940 telegram from the secretary of state for dominion affairs to the UK high commissioner in Ottawa, in AIR 46/8: "Training Schools—Move from UK to Canada," UKNA.

[32]UK high commissioner in Canada to the secretary of state for dominion affairs, 19 July 1940, in Hatch, *Aerodrome of Democracy*, 61.

[33]"Report of the chief of the air staff [to the members of the BCATP Supervisory Board]," 5 August 1940, in 73/1558, 11, DHH.

[34]Thomas Inskip, secretary of state for dominion affairs, "Reports for Month of July 1940 for the Dominions, India, Burma and the Colonies, Protectorates and Mandated Territories," 17 August 1940, The Cabinet Papers 1915–1982, in CAB 68/7/6, UKNA, http://www.nationalarchives.gov.uk/cabinetpapers.

[35]UK officials understood the political sensitivities surrounding RAF operations in Canada. Sore spots had been made abundantly clear in the negotiations leading to the BCATP agreement. For that reason, they proposed a group of four SFTSs as a "feeler." It was understood that they would follow-up with a request for the transfer of four more SFTSs if the feeler was favourably received. See "Notes of the 12th Meeting Held on Wednesday, 17th July, 1940," 1, in AIR 20/1379: "Empire Air Training Scheme Committee Minutes 1939–45," UKNA.

[36]"Supervisory Board—BCATP. Minutes of Meetings," in RG24, vol. 5231, LAC.

[37]By early 1941, enemy attacks on training aircraft had become routine. In the period between February and May of that year, fourteen training aircraft were attacked, most of them at night. See AIR 20/2956: "Enemy Attacks on Training Aircraft," UKNA.

[38]The secretary of state for air's Empire Air Training Scheme Committee conceded that "financial responsibility for these establishments [transferred schools] would be accepted by the United Kingdom Government." In the end, the transfer program cost $100 million. See "Empire Air Training Scheme Committee Minutes," 17 July 1940, 2, in AIR 20/1379: "Empire Air Training Plan Committee Minutes 1940–1945," UKNA.

[39]On 12 October 1940, the *Moose Jaw Times-Herald* announced the transfer of four RAF SFTSs to Canada. The Air Ministry's press release, on which this account was based, suggested that eight or more schools might ultimately be transferred. The press release affirmed the RAF view at the time that "[n]o elementary flying schools are being moved to Canada." A little over a month later in his address to Parliament on 18 November 1940, Minister Power indicated that he had the permission of the UK government to announce that the first transferred school had arrived in Canada. He was keen to point out that all transferred schools would be paid for by the British

government but would operate under the control of the RCAF. See *Dominion of Canada Official Report of Debates House of Commons*, 18 November 1940, vol. 1, 176.

[40]Air Ministry, *Notes on the History of RAF Training 1939–44*, 135, in AIR 20/1347, UKNA.

[41]See Air Ministry, "Code Names of Transferred Schools," 3, in AIR 20/1370: "Empire Air Training Scheme: Training Schools," UKNA. To avoid confusion with BCATP schools, the transferred RAF schools were assigned numbers ascending from 31.

[42]Air Ministry, "Transfer of RAF Flying Training."

[43]Ibid.

[44]"The trainer aircraft are our last reserve. In the last and decisive hour of battle, they might be decisive indeed." Lord Beaverbrook, in A. J. P. Taylor, *Beaverbrook: A Biography* (New York: Simon & Schuster, 1972), 427.

[45]Lord Beaverbrook, "Memoranda by the Minister of Aircraft Production," 20 August 1940, The Cabinet Papers 1915–1982, in CAB 66/11/3 and CAB 66/11/6, UKNA, http://www.nationalarchives.gov.uk/cabinetpapers.

[46]"Training Progress, July–Dec. 1940," in AIR 19/175, UKNA.

[47]Archibald Sinclair, "Memoranda to War Cabinet," 21 and 22 August 1940, The Cabinet Papers 1915–1982, in CAB 66/11/7 and CAB 66/11/8, UKNA, http://www.nationalarchives.gov.uk/cabinetpapers.

[48]Winston S. Churchill, "Training of RAF Pilots," 26 August 1940, The Cabinet Papers 1915–1982, in CAB 66/11/18, UKNA, http://www.nationalarchives.gov.uk/cabinetpapers.

[49]"Minutes of the War Cabinet," 30 August 1940, The Cabinet Papers 1915–1982, in CAB 65/14/27, UKNA, http://www.nationalarchives.gov.uk/cabinetpapers.

[50]Air Ministry, "Transfer of RAF Flying Training."

[51]Ibid.

[52]Keegan, *The Second World War*, 102.

[53]"Minutes of the War Cabinet," 21 November 1940, The Cabinet Papers 1915–1982, in CAB 65/10/13, UKNA, http://www.nationalarchives.gov.uk/cabinetpapers.

[54]Stacey, *Arms, Men and Governments*, 570. Operational training units (OTUs) were introduced by the RAF in 1938. Previously, pilots had moved directly from their advanced training (SFTSs) to squadrons conducting operations against the enemy. OTUs provided an intermediary stage. They furnished aircrew with training on specific operational aircraft and relieved fighting squadrons of the burden of providing on the job training for inexperienced aircrew. The RCAF was keen to host RAF OTUs. In the end, the RAF agreed to transfer some of its OTUs to Canada, in part because graduates could ferry aircraft from American factories to the UK on their trip home. See Hatch, *Aerodrome of Democracy*, 74.

[55]Gilbert S. Guinn, *The Arnold Scheme: British Pilots, The American South and the Allies' Daring Plan* (Charleston, SC: History Press, 2007), 198–99.

[56]It had been long understood by the Air Ministry that its advanced schools in Canada would require a corresponding EFTS feeder system in the same country. See, for instance, Air Ministry, "Memorandum on the Possibility of Increasing Training Capacity in Canada for the Royal Air Force," 2 September 1939.

[57]Archibald Sinclair, "Royal Air Force Training," 15 November 1940, The Cabinet Papers 1915–1982, in CAB 66/13/27, UKNA, http://www.nationalarchives.gov.uk/cabinetpapers.

[58]Telegram from UK high commissioner in Canada to the Air Ministry, 7 December 1940, in AIR 46/9: "Training Schools Transfer from UK to Canada," UKNA.

[59]Air Ministry telegram to the UK high commissioner in Canada, 23 January 1941, in AIR 46/9: "Training Schools Transfer from UK to Canada," UKNA.

[60]"Transfer of RAF Units for Training in Canada," in RG24, vol. 5173, LAC. On 21 February 1941, the RCAF Air Council approved a policy that reduced SFTS relief field requirements to one. See "Minutes of the Special Meeting of the Air Council," 21 February 1941, 8 in "Conferences, Conventions and Meetings—Air Council Meetings—28 November 1940–16 May 1941," in 96/124, box 6, file 2, DHH.

[61]"Conferences, Conventions and Meetings—Air Council Meetings—28 November 1940–16 May 1941," in 96/124, box 6, file 2, DHH.

[62]Air Ministry, *Notes on the History of RAF Training 1939–44*, 135.

[63]Fred Hatch indicates that the UKALM revised the number of additional schools to 9 SFTSs, 15 EFTSs, 10 AOSs, and 4 OTUs. This request appears in the 24 February 1941 correspondence between A/V/M McLean of the UKALM and Alfred G. R. Garrod, UK AMT. It did not, however, issue immediately in a formal request to the Canadian government. See Hatch, *Aerodrome of Democracy*, 67.

[64]"Dept. of National Defence for Air—BCATP—RAF Schools," in RG2, vol. 28, LAC.

[65]Hatch, *Aerodrome of Democracy*, 67.

[66]"Apart from one SFTS fed by one EFTS, there was no pilot training carried out in the UK after the end of 1941." See *History of Flying Training*, Part II, in AIR 32/14, UKNA.

[67]"Transfer of RAF Flying Training."

[68]"Notes of the 31st Meeting Held on Friday 28th March 1941," 5, in AIR 20/1379: "Empire Air Training Scheme Committee Minutes of Meetings, Jan. 1940—October 1945," UKNA.

[69]Air Ministry, Telegram from the UK high commissioner in Canada, 10 March 1942, in AIR 20/1825: "Canada—Transfer of Flying Training Schools," UKNA.

[70]Later that same year (1941), A. D. McLean would be awarded the McKee Trophy for his meritorious service in the advancement of aviation in Canada. Not only had he made a major contribution to the stupendous task of preparing aerodromes for the BCATP, but he had previously served as acting superintendent of airways and airports. See Ellis, *Canada's Flying Heritage*, 348, 366.

[71]A. D. McLean, "Letter to District Inspectors and Engineers, 15 March 1941, 1 in "Conferences and Committees—Interdepartmental—Aerodrome and Projects Development Committee," in RG12, vol. 368, LAC.

[72]McLean mentioned the new RCAF policy in a March 1941 letter. The relevant passage reads: "Future EFTS aerodromes are to be considered as full size schools each with a relief aerodrome." See A. D. McLean, "Letter to District Inspectors and Engineers, 15 March 1941, 1 in "Conferences and Committees—Interdepartmental—Aerodrome and Projects Development Committee," in RG12, vol. 368, LAC.

[73]"Dept. of National Defence Aerodrome Development Committee BCATP and Home War Establishment," minutes dated 13 May 1941, in "Conferences and Committees—Interdepartmental—Aerodrome and Projects Development Committee," in RG12, vol. 368, LAC.

[74]Document dated 4 April 1941 in DoT, "file 5168-913."

[75]Although this cost would prove much too high in the end, it was the amount set before the ADC when it approved the development of the Caron site. See "Dept. of National Defence Aerodrome Development Committee BCATP and Home War Establishment," minutes dated 8 July 1941, in "Conferences and Committees—Interdepartmental—Aerodrome and Projects Development Committee," in RG12, vol. 369, LAC.

[76]"Dept. of National Defence Aerodrome Development Committee BCATP and Home War Establishment," minutes dated 9 January 1941, in "Conferences and Committees—Interdepartmental—Aerodrome and Projects Development Committee," in RG12, vol. 368, LAC.

[77]DoT understood that its civil aerodromes should be sited in locations that permitted the expansion of runways up to 5,000 feet. Even though a limit of 1,800 or 3,000 feet might be necessary in some circumstances, the possibility of future expansion up to 5,000 feet was a major consideration. See Dominion of Canada, *Air Regulations 1938*, 83.

[78]The DoT inspector rounded this figure up. The actual amount is $4,462.50.

[79]Document dated 24 April 1941, in DoT, "file 5168-913."

[80]In a brief article on 8 May 1941, the *Moose Jaw Times-Herald* not only announced the school's location east of Caron but also that government inquiries had been made regarding acquiring 25,000 gallons of water per day from the city of Moose Jaw, which owned the nearby waterline.

[81]Document dated 30 June 1941, in DoT, "file 5168-913."

[82]Document dated 8 July 1941, in DoT, "file 5168-913."

[83]Document dated 11 July 1941, in DoT, "file 5168-913."

CHAPTER 3

Preparing Caron

Knowledge and timber shouldn't be much used until they are seasoned.[1]
—American Proverb

Throughout the late summer and fall of 1941, DoT, its partners, and contractors hastily built the Caron aerodrome, acquired its property, and resolved several compensation issues. The RCAF's Directorate of Works and Buildings (DW&B) concurrently planned its buildings, saw to their timely construction and, like DoT, responded to last-minute modifications. The RAF also had its share of tasks as it prepared to supply its six, double-sized EFTSs with staff and student pilots. No sooner had these preparations come to fruition than a surprise change in management roiled Caron's operations.

DoT's earliest sketch plan of the Caron aerodrome designated a site one half mile east of its final location (see Figure 2.3).[2] By June 1941, DoT planners had come to favour an adjacent site that required a portion of Charles McDowell's land, the former Little farm, and the dirt road that ran between them. Judging by their internal memoranda, DoT and CNR officials did everything possible to preserve McDowell's livelihood and farm buildings, despite many inconveniences. The former Little property could be handled much more easily since it no longer operated as a family farm. Issues surrounding the acquisition of the dirt road would not be resolved for almost two years.

By 24 June, DoT produced a plan that straddled and incorporated the dirt road. It preserved much of the McDowell farm, including a generous parcel to the north of the runway system and an additional seventy acres, including his farm yard, south and east of the same. However, since the dirt road would be closed, the plan landlocked the most northerly portion of McDowell's farm. And since all parties found this unacceptable, DoT recommended that a thirty-foot strip be left along the eastern edge of the runway system to allow McDowell access from the south. Despite the obvious complications, the CNR land commissioner believed that these accommodations were necessary and appropriate.[3] The formal papers filed on 11 September gave DoT title to the former Little farm (320 acres), two hundred acres of McDowell's land and the road running between them.[4] A month later, Charles McDowell agreed to this arrangement, being "very keen" to keep the northern parcel in his possession.[5]

Public tenders were never issued for the construction of the aerodrome at Caron. Prior arrangements had been made with the Evans Gravel Surfacing Company of Saskatoon, a company known to be reliable, capable, and suitably equipped. On 6 August, its workers and subcontractors entered the Caron site and commenced operations.[6] The contract, which would not be ratified for another six weeks, required that Evans shape, grade, and consolidate the entire aerodrome, erect a fence around the perimeter, and install a runway drainage system complete with manholes, pipe drains, and shoulder ditches. In addition, the company would install a six-inch, consolidated gravel base for the runways, prime the compacted gravel, and apply a 2" bituminous hot mix top and seal. DoT estimated the cost at $235,000.[7]

No sooner had the Caron aerodrome been approved than proposals to modify it (and its sister RAF EFTSs) began to appear. The first proposed revision, which came before the ADC on 22 July, called for a modification to the runways. Since EFTSs use the grass turf within their triangular runway system for takeoff and landing practice and they were now called upon to support double-size schools, DoT believed that it was imperative to increase the size of the interior turfed area. No. 2 Training Command (Winnipeg) recommended that this area be enlarged by pushing the runways out three hundred feet and connecting their former intersections with narrow taxiways. DoT estimated that Caron could be modified accordingly for $22,500. The ADC concurred and forwarded its recommendation to the minister for his approval.[8]

Figure 3.1. Evans' paving crew, fall 1941, Caron. Source: Author's collection.

Figure 3.2. Evans' construction camp, fall 1941, Caron. Source: Author's collection.

The original plan for the Caron aerodrome included $14,000 for a 125-kilowatt power supply and distribution system. Recent additions to the facilities and increased night flying operations elevated the expected demand to 230 kilowatts. This increase required substantial upgrading to the entire system including the supply line, substation, and transformers. On 19 November 1941, the ADC considered DoT's recommendation that a total of $27,000 be allocated for an enlarged power system at Caron. The committee approved and noted that the additional cost should be charged to the RAF.[9]

Caron's DoT projects continued through the fall. On 5 December, C. P. Edwards, deputy minister of transport, reported that the airfield was practically finished.[10] The two-inch hot mix had been laid and the runways were mostly sealed. The backfilled stone in the shoulder ditches had been treated with one coat of liquid asphalt; the final coat would be applied in the spring. The perimeter and interior of the airfield had been sown to grass.[11] The transmission and distribution power lines were almost complete. The water line would be completed by 1 December and the telephones two weeks later.[12] Mr. Edwards optimistically projected that all buildings would be finished by 1 December, except for those recently added to the plan. It seemed that Caron would open, as scheduled, on 5 January 1942.[13]

Retrofitting Caron to meet new demands continued. One of the first upgrades after the commencement of operations called for the installation of a telephone switchboard system. By late March 1942, the ADC had received a proposal from DoT to provide expanded telephone services including a common battery-type switchboard and trunk lines to Moose Jaw and the village of Caron. The committee approved the project at a cost of $2,370.[14] By late June, the ADC once again heard about the need for expanded telephone facilities at Caron (and elsewhere). This time, DoT proposed a telephone service linking the main aerodrome at Caron to its relief field at Boharm. The ADC concurred and authorized that the $1,540 expense be charged to the RAF.[15]

Beginning in the summer of 1942, several road improvement projects were recommended to the ADC by DoT. The dirt road to the Boharm airfield had been a continuing concern. At least two, $10,000 proposals to improve it had been broached. In early July 1942, the ADC considered a new $7,000 proposal to grade, drain, and gravel the approximately ten miles of dirt road that connected Boharm with its main aerodrome in Caron. It approved the request.[16]

Two final major projects were carried out by DoT in response to the changing operations at EFTSs. The night flying program at Caron placed considerable demands on its facilities and personnel. Although Boharm did not need power to illuminate its airfield or flight path (the latter only required flare pots), it did need electricity for the staff and equipment operating at the site. In mid-September 1943, DoT formally requested that electrical power be supplied to the Boharm airfield. The proposed line ran seven miles from the National Light and Power generating facility in Moose Jaw to the airfield at Boharm. The ADC concurred, charging the $5,900 expense to the BCATP.[17]

The RCAF's replacement of the de Havilland Tiger Moths with Fairchild Cornells in early 1943 exacerbated the problem of inadequate outdoor parking. These new aircraft were larger than the Moths and more were needed to support the increased number of student pilots. On 28 September 1943, the ADC reviewed a recommendation from DoT that additional parking and taxiing space be provided at Caron. DoT recommended cement-concrete for the new parking areas since it could better withstand extreme heat and spilled fuel.[18] Since significant grading, drainage, and surfacing work were required, the projected cost came to $69,000. The ADC approved.[19]

DoT originally estimated the cost for aerodrome-related projects at Caron at $393,100. In the end, this estimate closely matched the actual cost. Table 3.1 compares the projected and actual DoT costs as well as the cost of projects not included in the original proposal. Several entries require further comment. First, the grading, drainage, runway, and taxiing systems were initially estimated at about $93,000 more than the actual costs. Given the experience of DoT with similar projects, this sizable variance is puzzling. Further, the original proposal made no mention of water and sewer systems. For some reason, these expensive components were overlooked, although they had been part of the site plan from its earliest days. Most of the other additional expenses arose from the expansion of the EFTS program and could not have been foreseen.

Table 3.1

Estimated and actual aerodrome costs, Caron, 1941–43

Item	Estimate	Actual Cost
Land purchase (680 acres)	$32,000	$18,500
Grading, smoothing, seeding, etc.	$65,000	
Drainage	$55,000	
Construction of hard-surfaced runways & taxi strip	$170,000	
Construction of taxi strip & hangar aprons	$38,000	*$235,000
Expanded runway configuration		$22,500
Water supply	$15,000	$14,718
Revolving beacon	$1,300	$1,300

Item	Estimate	Actual Cost
Removal of local telephone line crossing airport	$2,000	$2,000
Re-routing Trans-Canada Telephone line	$800	$6,000
Power sub-station (125 kilowatt)	$5,000	
Power sub-station (230 kilowatt)		$18,000
Power line, two miles	$3,000	$3,000
Power distribution system on airbase proper	$6,000	$6,000
Power supply to R.1 at Boharm		$5,900
Water & sewer systems		$36,382
Easements		$85
Road improvements		$7,000
Crop/land damage claims		$1,925
Telephone upgrade, phase one		$2,370
Telephone upgrade, phase two		$1,540
Parking upgrade, partially completed (estimate)		$20,000
* includes grading, drainage, runways, taxi strips		
Totals	**$393,100**	**$402,220**

Once the primary land acquisitions had been settled, DoT had to settle several related property matters. Easements for the water and sewer works had to be arranged for the land that lay between the aerodrome and the water line to the south. Several claims for crop and other damages also needed to be settled. And finally, permission had to be obtained from the provincial highways department to close the dirt road, which now bisected the aerodrome.

As it turned out, DoT had to negotiate easement agreements with four property owners. Ernest McBride, who owned one of the parcels bisected by the water line, readily agreed to a twenty-foot easement for a single payment of fifty dollars.[20] It took longer to acquire an easement across Henry Muhle's land since he was a patient at the mental hospital in Weyburn, SK.[21] By 3 November, Arthur Spohn, the administrator appointed to oversee Muhle's affairs, agreed to an easement in the amount of twenty-five dollars.[22] By the time DoT reached an agreement for the third easement in early 1942, the rural municipality of Caron owned the property; it agreed to a token payment of ten dollars.[23] Acquiring an easement for the most northerly portion turned out to be the most complicated. Not only did the water line cross the property but the sewage treatment facilities were located on it as well. In the middle of negotiations, the North British and Mercantile Insurance Company foreclosed on the parcel. By spring of the following year, the company agreed to sell it to DoT for five-hundred dollars.[24]

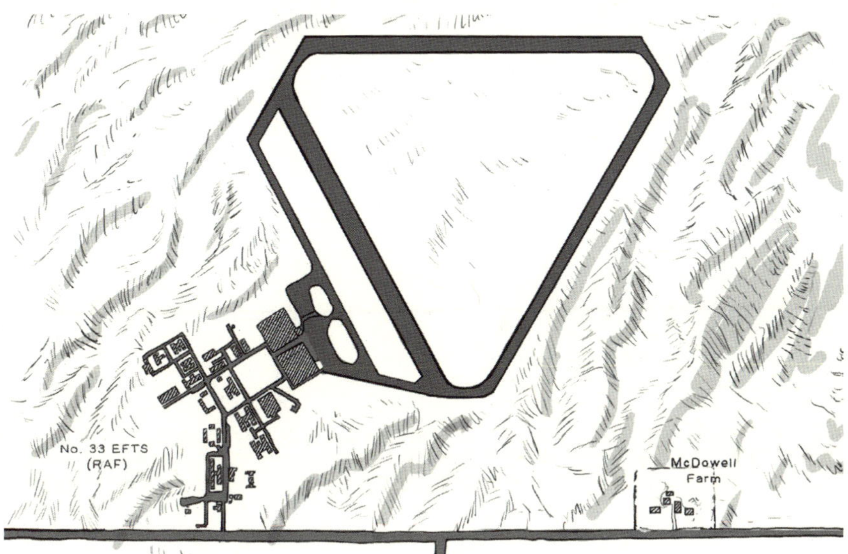

Figure 3.3. Final aerodrome plan, Caron. Source: DoT, "file 5168-913" (redrawn facsimile).

Compensating local farmers for damages also fell to the lot of DoT. Its investigation revealed that its contractors had rushed onto the site and ran roughshod over crops and ploughed fields. When the crews entered the land leased by Guy Clemens, they instructed him to swath his immature wheat. No sooner had he done so than they buried half of it with their earth-moving equipment and blanketed the rest with surveyors' stakes.[25] Charles McDowell received similar treatment. Here too, the contractors entered his land and forced him to cut his immature crop. They even burned a portion of it so that they could immediately commence grading operations.

When informed of the details, Commissioner Baird once again championed the interest of the farmer. He believed Clemens' claim. Not only had he lost his crop but his labour in summer fallowing an additional one hundred acres had been wasted due to the actions of the contractors. On 3 November, Guy Clemens agreed to eight-hundred dollars in compensation for his ruined crops and lost labour.[26] Commissioner Baird also sided with the resident DoT engineer in recommending that Charles McDowell be paid $325 for his losses.[27]

In a letter dated 28 February 1942, Philip Yates registered the final compensation claim. He noted that seventy acres of his crop had been trampled by surveyors and other workers with vehicles. He sought $280 in compensation.[28] Yates had an even more pressing complaint. In closing the dirt road, DoT had blocked his egress to the south. He sought five-hundred dollars in damages. DoT knew it would be difficult to find a basis in law for awarding road-access damages. But even if compensation could be offered, Yates had creditors who were entitled to a portion of the proceeds.

The CNR solicitor informed Commissioner Baird on 11 December that the power to close roads lay solely with the provincial highways department. The federal DoT had no such authority. Any claim that Mr. Yates might have to compensation arising from the road closure appeared to fall within the jurisdiction of the provincial government. By 18 December, Commissioner Baird believed that the best solution would be to simply pay the claim. He hesitated, however, when he considered the legal claims Mr. Yates' creditors had on compensation paid to him. By 9 January 1943, Baird believed that it was best to let Mr. Yates and his creditors "fight it out" as to their respective shares.

In early June (1943), Mr. Yates received word from DoT that it would pay him only if his creditors signed off on the deal. On 12 July, Commissioner Baird reported that final arrangements had been made. On 23 August 1943—a full two years after the road closure and crop damage—Privy Council authorized that Philip Yates be compensated for his loss of property value, inconvenience due to the road closure, and crop losses.[29]

Two years prior to the development of Caron, the DW&B, in conjunction with the Dept. of Munitions and Supply's Defence Construction Projects Branch, had hastily developed specifications, plans, and siting principles for BCATP, RCAF, and home defence facilities. R. R. Collard, former vice-president and general manager of one of Canada's most respected construction firms and now head of the DW&B, immediately enlisted some of the best engineering talent in the

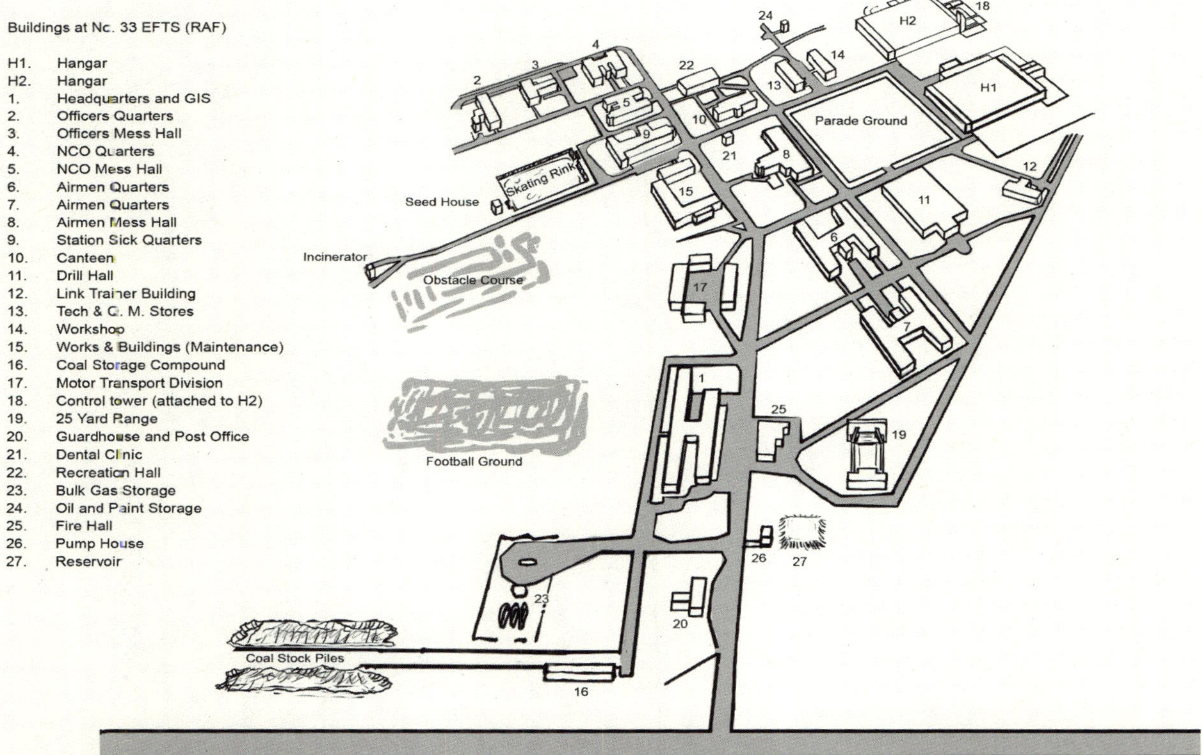

Figure 3.4. Buildings and identification numbers, Caron. Source: DoT, "file 5168-913" (redrawn facsimile).

dominion including those with experience in the layout, design, and assembly of wood, steel, and concrete structures as well as those capable of designing a great variety of heating, power, water and sewage, fuel oil distribution and storage, and refrigeration systems.[30] The RAF's Captain Balfour aptly summarized the design philosophy: "simplicity, adequacy, but no luxury."[31]

Once a suitable site had been identified by DoT, the DW&B's design staff oriented the main runway by directing its long axis into the prevailing wind. Fortunately, the Trans-Canada Airway had already conducted multi-year studies of wind direction and intensity at many western Canadian locations. The designers oriented the main runway (NW–SE) at Caron based on data gathered at nearby Moose Jaw.[32] The main runway now served as a baseline for the building area and the standard siting principles developed by the DW&B.

Since most of the airbase buildings in western Canada were constructed of wood, designers were deeply concerned about the spread of fire. Taller buildings had to be placed further apart given the greater risk posed by their elevated rooftops. Whereas one-storey buildings could be situated sixty feet apart, two-storey buildings had to be no less than one-hundred feet or, in the case of hangars, 150 feet apart. Buildings containing flammable or toxic fluids could be no less than one-hundred feet from adjacent buildings; above-ground gasoline storage units could be no closer than five-hundred feet from adjacent buildings.[33]

R. R. Collard aptly articulated an additional principle of site planning in evidence at Caron. "The generally accepted principle in laying out schools and designing buildings is that the officer quarters should be kept separate and distinct from the quarters of other ranks for the purpose of discipline."[34] This principle is clearly in evidence in the placement of the various residences, mess halls, and other amenities at Caron.[35] Like most RAF facilities, Caron had separate facilities for airmen, non-commissioned officers (sergeants), and officers.[36] Caron's site plan placed the officers quarters and mess hall at the extreme northwestern edge of the building area.[37]

The function of a building determined its location. Hangars were grouped together near the runways; parade grounds were adjacent to drill halls; canteens were in proximity to recreation halls, and mess halls were close to their respective barracks. Maintenance and motor vehicle buildings were clustered around their respective courtyards. Guardhouses, which also contained holding cells and post offices, were located just inside the main gate. Oil and paint storage buildings were situated near the workshops. And the tiny hose reel houses were naturally located near the fire hydrants.

Throughout the first years of the war, the number of requisite buildings at EFTSs had grown dramatically. In a speech before Parliament on 13 June 1940, the acting minister of national defence, listed the *seven* buildings necessary to support EFTSs at that time (see Table 3.2). These tiny schools, with their forty-eight students, were scarcely comparable to their successors. By 1942, the new, double-size elementary schools were fully five times the size of the originals, both in terms of facilities and student pilots under training.[38]

Table 3.2

Initial EFTS facilities requirements, BCATP, 1940

Building	Number
Hangar (112' by 160')	1
Airmen quarters	1
Officers and NCOs mess/quarters	1
Ground Instructional School	1
Mechanical transport section	1
Tech. and quartermaster stores	1
25-yard range	1

By late July 1941, eight qualified firms had been invited to submit bids for the erection of buildings at Caron. In late August, Smith Bros. & Wilson (Regina) had been unofficially awarded the $514,277 contract.[39] Due to the press of time and "the military urgency of the moment," they commenced their work well before signing the contract.[40] As was often the case, changes were introduced between the original tender and the final contract. (A complete list of the buildings and related facilities erected at Caron can be found in Appendix A.) The buildings called for in the contract were to be completed by 20 October 1941, an unimaginably aggressive deadline. Appendix A itemizes the supplementary contracts that were added to the original contract. In the end, these new projects, totalling some $197,840, added about forty per cent to the cost of DW&B projects at Caron.

Since steel could not be acquired during the war, most BCATP hangars and drill halls relied on Douglas fir structural components. The design of these superstructures, with their distinctive W-shaped cross supports, had been adapted from the Warren truss system, which had been used on wooden bridges in the United States for a century. The specifications for these large hangars included one-hundred-foot spans and a roof system rigid enough to resist snow loads and violent air pressure changes.

By the mid-1930s, the Timber Engineering Company (TECO) of Washington, DC had acquired the rights to a German invention, the split-ring connector. This simple device greatly increased the strength and rigidity of the superstructure joints. After the timbers were laid out in a templated pattern, holes were drilled through their intersections. Two- or four-inch circular slots were bored out around the drilled holes and TECO split-rings were pressed into the grooves. When the bolt compressed the entire joint, the split-ring lodged in the matching grooves in the adjoined timbers.[41] This simple device greatly increased the load-bearing capacity of timber superstructures by spreading the forces across the entire surface of the joint. It also prevented the joints from slipping when they inevitably shrank in the dry prairie air.[42]

Figure 3.5. Hangar No. 1 (background); drill hall (foreground), fall 1941, Caron. Source: Author's collection.

Once the rafter and support-post assemblies were bolted together, they were erected with cranes. In the case of a double-landplane hangar, like Hangar No. 1 at Caron, each of these bolted assemblies were over two-hundred feet long and about thirty-five feet high. After they were erected, and their support posts bolted to the footings, they were cross-braced until the side panels, fascia, and roof decking could be installed. This erection system did not require a great deal of skill and could be learned quickly. Wilf Crosbie, who helped assemble the hangars at Caron, recalled that his status as a carpenter arose from the fact that he knew how to hold a hammer.[43]

Figure 3.6. Assembling drill hall, fall 1941, Caron. Source: Author's collection.

Several important facilities were added to Caron in late 1941. Well after construction began, the Dept. of Munitions and Supply recommended that Smith Bros. & Wilson (Regina) provide a recreation hall (building no. 22), a bulk gasoline storage system (building no. 23), and a gasoline dispensing system (pump and underground tank) at the motor transport garage (building no. 17).[44] Since Smith Bros. & Wilson were still on the site, they were invited to undertake these new projects. As usual, Privy Council acquiesced in their $28,340 bid.[45]

Although not part of the original plan, the DW&B erected a fire hall across the street from the headquarters/GIS building in December 1941.[46] (Fire halls were not typically specified for EFTSs prior to this time.) The fire hall at Caron seems entirely typical of these new installations and included two bays for firetrucks, a workshop, an office with a coded fire alarm panel, a hose-drying room, a washroom/shower, a recreational room, and an open barracks.[47] Because the lumber for the fire hall had been shipped from BC when still wet, it arrived in Caron as a frozen agglomeration. Hank McDowell, who hauled it to the airbase from the train station, recalled that it took some doing to break it apart for transport.[48]

By late spring 1942, plans were underway to upgrade the de Havilland Tiger Moths with mono-wing Fairchild Cornells. In June of the same year, the ADC considered the accommodation needs of this new airplane. It seemed that each double-sized EFTS would now need at least two double-size hangars. By October, the Dept. of Munitions and Supply had entered into negotiations to provide extra hangar accommodation at Caron.[49] P. W. Graham & Sons of Moose Jaw won a contract for $51,484 to construct an additional one-half, double-landplane hangar.[50]

As the Caron airbase rose from the prairie in the fall of 1941, Canadian lumber shipments surpassed all previous levels. Timber companies on the west coast of BC shipped some seven million board feet every week. An article in the *Vancouver Sun* noted that the CPR—one of four railways transporting lumber—shipped an astounding 616 carloads of lumber in the week ending 20 September. Approximately half of this lumber hailed from old-growth forests on Vancouver Island. The reporter noted in astonishment that some of the Douglas fir timbers were sixty feet in length, sixteen inches square, and entirely knot-free. Many of these shipments were destined for army camps and airbases on the prairies.[51]

In the fall of 1942, it became clear that BC timber would not be available for up to five months.[52] All projects that relied on Douglas fir or Sitka spruce would be delayed. Despite the urgent demand, sawmill production in Canada declined as the war progressed. The departure of several thousand forestry workers who volunteered for overseas service with the Canadian Forestry Corps significantly reduced the skilled workforce.[53] To keep the timber moving, the federal government granted a special priority to the lumber industry and endeavoured to persuade prairie farmers to spend a winter working in the western forests. It even recalled a portion of the Forestry Corps to assist in domestic lumber operations.[54]

None of these provisions improved the prospects for a timely timber delivery at Caron. The BCATP Supervisory Board heard discouraging reports throughout the winter of 1942–43. In December, it learned that only one hangar a week should be expected. (By comparison, hangar deliveries occurred at the phenomenal rate of one per day in 1940–41!) The contractors at Caron would have to wait until spring or even summer to erect the hangar addition.[55] As late as August 1943, the board learned that extremely wet conditions and a shortage of workers would only add to the delay. The hangar addition at Caron was only ten per cent complete by early June.[56]

While it awaited the completion of its hangar extension, Caron received approval for additional storage and refrigeration accommodation. It, along with several other EFTSs, had experienced a food crisis during a period of prolonged poor weather. As it stood, the tiny storage facilities at the enlarged EFTSs could only hold enough foodstuffs for a single day! On 7 June 1943, the BCATP committee authorized new storage accommodation for all EFTSs distant from the nearest supply depot.[57] It would be late November before the storage depot at Caron would be ready for use—a mere six weeks before its training operations were suspended.[58]

Rapid improvements were made to the accommodations at Caron when news came that male and female civilians would be living on site beginning in spring 1942. Renovations to the airmen barracks closest to the mess hall (building no. 6) included the construction of a lounge, recreation room, and canteen for the female staff. Given the significant cost of these improvements, it is likely that further amenities, including private or semi-private rooms and partitioned washrooms, were also included in the project.[59] The cost of these renovations was pegged at $29,766—more than fifty per cent of the original cost of the building itself.[60]

The summer of 1942 saw several other proposals intended to improve facilities at RAF and BCATP sites.[61] On 11 August, the Works and Buildings Committee of DND recommended improvements in the postal accommodations at RAF EFTSs. Since double-size elementary schools now supported between 180 and 240 trainees, to say nothing of their permanent RAF and civilian staffs, the guard houses (building no. 20) were proving to have inadequate postal accommodations. Further, there were no washroom facilities for the largely female staff now operating the post offices. Although these modifications were approved, they were not carried out at Caron before it disbanded.

As preparations at Caron proceeded with all haste, the RAF assembled a staff for No. 33 EFTS (RAF). Its members would arrive in the Caron district in early December 1941 after a two-week journey. Contrary to some overly optimistic reports, the airbase needed a great deal of work before the RAF contingent could occupy it and welcome the first cohort of students in early January. The final section of this chapter recounts some of their earliest experiences at Caron and the rather surprising news that came in mid-May.

Herbert Vernon Peters was born in Streatham, South London on 9 October 1912. As a young adult, he worked as a taxation officer for the Somerset County Council before volunteering for the Royal Air Force. The air force released Peters into the RAF volunteer reserves due to colour blindness, which disqualified him from pilot or observer training. He was ordered to report to No. 4 Reception Centre in Bridgnorth on 7 February 1941. While on leave, he married Vera Cottrell. Later that fall, he wrote his new bride from RAF Padgate (No. 5 Personnel Dispersal Centre) while he completed his training and awaited posting to Canada.

In late August 1941, the Air Ministry officially established No. 33 EFTS (RAF). Its initial staff consisted of thirty-two officers and 304 airmen of other ranks. It would be equipped with fifty-six Fairchild 19A aircraft, with another eighteen held in reserve.[62] As a double-size school, it would concurrently train four cohorts of forty-five student pilots. The staff assembled at Padgate left Britain in late November. Just prior to departure, No. 33 EFTS (RAF) was redirected from Assiniboia, SK to Caron because the former could not be readied in time.[63]

Vernon Peters, and the rest of his Caron-bound colleagues, left Padgate on the evening of 20 November. Other RAF personnel who were also headed to Canada joined them for the train ride north to Scotland. Gerald Roberts kept a diary of the journey.[64] Their train departed at about midnight and travelled uneventfully until it stopped abruptly at Belford. Word soon spread that just a few miles ahead in Berwick-upon-Tweed the previous train had been machine-gunned by a German air raid. Many of the houses in the small hamlet had also been severely damaged.[65] After a sobering look at the damaged rail cars, Peters and his colleagues proceeded to Edinburgh, Glasgow, and the port of Gurock at Greenock. There they were ferried out to the *Pasteur* then taking on some 4,100 army, navy, and air force personnel bound for Canada.[66]

After breaking free of the Scottish coast, the *Pasteur* turned west towards North America. The North Atlantic seas were very rough; even this large ship pitched and rolled constantly, her sturdy frame heaving and groaning as waves crashed across the decks. Rumour had it that her stabilizers had been removed to make additional room.[67] Partway through the journey Peters (and Roberts) learned that the famous British scientist, Sir Julian Huxley, was aboard. In a letter to his wife, Peters noted that he knew Huxley from the BBC program, *The Brains Trust*.[68] They finally docked at Halifax on 2 December after ten days at sea.

Figure 3.7. Pilot Officer H. Vernon Peters, June 1943.
Source: Sylvia Lindridge collection. Used with permission.

Many of the RAF personnel who landed at Halifax made their way north to No. 31 Personnel Depot in Moncton, NB where they were typically given a few days leave. After a brief stay, most would be posted to one of the RAF training centres in Canada or the United States. The No. 33 EFTS contingent had no such luck: they were immediately hustled aboard a westbound train. Their four-day trip ended abruptly in Moose Jaw, SK on 6 December, a full two weeks after their departure from the UK. When they arrived, they learned that the facilities at Caron were not ready.

The following day, the No. 33 group met their new commanding officer, Wing Commander A. N. Worger-Slade. Worger-Slade, who had been born in London, ON, had gone to England in 1928 to join the RAF.[69] After a stint with the air force, he flew with Sir Alan Cobbam's air circus and with the government of India's Civil Aviation Directorate. When he returned to England, he took up charter flying and private instructional work. At the outbreak of the war, Worger-Slade had been recalled to active duty and served at several air training schools in the UK. In May 1941, he arrived in Canada as the chief ground instructor (CGI) at No. 31 EFTS (RAF) in De Winton, AB.[70] Within six months, he received a promotion and orders to take charge of Caron.

Later that same day, CO Worger-Slade, the equipment officer, and several airmen moved to Caron. Over the next ten days, working parties of No. 33 personnel commuted to Caron to assist the advance party already in residence. Vernon Peters described their rather inauspicious start:

> So we came to Caron. A bleak, uninviting, hopeless expanse of dreariness, icebound and snowbound as far as eye could reach. Workmen were still labouring to complete the camp, and the barracks blocks were mere shells of timber framing. There was no place to put our heads, and we perforce returned to Moose Jaw nightly to sleep.[71]

The first few weeks were challenging. The ground school's classrooms, which had the luxury of pot-belly stoves, became the temporary headquarters. Disorganization reigned: piles of *matériel* and paperwork were strewn about. Even the weather refused to accommodate: the temperature dropped to -15°F on the night of 9 December. Perhaps Peters had that night in mind when he later recalled that during their first days at Caron the glue and ink froze solid and had to be thawed on the stoves.

By 17 December, about fifty RAF personnel had moved to the base. Since only the NCO barracks had heat, it served as the common dormitory for all ranks. The NCO mess became the communal eating centre and housed a temporary medical clinic. The following day Peters wrote his wife indicating that he too had moved to Caron. He also reported that a bus ran to Moose Jaw for a roundtrip fare of $0.72 (the fare would soon be reduced to $0.60).[72] At least he wouldn't be stranded! By 20 December, the entire RAF staff resided at Caron.

During that same eventful month, the de Havilland Company crated and shipped more than fifty 82C Tiger Moth aircraft from its plant in Toronto, ON to No. 10 Repair Depot in Calgary, AB.[73] The Canadian model of this British aircraft had been modified for local conditions and featured a two-piece cowling, enclosed cockpit, wheel brakes, a tail wheel (in place of the standard tail skid), and a cockpit heating system.[74] After the staff at Calgary assembled and tested the aircraft, pilots from Caron ferried them four hundred miles east to their new base. By the end of December, twenty-one units had arrived in Caron where the local staff logged an additional two-hundred flying hours readying them for training operations.[75]

On 23 December, a group of pilots attached to No. 33 EFTS (RAF) departed Calgary for Caron aboard five new Tiger Moths. Five miles west of Medicine Hat, AB P/O Reginald Littlewood broke formation and descended into the inviting South Saskatchewan River valley. At 13:10, he struck a high-tension power line, which killed him instantly.[76] P/O Littlewood left behind his parents, his wife, Alysse, and a son.[77] His colleagues laid him to rest in the Caron municipal cemetery four days later.[78] The board of inquiry convened to examine the circumstances leading to his death would later conclude that Littlewood's "deliberate unauthorized low flying" caused his fatality.[79]

Vernon Peters recalled that the people of Moose Jaw and Caron were exceptionally generous to these "strangers in their midst" that first Christmas. Many airmen enjoyed dinners in private homes. The officers also pitched in and served Christmas dinner for all ranks. The newly-opened canteen hosted an impromptu concert "of extremely local talent" the following evening. The canteen would continue to serve as the primary centre of after-hours activity until spring when the recreation hall finally opened.

The new year found all parties labouring under less than ideal conditions. Most buildings were incomplete—many would not be finished until spring. Even the canteen would not have its dark oak and cream trim applied until early March.[80] The parade ground was little more than "a heap of rubble."[81] The spring thaw would soon expose the sorry state of the roads and walkways. Even the weather did its best to interfere with final preparations. On several occasions during the first ten days of January, the overnight temperature dropped to -30°F. During the day, the temperature rarely exceeded 0°F.[82]

Eighty-nine student pilots, dubbed course no. 40, arrived on 8 January. Leonard Smith recalled that they de-trained at the small railway station in the village of Caron just after dark. Lacking mechanized transport, they marched two miles east to the aerodrome. That evening they enjoyed a superb supper and immediately noticed that there was no shortage of meat, butter, or eggs. After eating, they got their first full night of sleep in three weeks. The following morning, they awoke to the "huge mantle of prairie sky" and the total absence of trees.[83]

An event in the early spring left an indelible impression on many at Caron. On 17 April, a frightening dust storm blew across the aerodrome and surrounding region. The official record in the *Daily Diary* indicates that the cloud of choking dust rose to a height of 4,000 feet and reduced visibility to nil. Flying operations were suspended. And although the storm was a far cry from the "black blizzards" of the preceding decade, it furnished a lasting memory for those new to the prairies. The *Daily Diary* reported that the administrative offices had to be dusted three times that day; each dusting removed a thick layer of wind-borne material.

By the end of April, Caron reached full operating capacity with an established strength of 56 Tiger Moths (plus 18 in reserve), 29 officers, 92 NCOs, 357 airmen of other ranks, 11 civilians, and 180 pilot trainees. Most buildings were complete; even the glutinous spring mud had released its final captives.[84] Even with seven or eight days of unsatisfactory weather, the flying instructors and students logged 3,522 hours in the air, more than double January's total. Yet, unbeknownst to all, big changes were afoot.

Within two weeks, everything would be tossed into the air. Vernon Peters later recounted that they were seated around the radio on 11 May when the following announcement stunned them: "A civilian company has arrived in the city to take over No. 33 EFTS at Caron." Peters continued:

> A strange man in civvy clothes appeared at the main guardroom and demanded admittance, saying that he was there to take over. Confusion reigned. There were hurried conferences among the senior officers. Interviews with the press. Strange men and women began to arrive in queer [civilian] uniforms and depart again as soon as they learned there was no accommodation on the camp for them. Four mysterious freight-cars were noted standing in the siding at Caron.[85]

It appears that not even the senior officers at Caron had been informed of an impending management change. Many decades later, SGT "Jock" (Robert) Brown recalled that "consternation reigned."[86] The *Moose Jaw Times-Herald* prognosticated on what this might mean and pointed out that railway cars were not only biding their time in Caron but further west in Swift Current as well. It also reported that civilian personnel from Boundary Bay, BC, Peters' "strange men and women," had taken up lodging in Moose Jaw hotels, the YMCA, and the YWCA.[87]

On 15 May, CO Worger-Slade could finally and officially inform his staff that No. 33 EFTS (RAF) would be broken up and its personnel dispersed. The civilian staff from the former No. 18 EFTS in Boundary Bay were ready to take over in ten days.[88] Vernon Peters vented his frustration in a letter to his wife that evening.

> Everyone, from the CO down, is wandering around looking thoroughly lost and fed-up... It is rotten when you get used to a dump like this, make up your minds to make the best of it, succeed up to a point and get towards making a rattling good home of the place, all the entertainments and games and fun organized for spare moments, and then BANG out of the blue you get the boot.[89]

Despite their disappointment, Peters and his RAF colleagues had little time for self-pity. They had to work "at full pressure" to get everything ready for takeover. Everyone surmised that the RAF staff would be split up and posted away.[90] Only the student pilots could expect to stay and complete their courses under the new management.[91]

Although it was by no means apparent at Caron, the RAF had compelling reasons to civilianize its Canadian EFTSs. First, it desperately needed its tradesmen back in the UK. Turning these tasks over to Canadian civilians would alleviate the escalating domestic crisis. Second, civilian-run EFTSs had worked well in the UK, and they were apparently working well in the BCATP too. Third, many of the flying instructors at Caron were overqualified as elementary instructors. At least five had seen operational duty in the Battle of Britain—several earning distinctions—and some thirty per cent were very experienced pilots.[92] Placing elementary training in civilian hands would allow them to serve at more advanced schools or even return to operations. And finally, this transfer would put the experienced staff from No. 18 EFTS to good use. The management team from Boundary Bay, which had operated the largest EFTS in Canada, would soon be asked to expand Caron up to a category-leading 240 student pilots.

Vernon Peters acquiesced in the fact that he had been selected to stay behind to clean up the place. Nevertheless, he and his good friend, F. F. Le B. Crankshaw, both of whom had done so much to get things going at Caron, were deeply saddened. As expected, over the next few days many of the original cohort were transferred to other RAF bases in Canada. Since the Boundary Bay group had brought some of its own aircraft, even the Tiger Moths were being shuttled here and there, into and out of storage. On the eve of the new civilian era, Peters found out that he too had been transferred to No. 33 ANS (RAF) near Hamilton, Ontario.[93]

Endnotes

[1]Mid-nineteenth-century American proverb, in *Little Oxford Dictionary of Proverbs*, 200.

[2]Sketch, dated 24 April 1941, in DoT, "file 5168-913."

[3]In a 5 August 1941 letter, Commissioner Baird insisted that access to this northern portion be preserved since it was by far the best parcel on McDowell's farm. In fact, it was appraised at ten times the value of the sandier land at the southern end of his holdings. James Macmillan's 1882 characterization of the Caron township nicely describes McDowell's portion of it: "The soil changes from clay to sand." See G. G. Baird, CNR land commissioner, to Mr. F. Thomas, DoT Real Estate Branch, 5 August 1941, in DoT, "file 5168-913."

[4]The Imperial Life Assurance Company readily accepted the $25.00 per acre ($8,000 in total) offered for the former Little farm. See document dated 21 August 1941, in DoT, "file 5168-913." Charles McDowell was compensated at the rate of $50.00 per acre. His price reflected the superior productive value of his land plus the fact that the residual value of the rest of his land had been adversely affected by the removal of this choice 200-acre portion. See letter from CNR Land Commissioner Baird to DoT, dated 18 October 1941, in DoT, "file 5168-913."

[5]McDowell would not receive a penny of the $10,000 purchase price. By the end of the 1930s, the balance of his mortgage in favour of the Toronto General Trusts Corporation came to approximately $11,000. After several months of negotiations with the government and McDowell, the trust company agreed to accept $10,000 as payment in full. Although he lost two hundred acres of productive land in the deal, at least and at last, McDowell was debt-free. See document dated 8 October 1941, in DoT, "file 5168-913."

[6]Guy Clemens mentioned this start-up date in his letter of complaint to the CNR land commissioner. See document dated 20 September 1941, in DoT, "file 5168-913."

[7]"PC 7496," 25 September 1941, in RG2, vol. 1732, LAC.

[8]Document dated 22 July 1941, in DoT, "file 5168-913."

[9]Document dated 21 November 1941, in "Conferences and Committees—Interdepartmental—Aerodrome and Projects Development Committee," in RG12, vol. 369, LAC.

[10]Letter to S. L. de Carteret, deputy minister of national defence for air, 5 December 1941, in "Airports & Airharbours [*sic*]. Construction and Maintenance—Aerodrome Development: RCAF Training Centres," in RG12, vol. 1836, LAC.

[11]Hank McDowell sowed the turf grass seed into a snow cover in the (very) late fall. See Hank McDowell, interviews by the author, Moose Jaw, SK, 4 June, 7 June, 20 August 2010.

[12]In late August 1941, DoT, through the agency of the Dept. of Munitions and Supply, solicited bids for the water and sewer works at Caron. In late October, Privy Council approved the bid of R. B. MacLeod of Saskatoon for $36,382.50. MacLeod was given a mere forty working days to complete the water distribution and sewage system. A separate contract for the supply line from the city of Moose Jaw water pipe (about 1.5 miles to the south) was subsequently awarded to the Saskatoon Contracting Company. It called for the installation of a six-inch pipe. See "PC

8230," 24 October 1941, in RG2, vol. 1735, LAC and "PC 8634," 7 November 1941, in RG2, vol. 1736, LAC.

[13]By 11 December 1941, this revised opening date appears in the record as the establishment date. See document dated 11 December 1941, in "Airports & Airharbours [*sic*]. The first group of student pilots arrived on 9 January and began their training two days later. See *Daily Diary*, No. 33 EFTS (RAF).

[14]Document dated 26 March 1942, in "Conferences and Committees—Interdepartmental—Aerodrome and Projects Development Committee," in RG12, vol. 370, LAC.

[15]Document dated 25 June 1942, in "Conferences and Committees—Interdepartmental—Aerodrome and Projects Development Committee," in RG12, vol. 370, LAC.

[16]Document dated 7 July 1942, in "Conferences and Committees—Interdepartmental—Aerodrome and Projects Development Committee," in RG12, vol. 371, LAC.

[17]Document dated 14 September 1943, in "Conferences and Committees—Interdepartmental—Aerodrome and Projects Development Committee," in RG12, vol. 373, LAC. By this time, expenses at the RAF airbases were charged to the BCATP account. The May 1942 renewal agreement stipulated that commencing 1 July 1942, the UK would pay a fixed percentage of the combined air training costs.

[18]This change in policy in favour of cement-concrete for parking areas is still apparent in the apron in front of the 1943 addition to Hangar No. 2 at Caron(port).

[19]Document dated 28 September 1943, in "Conferences and Committees—Interdepartmental—Aerodrome and Projects Development Committee," in RG12, vol. 373, LAC. Even though this work was authorized, very little was carried out before No. 33 EFTS (RAF) closed in January 1944.

[20]Ernest McBride, 8 October agreement, in DoT, "file 5168-913."

[21]This is confirmed in a 22 January 1942 letter from G. G. Baird, CNR land commissioner, in DoT, "file 5168-913." Based on data in the 1906 and 1916 censuses, Muhle would have been eighty-three years of age in 1941.

[22]3 November agreement, Thomas Spohn on behalf of Henry Muhle, in DoT, "file 5168-913."

[23]6 February 1942 acceptance, the RM of Caron, in DoT, "file 5168-913."

[24]1 April 1942 acceptance, the North British and Mercantile Insurance Company, in DoT, "file 5168-913." See also the 9 April 1942 letter from G. G. Baird to Col. F. F. Clarke, CNR chief land surveyor, in this same file.

[25]Letter in DoT, "file 5168-913."

[26]See documents dated 24 November 1941, 16 December 1941, and 26 December 1941, in DoT, "file 5168-913."

[27]See documents dated 2 March 1942, 4 April 1942, 17 April 1942, 13 May 1942, and 15 May 1942 in DoT, "file 5168-913."

[28]Letter, dated 28 February 1942, in DoT, "file 5168-913."

[29]Documents related to this compensation case can be found in DoT, "file 5168-913."

[30]"History of Construction Engineering," 2, AIR 74/20, DHH.

[31]H. H. Balfour, "Report to the [UK] Secretary of State," 10 September 1940, in AIR 19/469: "Empire Training Scheme. Report by the Under Secretary of State," UKNA.

[32]The main runway at Regina (some 95 kilometres east of Caron), which had been used by the Trans-Canada Air Lines and later, by the BCATP and the Regina International Airport, has an identical NW–SE orientation.

[33]See "Conferences and Committees—Interdepartmental—Aerodrome and Projects Development Committee," in RG12, vol. 372, LAC.

[34]R. R. Collard, memo to AMT, in "General Policy Re: Works and Bldgs.—BCATP," in RG24, vol. 4778, LAC.

[35]The RCAF policy allotted twice the floor space for officers as for airmen in both their sleeping quarters and mess halls. See "Accommodation—Policy Governing," in RG24, vol. 4782, LAC.

[36]Canadian air force personnel were put off by the strict separation of ranks in the RAF. David Bashow argues that Canadians were much more comfortable with their American and Australian colleagues who were more egalitarian and who ate at shared mess halls and had a stronger predilection for all-ranks social functions. See Bashow, *No Prouder Place*, 87.

[37]The siting principles at Caron, namely, the airmen closest to the airfield, the NCOs further away, and the officers at the greatest distance, were widely followed by the RAF at the time. The typical RAF airbase layout is associated with Sir Edwin Lutyens, one of the UK's foremost architects, who played an important role in standardizing site plans in the mid-1930s. See John James, *The Paladins: A Social History of the RAF up to the outbreak of World War II* (London: Macdonald, 1990), 168–73.

[38]The new 'D' class EFTSs (like Caron) were rightly denominated double-size. They were twice as large as the EFTSs called for in the original BCATP agreement. At the commencement of the BCATP, the Flying Clubs Association pressed the Canadian government to reduce the original EFTSs by half, that is, to forty-eight students, in order to accommodate the wishes of its twenty-two members. 'D' schools such as Caron were designed for 180 students but were soon expanded to accommodate 240. This meant that the expanded 'D' schools were five times as large as the first generation EFTSs.

[39]"Formal Contract. Smith Bros. & Wilson, Ltd., Regina, Sask," in RG28, vol. 402, LAC. It wasn't until 10 September 1941 that Privy Council formally authorized this contract. See "PC 7095," 10 September 1941, in RG2, vol. 1731, LAC.

[40]"PC 7095."

[41]J. E. Myer, *Fabricating TECO Timber Connector Structures* (Washington, DC: Timber Engineering Co., 1942), 1–5.

[42]Almost from the beginning, the bolts in the hangar and drill hall trusses at Caron (and elsewhere) had to be tightened as the timber dried and shrank. Hank McDowell recalled crawling around in the hangar superstructure tightening loose bolts. He was required to attach a cord to his wrench

so that it wouldn't fall and damage the aircraft beneath. Strangely, no such precaution was taken for his own safety! Hank McDowell, interviews by the author, Moose Jaw, SK, 4 June, 7 June, 20 August 2010. Beginning in 1942, large contracts were issued to repair the trusses in BCATP hangars. See "Works and Buildings, RCAF. Financial Encumbrances—Policy Governing," in RG24, vol. 4770, LAC and "Progress Report No. 55 by the Chief of the Air Staff to the Members of the Supervisory Board, BCATP," Monday, July 17, 1944, 2, in AIR 20/1408: "Empire Air Training Scheme Committee," UKNA.

[43]Wilfred Crosbie, interview by the author, Caronport, SK, 26 May 2010.

[44]The addition of a recreation hall at Caron corresponds to the addition of the same at No. 23 EFTS in nearby Davidson. Likely the increased size and rural location of these enlarged EFTFs warranted the decision. See "Recreation Hall Added to Airport," *Regina Leader-Post*, 17 October 1941, 3.

[45]"PC 9572," 9 December 1941, in RG2, vol. 1741, LAC.

[46]Very few official records exist for the Caron fire hall. The cost of its development is derived from government sources at the end of the war where its original cost figure is mentioned.

[47]"History of Construction Engineering," n.p.

[48]Hank McDowell, interviews by the author, Moose Jaw, SK, 4 June, 7 June, 20 August 2010.

[49]"Progress Report No. 35 by the Chief of the Air Staff to the Members of the Supervisory Board, BCATP," Monday, November 16th, 1941, 2, in AIR 20/1376: "Empire Air Training Scheme Committee, 1942," UKNA.

[50]"PC 11250," 16 December 1942, in RG2, vol. 1785, LAC.

[51]"Greatest Lumber Shipments Ever," *The Vancouver Sun*, 27 September 1941, 31.

[52]"Supervisory Board—BCATP. Minutes of Meetings," 16 November 1942, in RG24, vol. 5232, LAC. This information was provided to the Supervisory Board by the CAS(C). See "Progress Report No. 35."

[53]G. W. Taylor, *Timber: History of the Forest Industry in B.C.* (Vancouver: Douglas, 1975), 159.

[54]Dept. of Trade and Commerce, "The Influence of the War on Forestry," in *Canada Year Book 1945* (Ottawa: King's Printer, 1945), 268.

[55]"Supervisory Board—BCATP. Minutes of Meetings," 21 December 1942 and 18 January 1943, in RG24, vol. 5232, LAC.

[56]"List of RCAF Constr projects underway 1 Sep 42 to 1 Jun 43," in 181.005 (D 80), DHH.

[57]"Works & Buildings RCAF. Financial Encumbrances—Policy Governing."

[58]*Daily Diary*, No. 33 EFTS (RAF), 25 November 1943.

[59]A site plan produced after Caron disbanded indicated that these barracks had been upgraded to "civilian NCO class accommodations" for both males and females. See DoT, 1941 site plan for No. 34 EFTS, amended 1944.

[60]"List of RCAF Constr projects underway 1 Sep 42 to 1 Jun 43."

[61]In addition to post office improvements mentioned in this paragraph, plans were drawn up to convert drill halls into major entertainment centres. The most elaborate of these proposals included lean-tos added to both sides of the long axis of the building as well as a two-storey lean-to within the building itself. The new space was carefully laid out to include a padre's office, lecture rooms, gaming rooms, officer and airmen showers, an equipment storage room, office for the educational officer as well as an officer lounge and a public reading room. It is not clear that anything this elaborate was ever constructed even though it was recommended to the UKALM at a cost of $40,000. See "Works & Buildings, RCAF. Drill Halls, Construction & Maintenance of—Policy Governing," in RG24, vol. 4764, LAC.

[62]This American-made monoplane would not see service at Caron. In its place, the de Havilland Tiger Moth, model 82C, would be sent to Caron.

[63]Document dated 17 September 1941, in "Transfer of RAF Units for Training in Canada," LAC. No. 33 EFTS (RAF) was redirected to Caron by Secret Organization Order No. 27. In his report in December 1941, the CAS(C) informed the BCATP Supervisory Board of the switch. See "Progress Report No. 24 by the Chief of the Air Staff to the Members of the Supervisory Board, BCATP," Monday, December 15th, 1941, 3, in AIR 20/1376: "Empire Air Training Scheme Committee, 1942," UKNA.

[64]Gerald Trevor Roberts, "Going Overseas: A Diary," in British Broadcasting Corporation, *WW2 People's War*, http://www.bbc.co.uk/history/ww2peopleswar/stories/98/a4119798.shtml.

[65]According to Derek Sharman, Berwick-upon-Tweed was subject to eleven air raids, the last of which took place on 10 February 1942. As a result of these raids, 25 lives were lost, 47 were injured, 25 houses were demolished, and some 1,000 houses were damaged. See *Berwick at War 1939–45: The experience of a North East coastal town* (self-published, 1995), 19.

[66]Peters and Roberts shared their transport ship with about eight hundred student pilots drafted into the Arnold scheme. This program funneled RAF student pilots into American primary (elementary) air training schools. After a short stay in Moncton, NB, Robert's group (class SE-42-G) proceeded to Maxwell Field, Alabama, for an acclimatization course and then to primary schools scattered throughout southeastern USA where they would train alongside American counterparts. See Guinn, *The Arnold Scheme*, 199, 529, 533.

[67]See the memoirs of George Stewart at http://www.aircrewremembered.com/stewart-george-lowe.html.

[68]Vernon Peters to Vera, 28 November 1941.

[69]Many would-be airmen from Canada joined the RAF in England in the inter-war period. There were essentially no openings for pilots in the RCAF at the time.

[70]*The Moth Monthly*, February 1942, 25.

[71]Vernon Peters, "Looking Backward," *The Tailspin*, July 1943, 3.

[72]According to Peter Conrad, these buses had already seen many years of hard service with Brewster Tours in Banff, AB. They were operated by Airport (Bus) Lines, a company with close ties to the Moose Jaw Transportation Company. Regular bus service was offered to No. 33 EFTS (RAF) as well as No. 32 SFTS (RAF), located just south of Moose Jaw. This company also provided service

from Weyburn, SK to its nearby No. 41 SFTS (RAF). According to *Henderson's Directory*, the company employed no fewer than eight bus drivers in Moose Jaw. After the war, several of these buses were renovated and brought back into service in the city of Moose Jaw. See *Henderson's Moose Jaw Directory 1942* (Winnipeg: Henderson Directories, 1942), 35, Peter Conrad, *Saskatchewan in War: The Social Impact of the British Commonwealth Air Training Plan on Saskatchewan* (master's thesis, University of Saskatchewan, 1987), 137 and *Moose Jaw Times-Herald*, 13 January 1949, 9.

[73]"Canadian Military Aircraft Serial Numbers, RCAF," www.rwrwalker.ca.

[74]Leversedge, "History of the Military Air Services in Canada," 133.

[75]"Operations Record Book and Appendices, EFTS, Canada, 33–36," in AIR 29/624, UKNA.

[76]This incident was reported in the *Moose Jaw Times-Herald* and as far away as the *Vancouver Sun* on 24 December 1941.

[77]Al Kennerley records that P/O Littlewood had a son named Barry. See his *History of Caron RAF WWII Flying School* (Caron, SK: Caron Legion, n.d.), 59.

[78]*Daily Diary*, No. 33 EFTS (RAF), 27 December 1941.

[79]"Quarterly Analysis of Flying Accidents—No. 4 Training Command, Calgary, Alta.," in RG24, vol. 3280, LAC.

[80]*Daily Diary*, No. 33 EFTS (RAF), various dates.

[81]Vernon Peters to Vera, 3 February 1942.

[82]Dept. of Transport, *Monthly Record: Meteorological Observations in Canada and Newfoundland, January, February, March, 1942* (Toronto: DoT Meteorological Headquarters, 1942), 11.

[83]Leonard Smith, letter to Henry Hildebrand, reprinted in the latter's *In His Loving Service* (Caronport, SK: Briercrest Bible College, 1985), 93–94.

[84]The editor of the *Moth Monthly* reported that the spring thaw in March 1942 left "a sea of mud." By mid-April, the mud had dried up but now the dust blew and temperatures reached 80°F or more. See the *Moth Monthly*, April 1942, 3. The *Moose Jaw Times-Herald* reported that the temperature in Moose Jaw reached 86°F on 21 April.

[85]Peters, "Looking Backward," 5.

[86]"Jock" Brown, letter to Gordon Elmer, 21 January 1981, 8, in "Correspondence 33 EFTS," Gordon Elmer collection, accession # 2015-132, box 16, PASK.

[87]*Moose Jaw Times-Herald*, 14 May 1942.

[88]RCAF Organization Order No. 191 officially authorized the relocation of No. 18 EFTS from Boundary Bay to Caron. Secret Organization Order No. 27, which had originally established No. 33 EFTS (RAF), was officially rescinded, effective 25 May 1942.

[89]Vernon Peters to Vera, 15 May 1942.

[90]Because the exact nature of the civilianized RAF EFTSs was still under discussion even as the BBFTS took over operations at Caron, there was widespread confusion as to who would instruct the incoming student pilots. In the first instance, it was surmised that the BBFTS instructors

would take up these posts at Caron. In the end, the UK Air Ministry retained an all-RAF flying instructional staff which helped preserve the RAF identity of the airbase.

[91]Robert William Pape, a student pilot at No. 33 EFTS (RAF) during the transition to civilian management, didn't fly for two weeks beginning 15 May. On 27 May, he resumed his airborne instruction. A copy of his logbook is in the author's possession.

[92]*Moose Jaw Times-Herald,* 18 May 1942.

[93]Vernon Peters to Vera, 24 May 1942.

CHAPTER 4

The British Columbians Are Coming

War is much too serious a thing to be left to military men.[1]
— Charles Maurice de Talleyrand-Périgord

The shortage of ground crew in the UK worsened in the months following the opening of the Caron airbase. When several flying training companies became available in early 1942, Canadian officials urged the RAF to acquire their services, thereby releasing UK ground personnel for home service. Canadian officials were especially keen to redeploy the services of the Boundary Bay Flying Training School (BBFTS), which, in the aftermath of Pearl Harbor, had been dislodged from its airbase south of Vancouver. They urged the RAF to move quickly lest this fine company be lost to the air training effort. In short order, the RAF authorized the BBFTS to take over the operation of No. 33 EFTS (RAF) at Caron.

With the departure of the RFC/RAF at the end of the First World War, Canada had been left with very little air training capacity. Since the diminutive RCAF could only offer a handful of commissions, young men from Canada who were interested in service flying sought short-term (five year) appointments with the RAF. In the late 1920s, Canadian aviation officials responded to the general decline in domestic air-readiness by enacting several initiatives designed to build up reserves of pilots, mechanics, and flight engineers against the possibility of another war emergency.[2]

In 1927, the almost total depletion of service-qualified pilots compelled the Canadian government to ally itself more closely with the civilian flying clubs. It offered to assist the clubs if they could demonstrate that they had an approved flying field, adequate repair and maintenance facilities, at least one qualified instructor, and thirty members who were interested in flying lessons. A club that met these conditions could expect a cash grant for every member who qualified for a pilot's licence as well as a loan of one or more trainer aircraft. That same year, five flying clubs, including the Aero Club of British Columbia, qualified for assistance under the program.[3] By the following year, sixteen clubs had joined.[4]

Figure 4.1. Aero Club of BC Fleet II trainer, ca. 1930. This aircraft was originally loaned to the aero club by DND. It later saw service as an instructional airframe at Boundary Bay and Caron. Source: City of Vancouver archives, James Crookall fonds, AM640–S1–CVA260–358.

Throughout the 1930s, DND underwrote many of the training activities of the flying clubs. In February 1937, J. A. Wilson, controller of civil aviation, spelled out the conditions under which federal grants would be issued: qualifying clubs had to be managed by their own executive committee, their instructors and air engineers had to be licenced, and, in addition to flying instruction, they had to offer an approved ground school curriculum. If these conditions were met, DND would provide aircraft and issue a grant of one-hundred dollars for each trainee who qualified for a pilot's licence.[5] The Aero Club of BC offered basic flying training as well as advanced instrument courses under these arrangements.[6]

In late spring 1939, DND awarded new contracts to eight members of the Canadian Flying Clubs Association.[7] These contracts replicated many aspects of the existing agreements but were intended to direct eligible pilots into the expanding RCAF. When Canada entered the war, the remaining fourteen flying clubs joined the program.[8] By March 1940, all twenty-two flying clubs were active in the new scheme.[9] Immediately after Canada declared war, Murton Seymour, president of the Canadian Flying Clubs Association, approached DND with an offer to sponsor BCATP elementary flying training schools at or near each of his clubs. In January 1940, DND accepted his offer.[10] While awaiting their local EFTS, the clubs agreed to continue their training activities and formally incorporate operating companies through which they could legally conduct BCATP operations.[11]

EFTS operating contracts clearly specified the duties of each party. The king (i.e., DND) would furnish the physical plant, aeroplanes, crash trucks, snow compaction equipment, medical services, curricular materials, flying clothing, parachutes, and routine equipment replacements. The king would also provide a supervisory staff to oversee the entire operation, including the evaluation and discipline of student pilots. For its part, the operating company would maintain and protect the physical plant, pay the utility bills, provide meals, supply aeroplane oil and fuel, hire and supervise the necessary staff, keep proper financial accounts, and deliver the standard RAF flying and ground school curricula.

The stringent review and renegotiation provisions within the EFTS contracts were crafted to eliminate profiteering and thus avoid the major public relations disasters of the previous war.[12] EFTS profits were strictly limited and, for the most part, reverted to the government. Much to the credit of the flying clubs, operating expenses were significantly reduced over the course of the air training plan. Joseph Apedaile, financial adviser to the flying clubs association, noted that these efforts reduced the cost per EFTS graduate by over a third.[13]

Leslie J. Martin, president of the Aero Club of BC, played a leading role in these economizing measures.[14] He believed that EFTSs should be run on a strictly non-profit basis, that is, their operating companies should refuse even the modest profits due them under the plan.[15] In the end, many other operating companies followed Martin's lead and turned over their entire profits to the government. Mr. Apedaile calculated that these remittances and other efficiencies pioneered by Leslie Martin saved the Canadian government five million dollars.[16] For their part, Martin's two operating companies refunded over $800,000 of their profits and cost savings.[17] It is little wonder that Leslie Martin received an Order of the British Empire for his contribution to the air training plan or that the flying clubs association later became the Royal Canadian Flying Clubs Association.[18]

By the spring of 1940, the flying clubs were fully apprised of their role in the BCATP.[19] In a speech delivered before the Vancouver Kiwanis Club, Leslie Martin claimed to have gone to Ottawa in late May only to discover that Vancouver would not receive its EFTS until the summer of 1941. In his words, the delay got "under my skin."[20] The original DND master plan projected that No. 5 EFTS would open in Vancouver on 14 October 1940. However, due to difficulties in negotiations with the City of Vancouver, which owned the airfield on Sea Island, and concerns over west-coast weather, congestion at a shared airfield, and the distance from other training centres, BCATP planners moved the opening date back to June 1941.[21]

In his account, Martin rushed home from a meeting in Ottawa and single-handedly solved the major problems. Within a few days, he allegedly arranged to expedite the construction of the necessary buildings, raised $35,000 in working capital, and received a federal charter for what became the Vancouver Air Training Company (VATC).[22] Even Martin's attorneys in Ottawa pressed the secretary of state, arguing that "there is great urgency in the matter."[23] That same day (5 June 1940), the secretary issued letters patent for the VATC.[24] In his telling, Martin had "spurred Ottawa to advance the plan more than a year."[25]

There is little doubt that Leslie Martin achieved a great deal in very little time. However, his timeline and purported influence in Ottawa seem overly flattering. We know, for instance, that Martin knew the reasons for the delay at least a month before his visit to Ottawa in late May. Further, in a meeting of his aero club the previous month, he indicated that plans were already in place to begin EFTS training at Sea Island in July. He also noted at that time that he and W. G. Mackenzie, past president of the club, had already shuttled back and forth between Ottawa and city hall in Vancouver, helping to resolve the "snags."[26] There is little doubt that both the city of Vancouver and DND needed reassurance, cajoling, or even prodding. However, only a myopic account of these negotiations would suggest that the difficulties were single-handedly resolved in a mere twenty-four hours.

It is much more likely that events in Europe accelerated the opening of the Vancouver EFTS. It might even be that Mr. Martin, rather than heroically goading officials into action, was, in fact, summoned to Ottawa and directed to proceed with all haste. By the time he arrived in Ottawa, the UK government had informed the Canadian minister of national defence that, given the severe war emergency in Europe, the BCATP should be accelerated "to the utmost."[27] And, to further complicate matters, the UK had just informed Canadian officials that they could no longer provide airframes or aero-engines for the BCATP. Despite these threats to the air training plan, the UK urged Canada to "continue to exert every effort to make it productive to the fullest practicable extent in the shortest possible time."[28] On 28 May, DND decided to bring six EFTSs into operation within the next seven weeks, a move prompted by the intensification of hostilities in Europe and, quite remarkably, a surplus of elementary training aircraft in Canada.[29] In his report to the BCATP supervisory committee, the CAS(C) indicated that the goal was "to place as many pilots as possible under instruction."[30]

It appears that the moribund negotiations surrounding the Vancouver EFTS were suddenly reinvigorated by the war emergency and the general acceleration of the BCATP rather than Mr. Martin's singular triumph over eastern mandarins. The "great urgency" the VATC's lawyers impressed on the secretary of state arose not from Mr. Martin's strident insistence but from the demands of the acceleration policy and the UK's dire situation. Mr. Martin himself tellingly admitted that negotiations were suddenly "easy" and that he operated "at the request of Ottawa."[31]

From its inception, Leslie Martin directed the VATC. He would eventually manage four EFTSs including No. 8 at Sea Island, No. 18 at Boundary Bay, No. 33 (RAF) at Caron, and No. 24 at Abbotsford. For a brief time, he oversaw both Caron and Abbotsford, the only manager to simultaneously oversee two EFTSs. In fact, he had previously performed the same feat when he managed both No. 8 EFTS and No. 18 EFTS during the latter half of 1941. At the time of his appointment to the VATC, Martin served as a director and general sales manager of Home Oil Distributors. He also served as president of the Vancouver Kiwanis Club and the Aero Club of BC, as well as governor of the Vancouver General Hospital, director of the Vancouver Symphony Orchestra, vice-president of the Vancouver Tourist Association, and chairman of the board of the Columbia Coast Mission.[32]

Leslie John Martin had been born in Bilston, Staffordship, England on 25 May 1898.[33] His parents, John and Rebecca, and their children immigrated to Canada that same year.[34] By late 1899, the Martin family lived in Montreal. In or around 1909, John Martin died. Later accounts suggest that Leslie quit school shortly after his father's death and went to work as a messenger boy at the CPR's Windsor Street station.[35] On 15 March 1915, he applied to the Canadian Overseas Expeditionary Force. In his sworn attestation, he alleged that his birthdate was 24 May 1896, a date which inflated his true age (16) by two years.[36]

Private Martin departed Montreal for England with his unit, the No. 3 Canadian General Hospital (McGill).[37] By mid-June, the unit operated a busy hospital in Dannes-Camiers and later, Boulogne, France.[38] On 10 August 1916, Martin received a promotion to Lance Corporal and on 17 March 1917, a good conduct badge.[39] On 28 September 1917, he "reverted to ranks" at his own request, that is, he voluntarily relinquished his corporal stripes so that he could be posted away from No. 3 General Hospital. The following day, he was posted to the 7th Canadian Siege Battery where he served until he was transferred to the 24th Canadian Infantry Battalion in August 1918.[40] He received his discharge in Vancouver on 19 February 1919.[41]

Leslie Martin became the general manager at Caron when the BBFTS officially took over No. 33 EFTS (RAF) on 25 May 1942. In July of that year, the station magazine, *The Moth Monthly*, published a glowing account of Martin's military career. Much of the same content appeared a year later in the *Moose Jaw Times-Herald*. Unfortunately, his official service record is at variance with several claims in these articles. *The Moth Monthly* claimed that Martin spent his sixteenth birthday in the mud and trenches of France. In fact, he turned sixteen several months before the war began.[42] It further claimed that he served with Montreal's 24th Canadian Infantry Battalion (the Victoria Rifles of Montreal) at the time. In fact, Martin joined the 24th Battalion much later in the war (August 1918) at age twenty. Further, and contrary to these accounts, his official record makes no mention of any battlefield wound or gassing injury. Nor does it support the *Times-Herald's* contention that he held the rank of lieutenant when he was discharged at the end of the war.[43]

The Moth Monthly claimed two decorations for Mr. Martin: one for service in France in 1914 and another with the 24th Battalion at Canal du Nord in September 1918. His official service record makes no reference to these or any other meritorious awards (apart from the good conduct badge). Further, Martin was not eligible for the so-called Mons Star, the first of these honours, since he did not join the Canadian Expeditionary Force until March 1915 and this award was only given to those who served in France and Belgium between August and November 1914. The *Times-Herald* article claims, falsely as it turns out, that Martin was the youngest Canadian to receive the Mons Star.[44]

Figure 4.2. Leslie John Martin, general manager, No. 33 EFTS (RAF). Source: *The Tailspin*, June 1943, 16 (redrawn facsimile).

For four years beginning in 1923, Martin worked for the Powell River Company, which operated a major newsprint mill north of Vancouver.[45] In 1927, he joined Home Oil (later, Home Oil Distributors) as a director and vice-president. (He would be seconded from this position to serve the interests of air training during the war.) In 1927, Martin and five other flying enthusiasts organized the Aero Club of BC.[46] By 1940, he would be president of the club and general manager of an operating company charged with training pilots for the BCATP.

RCAF Organization Order No. 32 officially established No. 8 EFTS on Sea Island near Vancouver. The first cohort of student pilots graduated on 5 September 1940. Of the twenty-four who commenced training, only one failed.[47] Routine training operations were carried out at Sea Island until 7 December 1941 when the Japanese attacked Pearl Harbor. Because of its location on the Pacific coast, the RCAF immediately imposed strict limitations on No. 8 EFTS's operations. Personnel were confined to base. Barricades appeared on the highway leading to the base. Persons of Japanese descent were refused admission. Armed guards patrolled. The following day a blackout was imposed on the entire area.[48]

These emergency measures impeded air training: night flying operations ceased. It became extremely difficult to conduct overnight maintenance in the hangar without light escaping in violation of the blackout. Further, since the VATC's compensation depended on the total hours flown, any interference with its flying hours hurt the revenue of the company. On 18 December, the RCAF ordered that No. 8 EFTS be relocated to No. 18 EFTS in nearby Boundary Bay. The Sea Island facility would henceforth serve as an operational base under the RCAF's Western Air Command.

The VATC did not receive this sudden dislocation with grace. Leslie Martin happened to be in Ottawa when the order to terminate training operations arrived. His assistant manager, Charles Clark, refused to relocate their operations until Mr. Martin had authorized the directive. Later that day, Clark received a phone call from Leslie Martin indicating that the move should not take place until 2 January. Later that evening, A/C L. F. Stevenson, of No. 4 Training Command, reasserted the original moving date despite Mr. Martin's recalcitrance.

Things heated up the following day. The VATC dug in its heels and refused to move until authorized by its president. Mr. Clark insinuated that RCAF officials would not be welcome at No. 18 EFTS.[49] Caught in the middle, the RCAF's chief supervisory officer reported that "officials of the VATC endeavoured in every way to obstruct orders." They did this by "confusing the pupils with countermanding orders, refusing to accept equipment returned to Stores, and threatening that the pupils would not be fed at Boundary Bay when they arrived."[50] Notwithstanding the bluster and confusion, the RCAF moved its personnel without incident.

No. 18 EFTS sat on the edge of Boundary Bay, some twenty miles south of Vancouver. It had been formally established on 12 February 1941 as the first of a new class of 'D' or double-size EFTSs. As such, it could accommodate 180 student pilots.[51] It dwarfed first-generation EFTSs such as No. 8 on Sea Island, which could only accommodate two cohorts of twenty-four students. No. 18 EFTS began operations on 10 April 1941 under the management of the Boundary Bay Flying Training School.[52] For all intents and purposes, the BBFTS and the VATC were the same organization.[53] Leslie Martin served as the BBFTS's managing director; the other directors were the original VATC directors, including Austin Taylor, William MacKenzie, and Wendell Farris. The only newcomer, Sheldon Brooks, chaired the board of the Powell River Company.[54]

Prime Minister Mackenzie King attended the official opening of No. 18 EFTS on 2 July 1941. King confided to his diary that he felt out of harmony with the "[Wendell] Farris Gang" and the bitter, arch-Tory, Austin Taylor. King, put off by the group's publicity-mindedness, felt miffed that he had not been notified that his speech would be broadcast live. Notwithstanding, the five thousand celebrants impressed him.[55]

That same day, Leslie Martin revealed the reason behind his involvement in this new venture. He reported that shortly after No. 8 EFTS opened, he and his associates became restive to do more than produce a mere twenty graduates every four weeks. At the suggestion of Charles Power, minister of national defence for air, Martin and his co-directors undertook to operate a new, double-size EFTS at Boundary Bay.[56] They were encouraged in this by a recent air supremacy fundraising drive in the region. The *Vancouver Sun* opined that officials from across Canada were impressed with the funds raised on behalf of the air training plan. Such results supposedly showed that "British Columbia is the most air-minded province in Canada."[57] It thus seemed appropriate that No. 18 EFTS would be the largest elementary flying training school in the dominion.[58]

The Japanese attack on Pearl Harbor had deleterious effects on the operations at No. 18 EFTS just as it had on No. 8 EFTS. When the AOC of Western Air

Command ordered a general blackout of the entire Pacific coast on 8 December, Mr. Len Hawkridge, chief flying instructor (CFI) at Boundary Bay, refused to curtail his night-flying operations. He brazenly left his flares and obstruction lights burning in the darkness. When confronted about the matter, Leslie Martin supported his CFI and ordered night flying to continue. Further discussions with the RCAF's supervisory officer, however, resulted in the cancellation of night flying. The *Daily Diary*, whose entries were composed by a member of the RCAF staff, lamented that "[o]bstruction on the part of the Civilian personnel caused a regrettable delay in carrying out the [blackout] operation."[59]

Within a year of its opening, No. 18 EFTS would also be dislodged due to the defence needs of the Pacific coast. Organization Order No. 191, dated 6 January 1942, officially relocated No. 18 EFTS to Caron, effective the end of May. The move to Caron created additional friction between the BBFTS and the RCAF supervisory staff in large part because the latter would not be officially notified of the relocation to Caron until the end of May. In the meantime, the BBFTS prepared to move. Mr. Martin informed the RCAF's chief supervisory officer, F/L Frank Fredrickson, that food service and accommodations at No. 18 EFTS would be shut down effective 30 April. F/L Fredrickson, who still had no official word from his superiors at No. 4 Training Command, could not cooperate.

The situation and its many ambiguities left the resident RCAF officials embarrassed and confused. All the while, the BBFTS continued to pack, take up the linoleum, carpets, and furniture and leave everything untidy. On 29 April, Mr. Martin ordered that some of the Tiger Moths be dismantled. No. 4 Training Command seemed paralyzed and could only tell its supervisory staff to stand by. To make matters worse, BBFTS officials were not reticent to assert that they were not taking orders from the air force.[60] On 2 May, the RCAF staff learned that today's lunch would be the final meal served at Boundary Bay. By late afternoon, the civilians had left the facility and moved into temporary quarters. Shortly thereafter, they were issued train tickets to Moose Jaw and by 23 May all had departed by private car, rail, or air.

Meanwhile, the RCAF supervisory staff at No. 18 EFTS fumbled about. At the end of May, they finally learned that No. 18 EFTS had been officially disbanded and absorbed into No. 33 EFTS (RAF) at Caron. Even here, they received the news indirectly and not through official channels. In most matters, Mr. Martin had acted on his own authority and ignored the supervisory role assigned to the

RCAF in the EFTS contract. In early June, F/L Fredrickson complained yet again of his treatment at the hands of both the BBFTS and the training command. He concluded that these lapses in communication were designed to keep his staff in the dark. He also suspected that the lack of cooperation on the part of the civilian manager played no small part in the general confusion.[61]

F/L Fredrickson could not have known that the supervisory structure at Caron would be quite different than the BCATP model. These new arrangements were under discussion at a major air training conference in Ottawa and at the highest levels of the RAF even as No. 18 EFTS made its way to Caron.[62] One could say that Mr. Martin acted prematurely but nonetheless in conformity with the new organizational structure which would dispense with air force supervisory personnel at RAF EFTSs. The new arrangement placed executive power in the hands of the civilian manager; henceforth, all supervisory work would be carried out under his direction and through his staff. The CFI would be the senior RAF officer on site and would be responsible for the deportment of the RAF administrative staff, student pilots, and flying instructors as well as the quality of the flying instruction. All else would fall under the executive direction of the civilian manager. In case of an irresolvable dispute between the CFI and the manager, a resolution process would be carried out by training command.[63]

Until these matters were officially ratified, things were unsettled. The UK high commissioner regularly informed the Air Ministry about matters related to their EFTSs in Canada. He reported that the BBFTS's displacement from Boundary Bay greatly concerned their Canadian counterparts who were keen to retain the services of this efficient company by offering it to the RAF. The Canadians noted that any delay in redeploying the BBFTS would make it difficult for Martin to retain his experienced staff.[64] This same urgency is likely what motivated Martin to pack up and move rapidly. The high commissioner urged the Air Ministry to move quickly.[65]

On 8 May, the Empire Air Training Scheme Committee met in a special session to consider the high commissioner's pleas. The committee concurred that the RAF EFTSs in Canada should be put under civilian management. It also gave immediate approval to the BBFTS's management of Caron. It agreed with the high commissioner that it would be best to proceed with a new understanding (specified above) regarding the division of authority between the senior RAF officer and the civilian manager.[66] Even though there were several months of confusion yet to come as the various roles were clarified, Caron became the first RAF EFTS to be converted to civilian management.[67]

"Jock" Brown, who served as a flying instructor at Caron, recalled that not everything went smoothly during the transition to civilian oversight. Tensions immediately arose over whether BBFTS civilians or RAF instructors would provide the flying instruction. Since the school would continue to train RAF pupils, the Air Ministry and the local RAF flying instructors concluded that only the RAF could meet the highest standards. The civilians, however, were intent on operating the entire school under the No. 18 EFTS designation, which would clearly indicate its civilian character. By the end of May (1942), the No. 33 EFTS (RAF) designation prevailed. In the meantime, a dispute had arisen over the conduct of SGT Pryde, a RAF flying instructor. When Leslie Martin tried to discipline Pryde, he rudely refused to acknowledge the civilian manager's authority. CFI S/L B. H. Hayward, "a bull-dog of a man who brooked no interference," stood by his instructor. Things cooled off when Mr. Martin backed down. Thereafter, the new division of authority seemed to work well.[68]

Jessie Reagh lived with her parents in Ladner, BC when the Second World War erupted. By the time No. 18 EFTS opened just south of town, she had qualified for university entrance. Eager to serve her country, she set aside her educational plans and applied to work at the airbase. The BBFTS hired her as a waitress in the airmen mess. She would later be promoted to the NCO and then to the officers mess. She finished her service with the BBFTS as a switchboard operator. Jessie went along with the BBFTS staff when they relocated to Caron. Since she was still a minor, she had to have the written permission of her parents before she could leave for the prairies. A family friend, Agnes Green, promised to keep an eye on her.[69]

Peter (Pete) Rutherford and Louis (Lou) Piper were also recent high school graduates. Both had attended T. J. Trapp Technical High School in New Westminster, BC. Lou had been raised in Moose Jaw and had only recently moved to the Vancouver area.[70] The BBFTS snapped up their entire graduating class and put them to work as apprentice aircraft mechanics.[71] Jessie, Pete, and Lou were present in Caron on 25 May 1942 when the BBFTS officially took over No. 33 EFTS (RAF).

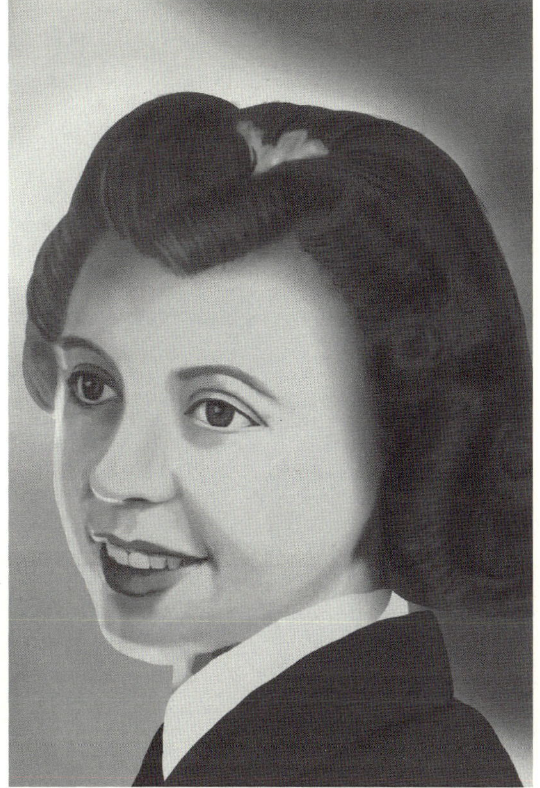

Figure 4.3. Miss Jessie Reagh. Source: Delta Museum and Archives, accession 1997-007 (redrawn facsimile).

LAC Vernon Peters, who had been assigned to help with the transition, described his initial impressions in a letter to his wife. He noted an immediate transformation issuing from the "spirit of Private Enterprise." Within a day of the civilian takeover, the entire place had been scrubbed clean. The professionalism of the kitchen staff impressed him (see Figure 4.4).[72] The cooks were no longer "ex-bus drivers" pressed into culinary duty.[73] Peters distilled all these changes into a grand lesson in the "difference between Private Enterprise & state control."[74]

The following day, he offered some further observations. He could not help but notice the change in atmosphere now that the loud, cheerful, and optimistic civilians had descended on the place. (Seventy years later, Jessie Reagh also recalled the buoyancy of those early days in Caron.) Neither the giggling females who scurried around the administrative building nor the disorderly dress worn by the civilians impressed Peters. He lamented, or feigned to, that the headquarters had become a madhouse.[75]

Figure 4.4. BBFTS kitchen staff, airmen mess, July 1942. Source: R-E-539, Esther Cooper collection, PASK. Used with permission.

In early July, Peters was posted to No. 33 ANS (RAF) near Hamilton, Ontario. Even before he left, he expected to be recalled to Caron due to the shortage of clerks in the headquarters.[76] Indeed, a flurry of telegrams between his Caron superiors and RCAF headquarters led to his immediate posting back to Caron.[77] Even though he was only in the Hamilton area for a day or so, he managed to meet with former colleagues from Caron. He discovered that they too wished they could return. When back in Caron, he exclaimed: "I feel I can breathe here." He paused to list the additional advantages of Caron: its cleanliness, the "happy atmosphere of this civvy unit," his pride in representing the RAF among the Canadian civilians, and last, but not least, the good food and the way it was served.[78] Compared with Hamilton, conditions at Caron were "simply perfect."[79]

In fairness to the staff in Hamilton, it is important to bear in mind the significant differences between the circumstances facing the civilians at Caron and the largely RAF staff at Hamilton. Many of the latter were deeply concerned with the welfare of their loved ones in the UK. More than a few felt guilty because they were enjoying relative ease, including an abundance of good food and electric lights, while their colleagues and kin at home were facing shortages, blackouts, and mortal danger. Further, no doubt some of Hamilton's instructors had fought during the Battle of Britain only to be posted to the trackless Canadian wilderness; it must have seemed like their valiant deeds were being punished. One can scarcely imagine the morale-crushing tedium that dogged battle-tested pilots turned instructors!

By fall 1942, Caron hosted the largest EFTSs in Canada. In May of that year, the Allies at the air conference in Ottawa determined that the RAF EFTSs should be enlarged.[80] Whereas double-size EFTSs were currently training 180 student pilots, by September, Caron had an enrolment of 240. Put another way, sixty new student pilots arrived at Caron every second week.[81] Caron now had five times the capacity of the first EFTSs sponsored by the flying clubs in 1940. As he had hoped, Leslie Martin could now do far more for the war effort than he could have imagined when he first became restive on Sea Island.

Figure 4.5. RAF officers and NCOs, June 1942, Caron. Note the civilian manager, Leslie Martin, seated in the middle of the front row. Source: Author's collection.

Early in the new year, new aircraft began appearing at Caron. On 12 January 1943, the first two Fairchild Cornells arrived. Over the next month or so, the entire fleet of Tiger Moths would be supplanted by these elegant mono-wing aircraft. The mechanics were happy to see the Cornells since they were equipped with electric starters; they would no longer have to risk their lives spinning propellers on slippery surfaces.[82] Lou Piper recalled that some of the Cornells were ferried to Caron by female pilots from the United States. The "colonialist" mentality of some of the American pilots, who patronizingly threw cigarettes to the benighted natives (the mechanics), left a lasting and unfavourable impression.

Whereas Tiger Moths were skinned with cloth, Cornells sported plywood laminate covered with cotton fabric (madapollam). The added stiffness provided by the laminate boosted overall performance, although experienced pilots still considered the aircraft underpowered. Lou Piper recalled that despite all their improvements, the Cornells increased certain maintenance costs. Whereas minor repairs could be carried out on the wings and fuselage of the Tiger Moth because of its simple design and cloth skin, damage to the Cornell's laminated surfaces required specialized repairs. Small holes in the Tiger Moths had been repaired with a cloth patch and a sailor's needle; no such repairs were possible when the Cornells received comparable damage.

Almost from the beginning, the Cornells had problems with their main structural components at the wing-fuselage junction.[83] On occasion, the wood adhesive (Kaurit glue) in this critical area failed when exposed to extreme temperature or humidity fluctuations or other severe stresses. Even though there is no record of any such problems at Caron, it is easy to see how temperature extremes in January 1943 may have had some effect on the glued components of these aircraft. In a span of a mere seven days, the temperature at Caron descended from a high of 43°F on 13 January to a low of -50°F a week later, a whopping 93°F variance.[84]

Problems with the Cornells were reported to the BCATP Supervisory Board throughout 1943.[85] Their structural problems rightly received most of the attention, especially after four fatalities in No. 4 Training Command were attributed to such. These sudden and catastrophic failures correlated with prior heavy landings as well as inadequate shock absorption by the oleo mechanisms in the landing gear. Rigorous inspections were routinely carried out to keep the situation from becoming worse. In the end, the board concluded that the Cornells' structural failures were due to a combination of poor design, substandard materials, and inferior workmanship.[86]

On 2 June 1943, Leslie Martin became an Officer (civil division) of the British Empire in recognition of his efforts on behalf of air training in Canada.[87] Vernon Peters reported that Mr. Martin's OBE made everyone at Caron excited.[88] Peters had some good news of his own. On 6 June, he was promoted to corporal. But even better news came the following week when he received his commission and promotion to the rank of pilot officer.[89] The commission had been long in coming. A full year earlier he had undergone a qualifying interview and had been recommended for a commission in the administrative and special duties branch.[90] Even though his superiors highly recommended his application, his commission had to await a suitable vacancy.[91] When the promotion finally came, it came with a transfer to No. 36 SFTS (RAF) near Penhold, AB.

Leaving saddened Peters. "I have become very much attached to Caron, for, as you know, I saw the original station formed and I watched it grow up. Consequently, I find a bit of a tug, coming away.... It was very sad to leave all the Caronites. They are such a grand crowd and I shed a silent tear."[92] In late July, he confided that he had hoped to finish his Canadian service at Caron. He wrote ruefully: "The chaps at Caron were all great fellows. I'd spend the next four years in a desert with them. And going back tomorrow would not wrong them or me."[93]

In October 1943, Leslie Martin again managed two EFTSs: No. 24 at Abbotsford (near Vancouver) and Caron.[94] He intended to alternate between the two and rely on his assistant managers to conduct operations in his absence. Sadly, this arrangement did not last the month. On 30 October, Leslie Martin died of apparent heart failure in Vancouver.[95] A local newspaper noted that he passed on shortly after attending the first graduation ceremony at No. 24 EFTS.[96] The *Vancouver Sun* added that he passed away in his suite at the Hotel Vancouver.[97] Although little is known of the specifics, Mr. Martin had been ill for a time the preceding winter.[98] The Abbotsford newspaper declared that Mr. Martin could almost be counted a war casualty since "he was a one-man all-out war effort, despite the fact that he had been in poor health for several months."[99]

Leslie Martin left behind his wife of twenty-one years, a daughter, Beverley, who worked at No. 24 EFTS, and a son, Leslie Charles, a pilot with the RCAF.[100]

Three days later, full military honours were afforded Mr. Martin at Christ Church Cathedral in Vancouver. A/V/M G. R. Howsam, AOC, No. 4 Training Command and A/V/M Stevenson, AOC, RCAF Western Air Command were in attendance as was Dean Cecil Swanson, Rev. Larmouth, and the Rt. Rev. Sir Francis Heathcote, bishop of the diocese of New Westminster.[101] After the service, a RCAF band, firing party, and escort party led an impressive parade from the cathedral to Mountain View Cemetery. Six pallbearers laid Sergeant Martin to rest in the field of honour.[102]

Within a matter of days, the operating company elected Austin Taylor to take Martin's place as president. On 7 November, Taylor announced that Stewart McKercher, KC, of Saskatoon, SK would assume the general manager's duties at both Abbotsford and Caron.[103] McKercher had flown with 11 Wing, No. 1 Squadron of the Royal Flying Corps in the First World War and had been severely injured in a crash in Ypres, Belgium in April 1917.[104] After the war, he completed a law degree at the University of Saskatchewan. He had been a longtime member of the Saskatoon Flying Club and the former managing director of No. 6 EFTS at Prince Albert, SK. At the time of his appointment, McKercher was a partner in a Saskatoon law firm and the president of the local bar association.[105]

The BCATP enjoyed a banner month in October 1943—over 2,000 pilots received their wings. In fact, far too many pilots were pouring out of the BCATP and RAF schools in Canada. As a stopgap measure, many newly-minted pilots were assigned guard duty and other extraneous tasks.[106] The RAF projected that the altered strategic situation in Europe meant that its Bomber Command would need an additional 2,300 navigators and 3,400 fewer pilots in the coming year.[107] Even though the BCATP responded to these new priorities by producing twice as many navigators in October as it had in July, the glut of pilots persisted.[108] Since RAF officials were increasingly concerned with the shortage of ground crew at operational bases in the UK and elsewhere, reducing the number of RAF schools in Canada seemed to be the only way that these deficiencies could be alleviated.[109]

High-level deliberations eventually concluded that several RAF schools in Canada could be disbanded. On 2 December 1943, the RAF indicated that it planned to close five SFTSs and three EFTSs, including Caron.[110] The

RCAF suggested as early as November that the Caron airbase could henceforth serve as a subsidiary airfield (R.1) to No. 32 SFTS (RAF) in Moose Jaw.[111] In late December, the *Moose Jaw Times-Herald* reinforced a local rumour to this effect by noting that the expansion of No. 32's R.1 at Buttress had been abruptly suspended.

The RAF and civilian staffs at Caron were gradually posted away as the final courses graduated. For instance, flying instructors Featherby, Howitt, and Unwin proceeded to No. 32 SFTS (RAF) to sharpen their skills in preparation for a return to operational duties in the UK.[112] Many of the civilian staff who came from BC were offered similar posts at No. 24 EFTS in Abbotsford. By the end of January 1944, at least forty civilians from Caron had transferred to Vancouver.[113] By early February, Charles Clark, the long-time friend and assistant to the late Leslie Martin, took up similar duties at Abbotsford. Mr. Clark, who came out of retirement at the beginning of the war to join the VATC, would have to wait another year before he could re-retire to his Okanagan orchard.[114]

Course no. 94, the final cohort to graduate from Caron, completed its examinations on 7 January 1944 and its flying training two days later.[115] On 14 January, its members proceeded on leave.[116] In total, some 160,787 hours and 57 minutes of flying time had been logged at Caron over the course of twenty-four months. In April 1943, its highest monthly total of 10,330 hours and 40 minutes of flying time were logged on its fleet of 84 Cornells.[117] Some 1,837 of its student pilots graduated.

Beginning in early January 1944, No. 33 EFTS (RAF) began its orderly closure. Officers from surrounding bases and No. 4 Training Command arrived to supervise the disposal of documents and equipment. Weekly meetings were held between the department heads of the BBFTS and the ranking RAF officer. The *Daily Diary* reported that these cordial meetings were in no small part responsible for the smooth closure of the airbase. Unlike at Boundary Bay and Sea Island, the civilian company gave every consideration to the requirements of the air force. In the words of F/L J. H. McRitchie, "the spirit of cooperation which has always been a feature of this unit was maintained up to the final closing."[118]

On 1 February 1944, the assets at Caron were officially taken from the authority of the BBFTS and given over to a board of officers appointed for the occasion. The board, in turn, handed them over to representatives of No. 32 SFTS (RAF). Later that same day, Hank McDowell helped Slim Adames, the

BBFTS stores keeper, haul the final loads of the company's equipment to the train in Caron. Adames and McDowell were the last to leave on that cold winter evening. The blackout, which had threatened BBFTS operations on the west coast, now had its way with Caron's empty buildings and abandoned airfield.[119] The following day, a small advance party from Moose Jaw began preparations for Caron's next life.

Endnotes

[1]Cited in George Seldes, *The Great Quotations* (New York: Pocket, 1967), 970.

[2]Dept. of Trade and Commerce, "Pre-War Civil Aviation and the Defence Program," in *Canada Year Book, 1941* (Ottawa: King's Printer, 1941), 608.

[3]"Hewson to RCAF Liaison Officer, 14 December 1927," in "Aeroplane Clubs," RCAF File 13/5, 181.009 (D 1037), DHH.

[4]Ellis, *Canada's Flying Heritage*, 290.

[5]"Air Traffic—Operations Companies—Flying Schools and Clubs—Aero Club of British Columbia," in RG12, vol. 2268, LAC.

[6]Ibid.

[7]This new arrangement paid the flying clubs a total of $1,074 for each pilot who achieved the appropriate elementary flying and ground school competencies. See Hatch, "BCATP," 57–58.

[8]Roberts, *Canada's War in the Air*, 39.

[9]In 1939, the Aero Club of BC's aircraft flew 1,850 hours. Instruction was given to fifty pupils, including nineteen pilots who took refresher courses, fourteen who underwent instruction in instrument flying, four who took instructor courses, and twelve RCAF pupils who underwent primary training. See "Aero Club Has Record Year," *The Vancouver Sun*, 13 January 1940, 28.

[10]"History of Civil Flying Schools," 1.

[11]Wartime restrictions on private flying and the all-consuming demands of their EFTSs meant that, by 1941, most flying clubs had curtailed their activities for the balance of the war. See *Report of the Dept. of National Defence Canada for the Fiscal Year Ending March 31, 1942* (Ottawa: King's Printer, 1942), 22.

[12]Charles Power, minister of national defence for air, faced questions on this matter in the House of Commons. On 17 March 1941, he reassured parliamentarians that in one way or another all profits from air training operations were being returned to the government. See *Dominion of Canada Official Report of Debates House of Commons*, 17 April 1941, vol. 2, 1618.

[13]"Parts of Canada Attend Closing Function at No. 24, Abbotsford," *Abbotsford, Sumas and Matsqui (British Columbia) News*, 2 August 1944.

[14]In a 16 March 1944 speech before Parliament, Cyrus MacMillan, parliamentary assistant to the minister of national defence for air, noted that the operating companies under Mr. Martin's care led the way by returning all their excess allowances and profits to the government. See the official record of MacMillan's speech before the 19th Parliament, 5th session, at https://lipad.ca/full/permalink/1336651.

[15]In his annual report to the Aero Club of BC, Leslie Martin announced that the directors of the operating company had determined that it would function as a strictly non-profit organization: no dividends or profit of any kind would be taken. See Leslie Martin, "Annual Report of the President of the Aero Club of BC," 16 May 1941," 1–2, in Aero Club of BC archives, Pitt Meadows, BC.

[16]W. K. Sproule,"Annual Report of the President of the Aero Club of BC," May 1944, 1, in Aero Club of BC archives, Pitt Meadows, BC.

[17]"History of Civil Flying Schools," Appendix.

[18]"Parts of Canada Attend Closing Function at No. 24, Abbotsford," 1.

[19]The Aero Club of BC was prepared to act quickly when called upon to sponsor an EFTS-operating company. At a special meeting on 3 June 1940, the membership authorized Leslie Martin to incorporate a company for the purpose of "entering into a contract with the Dept. of National Defence." By policy, no fewer than two of its members would sit as directors of the new company. See "Minutes of a special meeting of the Directors of the Aero Club of BC held on Monday, June 3rd, 1940," Aero Club of BC archives, Pitt Meadows, BC.

[20]"Vancouver Air School Organized in 24 Hours, Sets Dominion Record," *The Vancouver Sun*, 5 July 1940, 19.

[21]See "Training Under Empire Plan to Get Underway Here in July," *The Vancouver Sun*, 20 April 1940. The 23 July 1940 revised opening date appears in Appendix A to the "Chief of Air Staff's Report to the Members of the BCATP Supervisory Board," 11 March 1940, in AIR 20/1374: "Empire Air Training Scheme Committee, 1940," UKNA. A careful reader may notice the various projected starting dates (and even EFTS numbers—no. 5 vs. no. 8) associated with the Vancouver airbase. The data given in Table 1.5 by Fred Hatch suggests an original starting date of 9 December 1940. Appendix A of the CAS's report suggests a starting date of 22 July 1940. And Mr. Martin reported a further-revised starting date of summer 1941. It is perhaps best to reconcile these varying claims by acknowledging that opening dates were routinely revised. In the end, No. 8 EFTS opened on or about what was likely its original start-up date, and some 20 weeks in advance of a revised December date and a full year ahead of the date apparently projected at the time Mr. Martin began his frenetic push.

[22]Although he was not free to divulge the details in his speech to the Kiwanis Club, the minutes of the aero club indicate that Austin Taylor subscribed $15,000, and Mr. Martin, W. G. Mackenzie, W. B. Farris and the club itself subscribed $5,000 apiece. See Leslie Martin, "Annual Report of the President of the Aero Club of BC."

[23]Letter dated 5 June 1940, in "Vancouver Air Training Company Limited," in RG95, vol. 984, LAC.

[24]Letters patent, 5 June 1940, in "Vancouver Air Training Company Limited."

[25]"Vancouver Air School Organized in 24 Hours," 19.

[26]"Training Under Empire Plan to Get Underway Here in July."

[27]UK High Commissioner Gerald Campbell, letter to Norman Rogers, 20 May 1940, in *The British Commonwealth Air Training Plan*, vol. 3, RCAF Headquarters file 927-1-1, in Hatch, "BCATP," 181.

[28]"Policy—British Commonwealth Air Training Scheme," vol. 1, RCAF file S-1-6, DHH, in Hatch, "BCATP," 181–82.

[29]Nos. 3 and 4 EFTS (London and Windsor Mills, ON) were to be opened on 24 June; Nos. 5–8 EFTS (Lethbridge, AB, Prince Albert, SK, Windsor, ON, and Vancouver, BC) were to be opened

on 22 July. See "Report of the Chief of the Air Staff to the Members of the Supervisory Board, BCATP, Monday, June 10th, 1940," in AIR 20/1374: "Empire Air Training Scheme Committee, 1940." UKNA. For the surplus of elementary trainers, see Hatch, "BCATP," 189.

[30]"Report of the Chief of the Air Staff to the Members of the Supervisory Board, BCATP, Monday, June 10th, 1940."

[31]"Vancouver Air School Organized in 24 Hours," 19.

[32]This information was presented to the House of Commons by the minister of national defence for air on 18 November 1940.

[33]His birth was registered during the period spanning July–September 1898. A facsimile of the register is available at: http://www.ancestry.co.uk.

[34]District: Westmount, Quebec, No. 155, d–2 in *1901 Census of Canada*, in microfilm: T–6523, LAC.

[35]There is some question as to when Martin went to work for the CPR. An article in the July 1942 issue of the *Moth Monthly* suggested that he left school and went to work at age eleven. A 2 November 1943 article in the *Moose Jaw Times-Herald*, however, reported that he began working for the CPR in 1911, when he would have been twelve or thirteen years of age.

[36]Parts A and B of Leslie John Martin's official attestation are available as portable document format (pdf) files through LAC. The Canadian military was none too vigilant in verifying the ages of its applicants. Martin's case may well have been aided by the fact that he was over six feet tall when he applied.

[37]Martin's name appears on the nominal list (roll) for this unit as it departs for Europe. See R. C. Fetherstonhaugh, *No. 3 Canadian General Hospital (McGill) 1914–1919* (Montreal: The Gazette, 1928), 260.

[38]Ibid., 19, 48.

[39]"Leslie John Martin," in RG150, vol. 5990, LAC. Martin's good conduct badge is also noted in Featherstonehaugh, *No. 3 Canadian General Hospital*, 88.

[40]All three units that Martin served with were originally formed in Montreal. Much like the No. 3 Canadian General Hospital, the officers and other ranks of the 7th Canadian Siege Battery were drawn from graduate and undergraduate students at McGill University. The original personnel for the 24th Battalion were also recruited from the Montreal vicinity. For information on the 7th Canadian Siege Battery, see G. W. L. Nicholson, *The Gunners of Canada: The History of the Royal Regiment of Canadian Artillery*, 2 vols. (Toronto: McClelland & Stewart, 1967), 1:397, 403.

[41]"Martin, Leslie John," in RG150, vol. 5990. LAC. Martin's mother, Rebecca, had apparently moved to Vancouver during the war. He listed his discharge address as 1709 Chesterfield Ave., Vancouver.

[42]The false date of birth given when he entered the Canadian army does not help here: he would have been eighteen years of age when the war began if that (fabricated) birthdate is assumed.

[43]Martin's gravestone in the Mountain View Cemetery in Vancouver indicates that he achieved the rank of Sergeant. Given the factual problems in these accounts, it is hard to know what to

make of the *Moth Monthly's* claim that he tried to get into the RCAF after the war but was turned down due to a heart flutter.

[44]Later accounts of Martin's First World War experience claimed that he won the military medal in 1918. Three accounts published immediately after his premature death also made this claim. There is nothing in his official service record, however, to support this contention. Cf. *Abbotsford, Sumas and Matsqui News,* 3 November 1943, the *Vancouver Sun,* 1 November 1943, and the *Vancouver Province,* 1 November 1943.

[45]*Moose Jaw Times-Herald,* 3 June 1943.

[46]Ibid.

[47]"Martin Address to the Vancouver Board of Trade," *The Vancouver Province,* 17 September 1940. In this speech, Martin challenged the view that west coast rain and fog would make training operations difficult. He pointed out that most of the delays in Trans-Canada Air Lines flights occurred east of Winnipeg. In his view, BC weather permitted more flying days than any other part of Canada.

[48]*Daily Diary,* No. 8 EFTS, 7–8 December 1941.

[49]The fact that Mr. Martin was also the general manager at No. 18 EFTS gave Mr. Clark some clout in the matter.

[50]*Daily Diary,* No. 8 EFTS, 19 December 1941.

[51]The CAS(C) referred to No. 18 EFTS at Boundary Bay as the first double-size school in Canada. See "Report No. 17 by the Chief of the Air Staff to the Members of the Supervisory Board, BCATP, Monday, May 12th, 1941," 4, in AIR 20/1375: "Empire Air Training Scheme Committee, Papers Related to Training in Canada, 1941," UKNA.

[52]*Daily Diary,* No. 18 EFTS. Like most EFTSs, No. 18 was by no means complete when it opened in April 1941. Its mechanics and apprentices were barracked at No. 8 EFTS on Sea Island; the first class of student pilots flew out of nearby Patricia Bay since the runways at Boundary Bay were not yet complete. See "New Air Training School to be Busiest in Canada," *The Vancouver Sun,* 3 April 1941, 27.

[53]Michael DesMazes, long-time historian of wartime aviation in BC, reports as per Fred Graham, who served as an accountant for both the VATC and BBFTS, that these companies were essentially the same company operating under two names. The latter was incorporated solely to meet the government's requirement of only one school per flying club/operating company. According to Graham, the BBFTS was just a bureaucratic convenience, a necessary evil. See Michael DesMazes, "Relation of VATC and BBFTS," Facebook group: BCATP, http://www.facebook.com.

[54]"Boundary Bay Flying Training School Limited," in RG95, vol. 498, LAC.

[55]W. L. M. King, *The Diaries of William Lyon Mackenzie King,* 2 July 1941, https://www.bac-lac.gc.ca/eng/discover/politics-government/prime-ministers/william-lyon-mackenzie-king/Pages/diaries-william-lyon-mackenzie-king.aspx. The *Daily Diary* for No. 18 EFTS reported on 2 July 1941 that some 5,000 were present at the official opening of the airbase.

[56]*Daily Diary,* No. 18 EFTS, 2 July 1941.

[57]"Large New Flying School for Valley," *The Vancouver Sun*, 25 October 1940, 21.

[58]"Largest Air Training Field to Be in Delta," *Ladner (British Columbia) Optimist*, 12 December 1940.

[59]*Daily Diary*, No. 18 EFTS, 8 December 1941.

[60]*Daily Diary*, No. 18 EFTS, 1 May 1942.

[61]*Daily Diary*, No. 18 EFTS, 6 June 1942.

[62]"Air Training Conference—May 1942—Conference Diary—Formal Minutes—Proceedings," in RG24, vol. 5389, LAC. See the minutes of the sub-committee on the civilianization of the RAF EFTSs.

[63]RCAF Secret Organization Order No. 65, 20 May 1942, (in AIR 29/624, UKNA), would be amended on 20 January 1943 (amendment no. 2) to clearly delineate the relationship between the civilian manager and the air force's CFI. It also described the grievance procedure to be followed in case of an irreconcilable dispute.

[64]See telegram from the UK high commissioner in Canada to the Air Ministry via the Dominions Office, 25 April 1942, in AIR 19/339: "Joint Air Training Plan + Discussions in Canada and USA," UKNA.

[65]See telegram from the UK high commissioner in Canada to the Air Ministry via the Dominions Office, 29 April 1942, in AIR 19/339: "Joint Air Training Plan + Discussions in Canada and USA," UKNA.

[66]"Minutes of the Empire Air Training Scheme Committee," 8 May 1942, in AIR 20/1376: "Empire Air Training Scheme Committee 1942," UKNA.

[67]"Progress Report No. 30 by the Chief of the Air Staff to the Members of the Supervisory Board, BCATP," Monday, June 15th, 1942, 1, in AIR 20/1376: "Empire Air Training Scheme Committee, 1942," UKNA.

[68]"Jock" Brown, letter to Gordon Elmer, 14 February 1981, 1, in "Correspondence 33 EFTS," Gordon Elmer collection, accession # 2015-132, box 16, PASK.

[69]Jessie (Reagh) Belcher, telephone interview by the author, Caronport and Campbell River, BC, 10 March 2011.

[70]Louis Piper, telephone interview by the author, Caronport and Ottawa, ON, 5 May 2011.

[71]Peter Rutherford, telephone interview by the author, Caronport and Vernon, BC, 27 April 2011.

[72]Peters could not have known the pains Audrey Strong of the BBFTS took with the menus. While at No. 18 EFTS, she submitted them to nutritional experts at the Universities of British Columbia and Alberta. They were also vetted by two physicians. See "The Feminine Touch Brings Comforts of Home to Air School," *The Vancouver Sun*, 15 November 1941, 12.

[73]Peters would likely agree with the New Orleans-born "Countess Morphy" (Marcelle Azra Forbes/ Hincks) who declaimed that "[t]he tragedy of English cooking is that 'plain' cooking cannot be entrusted to 'plain' cooks." See her *Recipes of All Nations* (New York: Wise, 1935), 17.

[74]Vernon Peters to Vera, 25 May 1942. Pete Rutherford recalled that the head janitor—"the major"—insisted that the entire place be cleaned before BBFTS personnel could move onto the

airbase. And indeed, it was spotless when they settled in. Apparently, the RAF personnel had not been so fastidious. According to Rutherford, the RAF used brooms to clean off the dining tables and some of the drains in the barracks had already been plugged with tea leaves.

[75]Vernon Peters to Vera, 26 May 1942. From all reports, Leslie Martin's teenaged daughter, Beverley, made a nuisance of herself with the RAF administrative staff. Although Peters grumbled privately about her meddling, an anonymous poem (written by F/L J. Cadell) in the September 1942 issue of the *Moth Monthly* portrayed her as a universal bother. Apparently, the entire headquarters staff had some complaint or other. See the *Moth Monthly*, September 1942, 36 and Vernon Peters to Vera, 17 November 1942.

[76]Vernon Peters to Vera, 21 July 1942, 1.

[77]Vernon Peters' daughter, Sylvia Lindridge, has the originals of these telegrams in her private collection.

[78]One of the advantages civilian cooks enjoyed over their air force counterparts was their ability to source local foodstuffs. Cecil Smith recalled that he delivered sixty bushels of fresh potatoes to the Caron airbase with his father. Since these potatoes were delivered in the early fall, they must have been sold to the civilian cooks since they ran the kitchens during the only two falls (1942 and 1943) Caron was in operation. See "Sold Spuds to Air Base," *The Senior Paper* (Penticton, BC), 36 (June 2013): 3.

[79]Vernon Peters to Vera, 21 July 1942.

[80]"Air Training Conference—May 1942—Training of Aircrew, United Nations—Statistics Of," in RG24, vol. 5388, LAC.

[81]No. 33 EFTS (RAF) began training four separate cohorts (courses) of sixty students as early as August 1942. The editor of the *Moth Monthly* was quite proud that Caron had been chosen for this "experiment." In an editorial published the following month, he noted that the flying schedule was quite demanding but with extra discipline things had been going well. See the *Moth Monthly*, September 1942, 3. Apparently the experiment went very well indeed. By March of the following year, the RCAF increased the capacity of seven of its EFTSs to 240 student pilots (Nos. 5, 6, 9, 10, 15, 23, and 24). See "Progress Report No. 39 by the Chief of the Air Staff to the Members of the Supervisory Board, BCATP," Monday, March 15th, 1943, 2, in AIR 20/1377: "Empire Air Training Scheme Committee, 1943," UKNA.

[82]"Aircraft—Fairchild Cornell, Technical Aspects of," in RG24, vol. 5017, LAC.

[83]Douglas, *The Creation of a National Air Force*, 283. Although no specifics were given, F/L Osler of No. 2 Flying Instructor School at Vulcan, AB visited No. 33 EFTS (RAF) on 21 May 1943 to investigate technical problems with the Cornell. See *Daily Diary*, No. 33 EFTS (RAF), 21 May 1943.

[84]Dept. of Transport, *Monthly Record: Meteorological Observations in Canada and Newfoundland, January 1943* (Toronto: Dept. of Transport Meteorological Headquarters, 1943), 11.

[85]The comments on the Cornell that follow are derived from the CAS(C)'s reports to the BCATP Supervisory Board. See his progress reports dated 20 December 1943, 17 January 1944, 28 February 1944, 20 March 1944, and 19 June 1944.

[86]"Minutes, March 19, 1945," 2 in "Supervisory Board—BCATP. Minutes of Meetings," in RG24, vol. 5233, LAC. After the war, War Assets Corporation sold off the BCATP's surplus Cornells. Its advertisements for the same were careful to point out that these aircraft would need a "centre Front Spar modification" before they would be eligible for a certificate of airworthiness.

[87]*Supplement to the London Gazette*, 2 June 1943, 2481.

[88]Vernon Peters to Vera, 3 June 1943. Hank McDowell recalled seeing a photograph of Mr. Martin with the King and Queen taken on this occasion.

[89]This promotion was announced in the *Supplement to the London Gazette*, 3 August 1943, 3489.

[90]Vernon Peters to Vera, 4 April 1942.

[91]Sylvia Lindridge has a document in her private collection that shows the tortuous progress of her father's commission recommendation. Inquiries submitted to training command throughout the year between his qualifying interview and the awarding of the commission were either not acknowledged or returned with a blunt "no vacancies." Then suddenly, on 12 June 1943, the commission arrived.

[92]Vernon Peters to Vera, 13 June 1943.

[93]Vernon Peters to Vera, 22 July 1943.

[94]RCAF Organization Order No. 296, dated 6 October 1943, implies that some other group (perhaps the RCAF itself?) operated No. 24 EFTS when it first opened on 6 September 1943. (This opening date had originally been authorized by RCAF Organization Order No. 288.) At some point in the fall, the VATC was re-activated to offer its management services at No. 24 EFTS.

[95]*Daily Diary*, No. 24 EFTS, 30 October 1943.

[96]*Abbotsford, Sumas and Matsqui News*, 3 November 1943.

[97]*The Vancouver Sun*, 1 November 1943.

[98]In its January 1943 issue, the *Moth Monthly* included a thank you from Martin to the personnel of No. 33 EFTS (RAF) who sent flowers during his recent illness.

[99]*Abbotsford, Sumas and Matsqui News*, 3 November 1943, 4.

[100]Eighteen months later, F/O Leslie Charles Martin was killed in action with RCAF Bomber Reconnaissance Squadron No. 162 near Iceland.

[101]*Daily Diary*, No. 24 EFTS, 2 November 1943. See also *Abbotsford, Sumas and Matsqui News*, 3 November 1943. SGT Leslie John Martin's grave is in the ABRAY section of the cemetery, plot 03-25-7.

[102]"EFTS President Dies Suddenly," *Abbotsford, Sumas and Matsqui News*, 3 November 1943, 3. See also *The Vancouver Sun*, 1 and 2 November 1943.

[103]*Moose Jaw Times-Herald*, 8 November 1943.

[104]"McKercher, Lieutenant Stewart," in RG150, vol. 6988–63, LAC.

[105]*Sky: Memories of Abbotsford, 1944* (Abbotsford, 1944), 2. Stewart McKercher assumed a directorship of the VATC at the time he assumed the general manager's position with the VATC/

BBFTS. His name appears under the former office in the VATC *Annual Report*, 31 March 1944, which was filed with the federal government. See "Vancouver Air Training Company Limited."

[106]Air Force officials responded to this surplus by increasing the duration of the EFTS and SFTS training course. Although No. 33 EFTS (RAF) did not have its standard eight-week curriculum lengthened, other EFTSs were soon offering ten-week programs.

[107]Malcolm MacDonald, UK high commissioner, letter to C. G. Power, minister of national defence for air, 15 November 1943, in "BCATP Schools: Re-Organization of," in RG24, vol. 3213, 2, LAC. See also "Minutes of the 97th (Special) Meeting Held at 10:30 a.m. on Thursday, 4th November, 1943," 1, in AIR 20/1379: "Empire Air Training Scheme Committee Minutes of Meetings, Jan. 1940—October 1945," UKNA.

[108]Leckie, *Final Report*, 50.

[109]A/V/M Robert Leckie, acting CAS(C), described the ground crew shortage in Britain in a 29 November 1943 memorandum. See "BCATP Schools: Re-Organization of." The RAF AMT noted that some 67,000 maintenance personnel were needed to bring them up to full strength. See the Air Ministry's "Proposed Revision of Over-All Aircrew Training Requirements: Notes by AMT, RAF," in AIR 20/1378: "Empire Air Training Scheme Committee, Papers Relating to Training in Canada, 1944–46," UKNA.

[110]Document dated 2 December 1943," in "BCATP Schools: Re-Organization of." Since Caron was civilianized, its closure did not directly release RAF ground crew. However, closing the five RAF SFTSs, to which Caron supplied student pilots, did free up ground crew.

[111]Document dated 18 November 1943, in "BCATP Schools: Re-Organization of."

[112]*Daily Diary*, No. 33 EFTS (RAF), 27 November 1943.

[113]*The Breeze*, 7 January and 28 January 1944.

[114]*The Breeze*, 4 February 1944.

[115]*Daily Diary*, No. 33 EFTS (RAF), 13 November 1943.

[116]*Daily Diary*, No. 33 EFTS (RAF), 6, 7, 14 January 1944.

[117]*Daily Diary*, No. 33 EFTS (RAF), 30 April 1943.

[118]*Daily Diary*, No. 33 EFTS (RAF), 31 January 1944. Several months after the BBFTS arrived in Caron to take over No. 33 EFTS (RAF), Leslie Martin noted that there was a "perfect harmony" between the BBFTS and the RAF personnel. It should be recalled that the relations between Mr. Martin and the RCAF at No. 8 EFTS and No. 18 EFTS had been anything but harmonious. This affirmation of his experience at Caron may well have gained something by way of contrast with these prior situations. See the *Moth Monthly*, August 1942, 40.

[119]Hank McDowell, interviews by the author, Moose Jaw, SK, 4 June, 7 June, 20 August 2010.

CHAPTER 5

Teaching Caron

We count on the training plan to supply a great tide of airmen. . . .
We'd prefer 1,000 pilots from you later than 10 to-day.[1]
—Sir Winston Churchill

Figure 5.1. LAC Abraham Lawrence.
Source: Author's collection.

Abraham Lawrence arrived at Caron on 1 May 1943. Three years earlier, with the German invasion of England looming, he and his father changed their Jewish surname, Levy, to Lawrence.[2] In or about October 1942, the RAF sent Lawrence to No. 17 ITW in Scarborough, North Yorkshire, where he received instruction in the standard pre-flight syllabus.[3] Many of the subjects, itemized in Table 5.1, were repeated in whole or in part at his subsequent grading course and again at Caron.

Table 5.1

Pre-flying subjects[4]

Subjects
Anti-Gas
Aircraft Recognition
Armament
Drill and Physical Training
Engines
Hygiene and Sanitation
Law and Discipline
Administration and Organization
Mathematics
Meteorology
Air Navigation
Principles of Flight
Signals

Student pilots like Lawrence were issued a set of printed lecture notes at the commencement of their training. They were required to read them and keep them handy for future reference. These notes not only had the effect of sparing "laborious note taking" but also standardized the curriculum across all RAF schools in the UK and beyond. Students were warned that their notes were for official use only: they were not to be communicated to anyone outside the RAF nor taken into the air.[5] Judging by his annotations and personal notebooks, AC2 Lawrence received instruction in air navigation, meteorology, engines, and theory of flight while at No. 17 ITW.

Lawrence's air navigation unit taught him how to determine his aircraft's position at any instant and guide it from one location to another. Toward this end, he received instruction in map-reading, navigating by the stars, dead reckoning, determining air and ground speed, and the proper use of compasses and altimeters. Rumour had it that if a fledging pilot did too well in this subject, he would be reassigned to navigation training and lose his opportunity to become a pilot. More than a few of the mathematically-gifted found themselves transferred to an AOS or ANS for this reason.

Lawrence's notebooks indicate that while he was at No. 17 ITW he also attended meteorological lectures on atmospheric pressure, temperature, wind, cloud types, fog, frost, visibility, and basic weather maps. A notation in the meteorology syllabus indicates that the second half of this subject would be taught during the EFTS phase of his training. Subjects covered in this latter portion were to include weather forecasts, meteorological codes, ice formation, flying in clouds, and the role of the meteorological officer. By the time Lawrence arrived at Caron, meteorology had been transferred to the advanced schools and no longer figured in the elementary curriculum.

For the two months or so that Lawrence was at Scarborough, he also studied the principles and subsystems of internal combustion engines. This unit intended to help the novice pilot understand the relation between his cockpit controls and the aircraft's mechanical and electrical systems and that "there are wrong and right ways of handling engine-controls." In addition, he learned about the timing, fuel, ignition, lubrication, and cooling systems of aero-engines. In preparation for his final exam on engines, Lawrence wrote a "dummy" exam and received a grade of eighty-three per cent.

Although printed notes on the principles of flight are missing from his binder, Lawrence produced two small exercise books on the subject.[6] This unit instructed him on the reasons why his aircraft performed as it did and how he might prevent mistakes arising from ignorance. His notes show that lift, drag, differences in air pressure, stability, stalling, trimming and control devices, and gliding were also covered. By the end of this course, Lawrence had practice questions to aid his preparation for the final exam.

Lawrence also assembled a scrapbook to bolster his aircraft recognition skills. It contained pictorial entries on over seventy aircraft used by British, American, German, and Italian air forces. He clipped and pasted illustrative materials from at least three published sources. A typical entry included a photo of the aircraft, a series of ink profiles, wingspan, length, height, engine, and armament specifications, and a list of its principal structural features and special recognition points. In a few instances, Lawrence resorted to his own line-drawings.[7]

Just into the new year (1943), Lawrence was posted to No. 4 EFTS at Brough, East Yorkshire where he underwent a grading or elimination course.[8] Pre-EFTS grading courses had been instituted in response to the high failure rate which dogged the first RAF cohorts sent to Canada.[9] By 1943, aspiring pilots like Lawrence spent six or more weeks at a UK elementary airfield demonstrating their basic aptitude. While at Brough, Lawrence practiced taxiing, straight and level flying, climbing, gliding, stalling, turning, spinning, as well as takeoffs and landings. He apparently passed even though he never flew solo.[10]

LAC Lawrence arrived in Caron in early May 1943. Some 240 students hustled in and out of the flight rooms and ground school (GIS). Table 5.2 itemizes the hours allotted to the various GIS subjects over the standard eight-week EFTS program.[11] The syllabus left little doubt about the purpose of elementary training. Students were to be appraised in three central areas: their mastery of the necessary knowledge, their aptitude for flying, and their "temperamental suitability as a Service pilot."[12] Since pupils who showed persistent nervousness, unsuitable temperaments, or who lacked confidence seldom made good operational pilots, they were to be "*eliminated at the earliest opportunity*."[13]

Table 5.2

GIS subjects and instructional hours, EFTS, May 1942

GIS Subject	Hours
Airmanship (including engines, principles of flight)	30
Aircraft recognition	10
Armament	24
Drill and physical training	35
Navigation	24
Signals (wireless & lamp)	23
Discussions/debates on service subjects & current affairs	8
Total GIS instructional hours	154

Student pilots entering their first day at EFTS could expect something like the following. After breakfast, drill and physical training would be conducted by a NCO and/or a physical training instructor on the parade ground. Trainees would then move to the GIS building for their first hour of signals (wireless) instruction. (After civilianization, the BBFTS employed at least three signals instructors: Mrs. Margaret Bowles, Mr. Hugh Barclay, and Mr. G. O'Leary.[14]) To succeed, student pilots were required to accurately interpret Morse code at the rate of six words per minute. The signals classroom (depicted in Figure 5.2) featured long rows of listening stations where student pilots practiced decoding signals sent to their headsets from a central desk.[15]

Figure 5.2. Wireless (radio) instruction, No. 19 EFTS, Virden, MB, October 1944. This room is similar to that at Caron. Source: LAC/DND fonds, PA-140653. Used with permission.

Later that first morning, students received their one and only hour of parachute instruction. They were introduced to the Irvin parachute and taught how to use, maintain, and inspect it. Even though others (typically, female staff) were charged with airing, examining, hanging, and re-packing parachutes, students were appraised on how they might minimize any unnecessary work.[16] Beyond this initial session, they could expect no further instruction in parachutes: henceforth, luck and instinct would be their guides.

Shortly after arrival, student pilots began their full complement of GIS courses in airmanship, air navigation, armament, and aircraft recognition. The airmanship curriculum at Caron combined theory of flight, airframes, and engines with the matters previously designated as airmanship. The BBFTS course notes acknowledged that this new, broader use of the term might be confusing, but students were assured that a unifying thread ran through the subjects now grouped together under the airmanship nomenclature. Thirty or more classroom hours would be dedicated to this subject area.[17]

The EFTS syllabus mandated that the airmanship unit provide instruction in flying regulations, local flying orders, aerodrome procedures, control tower and duty pilot signals, circuit routes, and flying boundaries. Students could expect additional instruction in engine-starting procedures as well as actions to be taken in the event of a fire or forced landings. The theory of flight also figured in this portion of the curriculum even though many students like Abraham Lawrence had covered its components—airflow, stability, controls, turning, and aerobatics—at their ITW or grading course in the UK.

The Caron airmanship curriculum also contained a subunit on airframes, that is, the study of all parts of the aircraft, save the engine. Student pilots were instructed on how the various components of the aircraft body were constructed and manipulated by their controls and given rudimentary insight into the art of repairing fabric tears. It is likely that the two aircraft engines brought to Caron by the BBFTS served as visual aids when aero-engines became the focus of instruction. A later inventory of instructional equipment at Caron indicated that it possessed two radial engines, two inline engines, and two airframes with rigging.[18] Students were given hands-on and eyes-on instruction in the various components of four-stroke internal combustion engines, including their fueling, timing, cooling, ignition, carburation, and lubrication systems.[19]

The EFTS curriculum also called for twenty-four hours of navigation instruction. Much of the material covered in the EFTS syllabus is identical to what LAC Lawrence had laboured over in the UK. Although his Caron notebooks include only a few terse entries on airmanship, he is alive to matters covered in the navigation course. He became keenly focused on navigational instruction when it finally turned to plotting flight paths and preparing for cross-country flying.[20]

In addition to courses on airmanship and air navigation, Caron offered instruction in armament and aircraft recognition. Unlike other GIS subjects which were taught by BBFTS civilians, uniformed air force personnel were responsible for armament instruction.[21] In October 1943, BCATP officials modified the EFTS syllabus to include the armament units and activities listed in Table 5.3.[22] In this course, student pilots were given an overview of the weaponry used by the RAF as well as brief lessons on Browning machine guns and ammunition, range estimation, and service rifles. Students were then escorted to the nearby 25-yard range (building no. 19) where they were briefed on proper shooting procedures and range discipline before they fired live ammunition. Although the original EFTS syllabus did not allot classroom time for aircraft recognition, by 1942, it dedicated ten hours to the skill. By October 1943, the hours allotted to aircraft recognition had risen to fourteen.[23]

Table 5.3

GIS armament instruction, EFTS, October 1943

Subject	**Classroom Hours**	**Range Hours**	**Total Hours**
Service rifle	2	8	10
Browning gun	5	4	9
Ammunition	1		1
Range estimation	4		4
Totals	**12**	**12**	**24**

In addition to their ground school curriculum, student pilots at Caron were assigned to the Link Flight Trainers. Although widely used to screen aspiring pilots, Link simulators also had their place in the EFTS and SFTS curricula.[24] In 1940, the EFTS syllabus mandated a mere five hours of Link exercises; by 1941, ten hours were called for.[25] By the time that Caron opened in 1942, student pilots were expected to log thirty hours in the trainers before their graduation from SFTS.[26] Many trainees disliked these unforgiving, mechanical tutors.

And although flying instructors occasionally complained that they taught bad habits, the Link instructors at Caron insisted that they were the "greatest mental disciplinarian in the world."[27]

Figure 5.3. Link Flight Trainer instruction, No. 19 EFTS, Virden, MB, October 1944. This room is similar to that at Caron. Source: LAC/DND fonds, PA-140658. Used with permission.

Edwin Link developed his flying trainer at his family's piano and organ factory in Binghamton, New York.[28] Using organ valves, bellows, and controls, he created a sophisticated system that allowed the simulator to produce rotation around all three flying axes (pitch, roll, and yaw). The instructor's control desk featured a bank of gauges that allowed him to monitor the student pilot as he responded to flying instructions. An ink plotter traced the pupil's flight path on a paper map, thus leaving a record of his navigational prowess (or not). Aspiring pilots who were confused by these simulated flying exercises were sometimes washed out even before they had been aloft.

The third component of the training at Caron occurred in what Ted Barris calls the "cockpit classroom."[29] It is here, of course, that aspiring pilots faced the most exacting scrutiny. The success of this component depended not only on the pupil's mastery of the specific flying skills but on the teaching competency and morale of his flying instructors. Five of the original flying instructors at Caron had flown operations during the Battle of Britain. Peter Boot, DFC, who served at Caron almost until the end, had been decorated for destroying several enemy aircraft. Alwyn Edgley who flew with 253 Squadron had sustained a serious shoulder injury during a crash landing. Walter Ellis fought with 92 Squadron and recorded several enemy kills. Glyn Griffiths, DFM, also earned distinction in the great air battle. After his return to England from Caron, Griffiths was badly burned during operations over France. And Isaac Howitt, who served with 42 Squadron, arrived in Canada shortly after he received his commission in October 1941.[30]

It is difficult to imagine the disillusionment that accompanied instructional postings to Canada in the aftermath of the excitement and terror of the air war. More than a few instructors pined for the heady days of mortal danger rather than the numbing peace and comfort of their instructional duties. Many of the flying instructors who had undergone their training in Canada also had reason to be disheartened. Their anticipation of conducting operations against the enemy had been crushed when they were posted to domestic instructional duties. A host of highly-skilled RAF and RCAF pilots would never see enemy operations or, if they did, they arrived in Europe just as hostilities were winding down. For many, the thousands of hours of instructional duty paled in comparison to the thrill of a single, real operation against the enemy.[31]

By early 1943, the BCATP could supply the requisite flying instructors from its own schools. During that year, dozens of flying instructors, chiefly from No. 3 FIS in Arnprior, ON arrived at Caron. Many were later transferred back to a FIS in posts that saw them training flying instructors rather than student pilots. Caron also witnessed a steady stream of incoming and outgoing instructors who moved easily between the EFTSs and SFTSs in No. 4 Training Command.[32] Some moved on from Caron to become staff pilots at B&GSs and ANSs.

The standard EFTS syllabus included four distinct flying competencies. The first developed the ability to carry out normal aircraft manoeuvres including takeoff, climbing, level flying, gliding, turning, and landing. The second taught emergency procedures, including forced landings, voluntary and involuntary spins, and stalls. The third included instruction in aerobatics such as loops, half-rolls, and slow-rolls.[33] The final aspect of airborne training aimed to develop navigational skills to the level that basic compass courses could be followed, and the student pilot could successfully plan and execute a cross-country flight of fifty miles or more.[34]

The original EFTS syllabus allocated fifty hours to air exercises, twenty-five of which were to be flown solo. However, by May 1942, BCATP officials expected that sixty flying hours would be allocated to air exercises. The revised curriculum appears in Table 5.4. The increase in hours did little to add new skills, although it did shift the emphasis towards navigational, instrument, and night flying. The flying instruction at Caron following the sequence of exercises in Table 5.5.[35]

Table 5.4

Revised EFTS flying instructional hours, 1942

Flying Instruction Type[36]	**Hours in 8-Week Course**
With instructor (dual)	
Clear hood	18
Instrument flying	7
Navigation	4
Night flying	3
Total dual	**32**
Solo	
Clear hood	24
Navigation	3
Night	1
Total solo	**28**
Minimum total (dual & solo)	**60**

Student pilots could expect to advance through the exercises in Table 5.5 as they mastered its elements. Pupils would be formally appraised after twelve, twenty, and fifty hours of air training. These progress tests were administered by the CFI or another senior officer not involved in the student's day-to-day instruction. The flight commander's test after twelve hours usually determined the fate of an aspiring pilot. Results from the initial GIS examinations were made available to the CFI and his senior colleagues as they deliberated on the outcome of this important test. LAC Lawrence had his career as a pilot terminated at this point.

Table 5.5[37]

Sequence, flying training exercises, EFTS, 1942

Exercise	Description
1a	Air experience
1b	Familiarity with cockpit layout
2	Effect of controls
3	Taxiing and handling of engine
4	Straight and level flying
5	Climbing, gliding, and stalling
6	Medium turns
7	Taking off into wind
8	Powered approach and landing
9	Gliding approach and landing
	Flight Commander's Test
10a	Spinning from a straight glide
10b	Incipient spin from a gliding turn
10c	Incipient spin from a turn with insufficient power
11	First solo
12	Side slipping
13	Precautionary landings
14	Low flying (dual only)
15	Steep turns
16	Climbing turns

Exercise	Description
17	Forced landings (dual only)
18a	Action in event of fire (dual only)
18b	Abandoning of aircraft
19	Instrument flying
20	Taking off and landing out of wind
21	[Intentionally left blank]
22	Aerobatics
23	Navigation exercises
	(1) Steering by compass
	(2) Turning from one course to another
	(3) Recognition of pinpoints
	(4) Use of time scale
	(5) Solo (turning from one course to another)
	(6) Pinpoints
24	Cross country test

Students like LAC Lawrence were carefully prepared for their first solo flight. In the days leading up to the flight, student pilots had to formally indicate that they had read and understood the flying orders of the school. Further, they signed off that they understood the hydraulic, braking, and gasoline systems of their aircraft, as well as its emergency procedures. And finally, they certified that they knew how to locate the authorized low flying and forced landing areas. LAC Lawrence dutifully signed off on these matters, even though he would never fly solo.[38]

The growing emphasis on night flying at the Canadian EFTSs mirrored the Allies' increasing emphasis on night bombing over Germany. This new strategy added complexity to the EFTS curriculum and the physical plant required to support these initiatives. Overnight accommodations, electric power, and telephones were now needed for the staff charged with supervising night flying operations at remote relief fields. The staff at Caron's R.1 near Boharm now had to set and maintain the flare path, a series of flaming markers that guided night flyers safely onto the grass field.[39] The first night solos at Caron were conducted in August 1942 when seven student pilots successfully completed the operation.[40] Night solos soon became commonplace.[41]

EFTS instructors struggled to provide sixty flying hours per student. With 240 students at Caron, an average of 1,800 flying hours per week were required. In many cases, the standard, eight-week course had to be extended to achieve the minimum flying time. And contrary to the view of some early detractors, No. 4 Training Command, which covered the southern half of Saskatchewan, Alberta, and British Columbia, lost the fewest flying days of any training command in Canada. A January 1943 study of the previous three Decembers revealed that the eastern Canadian commands lost an average of forty-three per cent of their flying time due to unsuitable weather whereas the commands in western Canada lost only twenty-five per cent.[42]

Course no. 44, which graduated in May 1942, had to be extended to ten and a half weeks because it included some twenty-eight days deemed unfit for flying.[43] The weather conditions in the early months of 1943 were particularly challenging. Courses nos. 67 to 71 were granted extensions totaling forty-nine days. Because of the backlog produced by these extensions, BCATP officials cancelled course no. 74 outright. Weather-related delays caused considerable variability in the number of flying hours available to the courses. For example, course no. 73 graduated with an average of 72:35 hours, whereas course no. 75 graduated with an average of only 50:55 hours per pupil.[44]

Robert William Pape arrived at Caron on 5 April 1942. Like Abraham Lawrence, he began his pilot training at No. 17 ITW in Scarborough.[45] He spent a month at No. 1 EFTS in Hatfield where he logged five hours of flying time before sailing for Canada. While at Caron, LAC Pape progressed smoothly through the air exercises. On 11 May, he underwent the flight commander's test. Two days later he executed his first solo flight. He slowly worked his way through the training sequence, adding instrument flying on 15 May. Due to the civilian changeover, Pape lost two weeks of flying time in mid-May. He resumed flying on 27 May, practicing low flying, side slipping, and instrument flying.

Figure 5.4. Course no. 65, 1 October 1942, Caron. Source: Author's collection.

On 2 June, F/O Geoffrey J. Wright administered LAC Pape's twenty-hour flying test. He passed. He then focused on turns, takeoffs, and landings whenever he was flying solo. During the first week of June, he practiced steering by compass and turning from one course to another. He passed his fifty-hour test on 21 June and planned and executed his cross-country test the following day. During the final week of June, he continued to perform solo aerobatics and undertook night flying, logging twelve landings.

LAC Pape passed out of Caron and was posted to No. 37 SFTS (RAF) in Calgary, AB. His final assessment noted that he logged sixty-seven and a half hours of flying time at Caron. His instructors rated his ability as average. CFI Hayward advised Pape's next supervisor that he "requires constant checking" since he is "inclined to get very careless." Unfortunately, LAC Pape washed out at Calgary but was re-mustered as a bomb aimer and transferred to No. 2 B&GS at Mossbank, SK. He would later fly operations with No. 10 Squadron (Melbourne). P/O Robert William Pape received the DFC in 1944.[46]

Figure 5.5. Course no. 65 (selected members), October 1942, Caron.

Source: Author's collection.

Corporal E. E. Fox arrived at Caron in late February 1943. By the time he finished, he had accumulated seventy-seven and a half hours of flying time, some of which appears to have been logged prior to his arrival. His logbook provides helpful information on his cross-country solo flights. On 12 April, he flew sixty miles east from Caron to Regina and then back again. During the flight, he practiced all six sub-elements of training sequence no. 23, except (5). The following day, he flew approximately fifty miles NNE to Liberty and then thirty miles NW to Davidson where he landed at No. 23 EFTS. His return flight from Davidson to Caron covered approximately sixty miles. Once again, he practiced sequence no. 23 (1)–(4).

Following custom, the BBFTS hosted a dinner in celebration of course no. 75's graduation at the CPR Restaurant Banquet Hall in Moose Jaw. Besides the usual good-byes and accolades, E. E. Fox and his fellows were treated to a roast turkey dinner, including ice cream and cake. Although the official record is silent in this instance, BBFTS officials likely honoured the top GIS student.[47]

(The first class to graduate from Caron in March 1942 awarded its top student, LAC W. Darbyshire, a small trophy and bracelet.[48]) It is also likely that Leslie Martin, BBFTS's general manager, hosted the celebration on that warm spring day as he had ever since the first class of twenty-three graduated from No. 8 EFTS some two and half years previous.[49]

Figure 5.6. Course no. 65 signatories, October 1942, Caron. Source: Author's collection.

Some of Caron's most demanding lessons were taught outside the formal curriculum. For instance, what were the airmen and officers to make of their prairie setting? How could its vast emptiness be assimilated to their previous experience? For many, it would remain an enigma. Some, however, came to more considered views once they recovered from the initial shock. Assumptions rooted in their experience as well as the influential views of the English romantics contributed to the numbing disorientation occasioned by their new environs.

The first contingent of RAF personnel to arrive at Caron travelled nearly five thousand miles in a span of two weeks.[50] It took ten days to cross the 2,600 miles of ocean between Scotland and Halifax.[51] When they arrived, they were immediately hustled aboard antiquated colonist railway cars for a four-day journey across the Canadian hinterland.[52] The enormity of the cumulative distance would have been unparalleled for most since they traversed a distance equivalent to the width of England—some three hundred miles—each day of their journey.

The seafaring leg of their journey pre-figured elements of their Canadian experience. Other than the oppressive waves that hounded them, there was little to see other than the featureless horizon and the drama played out in the skies. No doubt they would have concurred with William Quayle's apt observation that the "[p]rairie and sea plant no other hedgerows than the sky."[53] The tediousness of the ocean and its inhospitable, even violent, disregard for human comfort turned out to be a foretaste of the tutelage to follow.

The first two thousand miles of their overland journey into the Canadian heartland would have been disconcerting and alien. By UK standards, even Canada's larger centres were small, primitive, and remote. With few exceptions, the countryside must have appeared nearly as empty as the ocean itself. Table 5.6 highlights one aspect of their UK experience, which contrasted starkly with what they observed as they rattled westward across the frozen dominion. The singular paucity of human beings could only have heightened the lonely emptiness felt by those introduced to Canada's interminable landscapes.

Table 5.6

Population density by geographic unit, 1941

Geographic Unit	Land Area (sq. miles)	Population (1940/41)	Population Density (persons/sq. mile)
United Kingdom	94,247	48,216,000	512
England proper	50,346	41,000,000	814
Canada	3,855,101	11,506,655	3.0
Saskatchewan	251,366	895,992	3.6
Municipality of Caron	217	1,020	4.7

The central portion of their Canadian journey would have taken them north of the Great Lakes where a new type of monotony would have been almost as spirit-crushing as the ocean. For although this rugged region sports a myriad of small lakes, trees, and pre-Cambrian rock outcroppings, there is little else. Regardless of the picturesque vignettes offered up by what Pierre Berton called the "gnarled expanse of granite ridges and stunted pines," the endless recurrence of the same would have soon benumbed even the most attentive.[54] Vernon Peters, who journeyed with the first contingent and had so eagerly anticipated "seeing something of Canada's much-talked-of scenery" likely had reason to reconsider.[55]

After twelve, fatiguing days of sequential monotonies, the RAF group experienced yet another: the prairies. The topographical uniformity and continental scale of the region were disorienting.[56] Peters bluntly reported that the landscape around Caron was "bleak and desolate."[57] Several days later he fleshed out his complaint, noting that "the clean air gives you a horizon about 20 miles away & it is dead flat all the way except just to the southwest where a low range of hills breaks the monotony."[58] Several months later, he again complained that "the scenery around Caron is dim. Standing on any one spot within a hundred-mile radius, the view is the same: flat, deadly monotonous."[59] Eighteen months later, he recalled his initial impression of the area as a "bleak, uninviting, hopeless expanse of dreariness, icebound and snowbound as far as eye could reach."[60]

The station magazines at Caron documented the first impressions of those arriving from the UK. Typically, they characterized the region as "baldheaded," "naturally tedious," a "vast nothingness," or "flat and blank."[61] A particularly insightful account lamented that "[o]ne is quite naturally disappointed in the prairie. It seems impossible that the pioneers of those glorious Technicolor films actually trekked across these characterless wastes. Surely no Indians could ever have roamed here."[62] In the understated words of another, Caron was "not entirely a land flowing of milk and honey."[63]

From their first contact with the interior plains of North America, British explorers and adventurers often mistook the prairie's treelessness for non-arability or even sterility. In the early-to-mid-eighteenth century, when enduring impressions of Canada were first communicated to the British public, trees were taken as indicators of the soil's productivity. In well-watered, temperate England, this rule of thumb served well, but it could not be applied without qualification to the dry regions in the middle of North America. The prairies could easily be mistaken for a barren desert.[64]

Another motif surfaced from time to time in the views of the RAF staff and students, one which adopted a different stance towards the encompassing flatlands. Leonard Smith, who arrived with the first cohort of student pilots in January 1942, later recalled the "huge mantle of prairie sky."[65] *The Moth Monthly* noted that the vast extent of the country was a "source of wonderment."[66] Even Vernon Peters who, despite his initial disappointments, would become quite attached to the place, noted that he could breathe at Caron.[67]

Perhaps the best way to reconcile these varying experiences is to acknowledge a fundamental axiom: it takes time and attention to overcome the nullity of the prairie landscape. Student pilots were at a considerable disadvantage in this regard since they came and went within a mere eight weeks. Nevertheless, for some, the countryside slowly "assumed a definite shape." Some found that "there *are* details from which to navigate—once we have got used to the new terrain."[68] Others who were initially transfixed by the deadly power of the blizzards, the preternatural mid-winter thaws, or the unchecked reign of the midday sun, with time, also noticed the antic dance of the *aurora borealis* (northern lights), the luminous sun-dogs (concentric rings of refracted light surrounding the winter sun), or, on rare occasions, mirages of far-away buildings and lights.[69]

The prairie offered little to the uninterested or uninitiated.[70] At first, she only made demands. She insisted on a willingness to endure her moods. She abhorred the pretensions of the proud but gave her graces to the humble. A penetrating essay in the *Tailspin* mused that she was "a very sly creature. If you do not lie in wait for her and woo her, you may leave her without ever having seen her beauty . . . [She] only reveals her secrets to those who are looking for them."[71] For those who did pay attention, she unfurled her aerial benefactions, her thriving ravines and wetlands, her gophers, rabbits, coyotes, foxes, deer, and noisy convoys of migrating waterfowl. To those who bothered to make her acquaintance, she taught that not all topography rises above the horizon. Those who were particularly favoured might learn, as Vernon Peters did, to breathe her bracing air. And those willing to enroll in her post-graduate seminar and plumb her most subtle mysteries might learn something of "the emotional power of space."[72]

Something must be said about the prairie that greeted those who arrived in the Caron district. By 1940, the region and its grasslands had been scandalously degraded by ill-chosen farming methods. The deep tillage and summer fallow techniques passed along to inexperienced farmers left millions of tons of topsoil exposed to the winds and droughts of the 1920s and 30s. The native grasses over which the first settlers and Indigenous peoples roamed, and which could endure indefinite drought without losing their hold on the soil, had been systematically ploughed under. A period of prolonged drought easily eradicated nonnative cereal and forage crops and exposed vast areas of denuded soils to the unchecked winds. Millions of acres were thusly stripped of their meagre topsoil. Whatever vegetation survived faced perils from virulent Russian thistles, grasshoppers, and army worms. Soil drifting and dust storms redistributed a thousand years of hard-won topsoil along fence lines and sand-blasted farm buildings.

It is entirely appropriate, then, for the *Moth Monthly* to question why pioneers had trekked across "these characterless wastes" or even if Indigenous peoples had ever hunted in these parts.[73] The writer could not have known that the virgin prairie had been ravished by the misguided actions of these same pioneers. The nourishing, indestructible, native grasses that had attracted the interest of bison, Indigenous peoples, and settlers alike were now largely gone. The semi-arid wastes of the early 1940s were not the primordial prairies. The ranchers who knew the land well, the Indigenous peoples who rightly feared the encroachment of white settlers, the few government officials who loathed this great land-use experiment, as well as the judgement of careful afterthought can be summed up in Timothy Egan's clarion judgement: "This grass was never meant to be plowed."[74]

Nevertheless, even under ideal conditions, neither Caron nor the prairie could meet the expectations of those weaned on British notions of country living and landscape experience.[75] The Romantic Movement contributed in no small way to the cultural prominence of these ideals. This movement, which reached its zenith in the work of William Wordsworth at the beginning of the nineteenth century, postulated a unity between Nature, Infinite Spirit, and the human heart. Human faculties, chiefly the heart or imagination, were no longer fallen or corrupted but vessels through which the Infinite expressed itself.[76] Pristine, picturesque Nature put artists and poets in direct contact with the Infinite. Their deepest feelings purportedly pushed to the surface the great expressive current that flowed in and through every natural thing.[77] In Wordsworth's couplet: "To her fair works did nature link / The human soul that through me ran."[78] Only nature—of the English countryside variety—could resuscitate modern life.[79]

Romanticism made the tedious sameness of the dun-coloured prairie even more disconcerting.[80] The great romantics idealized the one-of-a-kind. The Infinite Spirit spoke most clearly through the misshapen, the singular, the picturesque, the grotesque, and especially, the solitary.[81] Wordsworth's poems are filled with vignettes celebrating the social peculiarity of shepherds, peddlers, hermits, woodsmen, travelers, and wanderers. His physical environment, too, is filled with idiosyncratic bowers, hedgerows, groves, lofty crags, solitary cliffs, lonesome peaks, and bejeweled sunsets. If these features of the English countryside were supposed antidotes to the crushing monotony of industrial and urban modes of life, how could the prairie withstand the romantic gaze?

The British experience at Caron can be analyzed bluntly: the prairie crushed their notions of nature and rurality. Its features were antithetical to the general belief in the regenerative power of country settings.[82] It offered little that was quaintly picturesque: there were no endearing, peculiar niches. It seemed to be entirely bereft of history; nothing had left "a clear cultural impress."[83] From all appearances, nothing reached out longingly to bygone eras; everything was less than a half-century old! Whatever might have captured the interest of a romantic sensibility had been, in the words of the nineteenth-century American poet, Emily Dickinson, "[g]athered into the Earth / And out of story."[84] For those weaned on such notions, the prairie proved intractable.[85]

There was little in romanticized notions of country life that could have prepared the RAF personnel for the sheer size and unrelenting uniformity of Canada's vast interior regions. The massive, geometric grid imposed on the prairie by the Dominion Land Survey must have seemed otherworldly, perhaps immoral, to those accustomed to tiny pasturages, irregular meadows, meandering stone fences, marshy fens, and land-use traditions evolved over a millennium. And, to top it all, this never-ending, mute, denuded land was empty.

The Caron airbase's parsimony and charmlessness did little to counter its environment. Its exterior surfaces—even its roofs—were monoliths of cedar shingles besmeared with a single drab colour. Only the simplest, most utilitarian geometries elbowed their way into its design. There were no trees, ornamental plants or decorative elements save for the whitewashed stones lining its paths. The clumpy grass, weeds, and sea of sandy soil that penetrated the place did little to diffuse the tedium. Even a blanket of fresh snow offered little respite.

Figure 5.7. Aerial view of No. 33 EFTS (RAF), fall 1943.
Source: CATP Museum, Brandon, MB. Used with permission.

The nearby village of Caron also had little to offer an eye attuned to the charms of British village and country life. Vernon Peters described it as "a typical 1 shack prairie township."[86] Student pilots commented that it did little to inspire;

they couldn't find much to say in its favour.[87] Compared to Moose Jaw, to say nothing of their homeland, the village's few stores, post office, Chinese laundry, and hulking grain elevator were of little interest.[88] But here again, it is important to recall that this disheveled, unkempt confluence of 150 residents had just come through the catastrophe of the 1930s.[89] Maintaining its plain wooden buildings and simple streets had been impossible in a period when tax revenues, commercial receipts, and personal incomes had fallen to nearly nothing. But even under ideal conditions, Caron's dirty-faced buildings could do little to counter the vapidity of the surrounding sandy pastures and fields.[90]

Given what must have seemed a conspiracy of blandness, it is no wonder that the glories of the rising and setting sun attracted more than a few starved sensibilities. The sunsets and sunrises of the early 1940s were spectacular. The large quantity of air-borne dust enhanced their splendour by an order of magnitude. In February 1943, the *Moth Monthly* included the following account of a winter sunrise over the prairie:

> Sunrise here is often more colourful than the sunset; to catch it right, from the crew-room window, is an amazing experience. A thin blood red streak bows from the horizon and melts into a pink glow, then yellowish-green, finally disappearing into the blue depths that night has left behind. The Tigers [Tiger Moths], arranged in lines and silhouetted against the snow and the sunrise, tick over almost joyfully. One is quite surprised to find that the place is beautiful.[91]

The author notes, however, that the sunrise is only one of two hours a day that are worthy of the lyricism of Wordsworth or the artistry of J. M. W. Turner, England's greatest landscape painter. Regrettably, the day itself is beneath the notice of these romantic worthies. In characterizing the midday, the author revealed his underlying sensibility. The sun, if not the prairie itself, is a romantic disappointment.

> But soon you see you were right after all. The sun gets up and in its hard and horizontal glare the countryside assumes a shabby, dim outlook, hum-drum and heartless, unloving and unloved by all save those who gripe their very existence from the living soil. And even they fear it.[92]

All is not lost, however. The evening sun once again offers something of note.

> Again, at night fall, this flat and uninteresting stretch of prairie dons a cloak of momentary glory. The long views, caught in the oblique rays of the descending sun, swim in a hazy sea of blue twilight. There are long shadows on the snow and the ground melts away into a distant panorama of light and shade caressed by the western glow. Soon the lights of distant villages twinkle, suspended in the dusky twilight, as if in answer to the stars. And then everything is plunged into darkness and the oblivion it deserves.[93]

Even the spectacular prairie sunset, which lit up the western sky with effusions of red, orange, mauve, and lavender, is scarcely more than a postmortem on the sun's otherwise dreary circuit. It is hard not to feel the disappointment and longing that permeates this account. At its best, the sunset is but a momentary respite; even it cannot sate the unquenched longings of the heart.

The *Daily Diary* for No. 32 SFTS (RAF) in nearby Moose Jaw offered a remarkable tribute to various glories manifest in the prairie sky.[94] But unlike the author of Caron's *Moth Monthly* account, this (unnamed) writer noticed that the glories of the sunset are complemented by the glories of the midday and night skies. After acknowledging the initial impression that the prairie was a "treeless unmysterious landscape," the *Diary* turns to praise the "vast overarch of the sky" and its "supernal blue." For those who are willing, the boundless sky can teach "the emotional power of space." This lesson had been lost on the *Moth Monthly* writer who saw only shabbiness, dimness, and unloveliness in the interregnum between sunrise and sunset.

The Moose Jaw account continues. "And when evening draws the clouds in a tangled skein the colour deepens in the wheat expanse till the tortured flames of mauve and scarlet that issue from the west come full circle and turn their intensity into the earth."[95] The descent of the evening sun is not fatally disappointing for there are other wonders at hand. After the sun set and the prairie receded into inky oblivion, another marvel appeared in the crisp clear air: "the infinite reaches of the stars." For this writer (and many others), the density of the star blanket can overwhelm. In Timothy Egan's phrase, on the prairie one can see the stars behind the stars. Infinity would never be an abstraction for those who gaze into the ever-receding depths of the prairie night sky.[96]

Although the Moose Jaw writer feels the romantic power of the sunset's spectacle and the disappointment of the landscape's midday tedium every bit as much as his colleague at Caron, he came to appreciate the surprising potency of the prairie sky itself. Like his Caron compatriot, he acknowledged the beauty of the evening lights that emanate from villages and farmyards near and far. After several years of blackouts in Britain, these earthbound lights catch his fancy as complements to those in the sky above. Although there may be monotony and uniformity aplenty, there are glories that even a romantic sensibility can appreciate once it is attuned to the scale of the region and the dominance of the sky.

Endnotes

[1]Sentiment attributed to Winston Churchill and the UK government, in Smith, *The British Commonwealth Air Training Plan*, 7.

[2]The official notice of this name change was published in the *London Gazette*, 9 April 1940, 2115.

[3]The author's private collection includes Abraham Lawrence's notebooks from No. 17 ITW. These exercise books contain handwritten notes on air navigation, meteorology, internal combustion engines, and the theory (or principles) of flight.

[4]Curriculum issued by the Air Ministry's Directorate of Flying Training, March 1942.

[5]*Air Crew Lecture Notes*, frontispiece.

[6]Lawrence's notes indicate that he was instructed in the standard RAF curriculum on the theory or principles of flight. Similar introductory materials can be found in the Air Ministry publication *Elementary Flying Training: Cadets' Handbook* (London: Stationery Office, 1943).

[7]Abraham Lawrence's aircraft recognition scrapbook is in the author's possession.

[8]In addition to ground school, grading programs required twelve hours of flying time. After six or seven hours of dual flying, the student pilot typically attempted his first solo flight. Long experience had shown that those who soloed quickest were most likely to succeed as pilots. One official estimate suggested that grading courses saved some 350 round-trip passages between the UK and Canada each month. See *History of Flying Training*, Part II, 96.

[9]In the case of the first course (no. 40) at Caron, some twenty-nine of the eighty-nine washed out, a rather startling thirty per cent failure rate. See *Daily Diary*, No. 33 EFTS (RAF), 13 March 1942.

[10]Abraham Lawrence's flying logbook is in the author's possession.

[11]"Air Training Conference—May 1942—Training of Aircrew."

[12]A 20 January 1941 letter from A/C Leckie to the BCATP training commands insisted that the primary question was not whether a given candidate could learn to fly an elementary aircraft. Rather, the question was, could he become "an efficient Service pilot?" On no account should a student to be babied along simply "because he is such a nice fellow." See RCAF HQ file 306-100-A65-1, vol. 1, in Hatch, "BCATP," 349–50.

[13]RCAF, *Elementary Flying Training School Syllabus*, 4th ed., 22 January 1941, 1, in Delta Museum and Archives, accession 2005–037. Emphasis is in the original.

[14]See the *Moth Monthly*, January 1943, September 1942, and October 1942.

[15]"RAF Standard Syllabus: EFTS," in "Supervisory Board—BCATP. Minutes of Meetings," in RG24, vol. 5233, LAC.

[16]Ground Instruction School schedule, No. 8 EFTS, July 1940. After Caron's civilization in May 1942, a staff of civilian females inspected, repaired, dried, and packed parachutes. See the *Moth Monthly*, November 1942, 31.

[17]See the No. 33 EFTS (RAF) printed lectures notes in the author's possession.

[18]Kennerley, *History of Caron RAF,* 20. One of the airframes at Caron was originally registered as CF-ANN. This Fleet II had been loaned to the Aero Club of BC by DND. It would later be used as an instructional airframe at No. 18 EFTS and No. 33 EFTS (RAF). By December 1943, the Aero Club could no longer locate its official registration certificate and asked Mr. Clark, assistant manager at Caron, to destroy it and notify them when the deed had been done. By January 1944, it had been reduced to spare parts. See "Aircraft Registers," in *Golden Years of Aviation,*" http://www.airhistory.org.uk/gy/reg_index.html and "Minutes of Directors meeting, Aero Club of BC (Vancouver) Branch, Wednesday, December 15, [1943]."

[19]It is not surprising that LAC Lawrence took very few notes on engines at Caron since most of the material had been covered at No. 17 ITW.

[20]By 1943, the RAF was in dire need of navigators. Huge surpluses of pilots were projected as were corresponding deficiencies of navigators. No. 4 Training Command's flying and specialized training unit sent its navigation officers to confer with the training staff at Caron no less than three times in 1943. See *Daily Diary,* No. 33 EFTS (RAF), 3 March, 17 October, and 22 October 1943. A SFTS navigation conference was held at No. 4 Training Command on 4 November 1943. An EFTS navigation conference was held two days later. See *Daily Diary,* No. 4 Training Command, 4 and 6 November 1943.

[21]On 26 August 1943, the *Daily Diary* noted the arrival of SGT Washburn who had been posted to No. 33 EFTS (RAF) as an armament instructor. On 11 October, the *Daily Diary* noted that CPL Ridgway had been posted away from Caron and CPL Brennan had replaced him as the resident armourer.

[22]The armament officer from training command visited No. 33 EFTS (RAF) on 26 November 1943 to discuss the revised curriculum with the armament instructor. See *Daily Diary,* No. 33 EFTS (RAF), 26 November 1943. An armament inspection team visited No. 33 EFTS (RAF) on 7 March 1943 as part of its regular inspection of armament instruction at BCATP schools. See *Daily Diary,* No. 33 EFTS (RAF), 7 March 1943.

[23]W/C L. G. Lewis, memorandum dated 27 October 1943, in "Organization & Establishment—Elementary Flying Training Schools," in RG24, vol. 4955, LAC.

[24]For a brief history of the Link Flight Trainer in Canada, see English, *The Cream of the Crop,* 34–37.

[25]RCAF, *Elementary Flying Training School Syllabus,* 4th ed.

[26]*The Moth Monthly,* February 1942, 10. Matthew Chapman indicates that by the conclusion of the BCATP in 1945, a full 48 hours of Link training was required. See his "BCATP Revisited: The Wartime Evolution of Flight Training in Canada," *Royal Canadian Air Force Journal* 5, no. 2 (Spring 2016): 15.

[27]Douglas, *The Creation of a National Air Force,* 242. See also the *Moth Monthly,* February 1942, 10.

[28]Some ten thousand trainers were produced by Link Aviation Devices during the Second World War. See *The Link Flight Trainer* (Binghamton, NY: Roberson Museum and Science Center, 2000), http://web.mit.edu/digitalapollo/Documents/Chapter2/linktrainer.pdf.

[29]Barris, *Behind the Glory,* 91.

[30]The information in this paragraph is taken from entries in: Kenneth G. Wynn, *Men of the Battle of Britain* (Norwich: Gliddon Books, 1989) and *Men of the Battle of Britain: Supplementary Volume* (Norwich: Gliddon Books, 1992).

[31]Of the 238 Canadian pilots who graduated from the BCATP in 1940, only twenty were posted to the UK. The rest were assigned to instructional, home defence, or headquarters duties in Canada. See "Minutes of the BCATP Supervisory Board, 13 January 1941," in Hatch, "BCATP," 214.

[32]The *Daily Diary* indicates that several who had graduated from Caron's EFTS and gone on to a FIS had now returned as instructors. For instance, William Harrison-Cripps graduated from Caron in January 1943. By July of the same year, he was back after successfully completing his instructor course at No. 3 FIS. As operations wound down at Caron, Harrison-Cripps was once again posted to No. 3 FIS to serve as an instructor of instructors. If, like most, Harrison-Cripps was keen to fly operations, his circuit must have seemed like a karmic wheel.

[33]The leading figure in the incorporation of aerobatics, side slipping, banked turns, cross-wind landings and other "dangerous stunts" into RFC/RAF flying training was Robert Smith Barry. The freedom he extended to flight commanders and even student pilots was quite disconcerting to many of his peers and superiors. His approach diverged sharply from its conservative antecedents and especially the tightly-controlled French training regime of the time. See Frank D. Tredrey, *Pioneer Pilot: The Great Smith Barry Who Taught the World How to Fly* (London: Davies, 1976), esp. 74–96, 116–17.

[34]"RAF Standard Syllabus: EFTS."

[35]For instance, Robert Pape's logbook entries from No. 1 EFTS in Hatfield, UK contain a sequence of training identical to the one used at No. 33 EFTS (RAF) at the time.

[36]By the fall of 1943, EFTS student pilots could also expect to conduct exercises in night flying, landings, and overshoots. Further, their sequence of training included five exercises in air navigation, which greatly expanded on the simple cross-country flight required previously. These additional requirements at No. 33 EFTS (RAF) can be seen in George W. Knox's pilot's logbook held at the RAF Museum in London (item no. X004-2396/001).

[37]Source: "Air Training Conference—May 1942—Training of Aircrew."

[38]Like many, after his career as a service pilot was cut short, Lawrence re-mustered into another air trade, possibly aerial photography. A letter to his father in June 1945 indicated that he was serving with 681 Photo Reconnaissance Squadron based in Mingaladon, Burma.

[39]By 1943, No. 33 EFTS (RAF) was equipped with modern circuit lights—including electric lights of various colours. Caron's R.1 at Boharm, on the other hand, was equipped with goose-neck, cast-iron, oil flares, which had to be aligned on the airfield and constantly re-fueled, re-set, and monitored. See Frank Broome, *Dead Before Dawn: A Heavy Bomber Tail-gunner in World War II* (Barnsley, South Yorkshire: Pen & Sword, 2008), 77.

[40]*Daily Diary*, No. 33 EFTS (RAF), 28 August 1942.

[41]Many of the adaptations to night flying at the EFTS level were introduced in 1941. In early spring, the EFTS curriculum was modified to include three hours of night flying. EFTSs were modified to include obstruction lights and in some cases, like Caron, to include revolving beacons.

Elementary aircraft were fitted with dashboard and navigational lights. Many of these policy changes were already in place when the specifications for Caron were developed in 1941. See "Report No. 18 by the Chief of the Air Staff to the Members of the Supervisory Board, BCATP," Monday, June 9th, 1941, 4, in AIR 20/1375: "Empire Air Training Scheme Committee, Papers Related to Training in Canada, 1941," UKNA.

[42]18 January 1943 minutes, in "Supervisory Board—BCATP. Minutes of Meetings," in RG24, vol. 5232, LAC.

[43]"RCAF Binder—BCATP—Statistics—Aircrew Training Summary—Dec. 1941 to Jan. 1942," in 181.005 (D1790), DHH. The CAS(C) reported that course no. 42 at Caron had also been extended two weeks due to adverse weather. See "Progress Report No. 28 by the Chief of the Air Staff to the Members of the Supervisory Board, BCATP," Monday, April 20th, 1941, 3, in AIR 20/1376: "Empire Air Training Scheme Committee, 1942," UKNA.

[44]"Air Training: Elementary Flying Training Schools," in RG24, vol. 3389, LAC. Course no. 59, which graduated at the end of August 1942, may well have had the highest average flying time of any course at Caron. Student pilots averaged 75:30 hours of flying time. See *Daily Diary*, No. 33 EFTS (RAF), 28 August 1942.

[45]According to his logbook, Robert Pape was at No. 17 ITW from 12 October 1941 through 9 January 1942.

[46]*Supplement to the London Gazette*, 17 November 1944, 5284.

[47]Very few student pilots averaged above ninety per cent in their GIS studies. For instance, the highest average between course no. 40 and no. 59 was 91.8 per cent. See *Daily Diary*, No. 33 EFTS (RAF), 18 August 1942.

[48]*The Moth Monthly*, April 1942, 6.

[49]*Daily Diary*, No. 4 Training Command, 5 September 1940.

[50]The RAF security guards arrived several weeks prior to the main contingent. They were on duty no later than 1 December 1941. See *Daily Diary*, No. 4 Training Command, 1 December 1941.

[51]This is the shortest distance between these ports. It was not uncommon for personnel ships to plot courses that led them far afield to avoid submarine attack. It is not known if or by how much the *Pasteur* may have deviated from the shortest course.

[52]The distance by railway from Halifax, NS to Moose Jaw, SK is 2,409 miles. See See "Distances Between Principal Points in Canada (by railway)," https://www66.statcan.gc.ca/eng/1943-44/194300120000_Distances%20Between%20Principal%20Points%20in%20Canada.

[53]William A. Quayle, *The Prairie and the Sea* (Cincinnati, OH: Jennings and Graham, 1905), 49.

[54]Pierre Berton, *The Promised Land: Settling the West 1896–1914* (Toronto: McClelland & Stewart, 1984), 50.

[55]Vernon Peters to Vera, 27 November 1941, 16.

[56]Several phrases in this sentence are derived from John C. Lehr, John Everitt, and Simon Evans, "The Making of the Prairie Landscape," in *Immigration and Settlement,1870–1939*, ed. Gregory P. Marchildon (Regina, SK: Canadian Plains Research Center, 2009), 13–14.

[57]Vernon Peters to Vera, 14 December 1941. Rudyard Kipling travelled through the region a generation prior. He remarked that "the tedium of it was eternal." See Rudyard Kipling, *Letters of Travel 1892–1913* (London: Macmillan, 1920), 26.

[58]Vernon Peters to Vera, 18 December 1941. The hills seven miles southwest of the airbase are the edge of the Missouri Coteau, a large elevated plateau or steppe. They rise some four hundred feet above the village of Caron. Contrary to popular opinion, the area around Caron is by no means flat; the scale of its open vistas somehow neutralizes the effect of its topographical variance. If the Coteau Hills were somehow pressed up against the airbase, they would no doubt banish the perceived flatness that so easily overwhelms visitors.

[59]Vernon Peters to Vera, 30 March 1942, 5.

[60]Peters, "Looking Backward," 3.

[61]These descriptions appeared in the *Moth Monthly*, August 1942 and February 1943, and the *Tailspin*, March 1943.

[62]"First Letter Home," *The Moth Monthly*, February 1943, 19. Although it is not part of this study, it would be interesting to analyze the influence of Hollywood movies on the expectations and experiences of RAF personnel. This quote suggests that the stock of prairie images brought from Britain were derived from this source. Awareness of the Royal Canadian Mounted Police, which appears in the record from time to time, likely also came from these same sources. Vernon Peters' letters to his wife are replete with dashed expectations of free-roaming cowboys and Indians, sage brush, purple-hazed mountains, log cabins, and coyotes. It is also likely that the (mis) understanding of the Canadian west derived in no small part from the promotional literature produced by the Canadian government, railways, and steamship lines. These parties were clearly interested in depicting the region as a dreamy land of quaint cottages, lush groves, gentle breezes, plump babies, glowing women, and contented cattle.

[63]"75 Course Notes," *The Tailspin*, May 1943, 30.

[64]D. W. Moodie argues that the earliest accounts of the prairie region, beginning in the late seventeenth century, were shaped by the interests of the reporting parties. Those who wished to discourage English settlement in the region (i.e., fur traders) tended to downplay its agricultural potential by calling it a desert; those, like Arthur Dobbs, who wished to stimulate English settlement, referred to the grasslands as a flat country, full of meadows. The latter's 1744 report gave tacit approval to the longstanding treelessness-equals-infertility tenet by overtly ignoring any complaint that the region was bereft of trees. It was, in Dobbs's studied idiom, full of meadows. See D. W. Moodie, "Early British Images of Rupert's Land," in *Canadian Plains Studies 6: Man and Nature on the Prairies*, ed. Richard Allen (Regina, SK: Canadian Plains Research Center, 1976), 1–20.

[65]Leonard Smith, in Hildebrand, *In His Loving Service*, 93–94.

[66]*The Moth Monthly*, February 1942, 21.

[67]Vernon Peters to Vera, 21 July 1942. Peters' growing appreciation for the prairie was enhanced by his first flight on 18 September 1942. In a memorable phrase, he later suggested that his airborne experience was like "standing over a huge map." This same phrase had been used previously to describe the experience of looking down on the English countryside from a mountain top or, more recently, by those privileged to glide over the landscape in a hot-air balloon. See Rachel Hewitt, *Map of a Nation: A Biography of the Ordnance Survey* (London: Granta, 2010), 130, 168–69.

[68]"First Letter Home," *The Moth Monthly*, February 1943, 19.

[69]In its first issue (February 1942), the *Moth Monthly* featured a report on a mirage of the city of Regina that was observed from some forty-seven miles away. In that instance, the major buildings of the provincial capital were clearly identifiable.

[70]The great German poet, Johann von Goethe, suggested much the same of nature in general: "We snatch in vain at Nature's veil, / She is mysterious in broad daylight, / No screws or levers can compel her to reveal / The secrets she has hidden from our sight." See Goethe, *Faust: Part I*, Act I, Night, lines 672–75, trans. David Luke (Oxford: Oxford University Press, 2008), 23.

[71]"First Letter Home," *The Moth Monthly*, February 1943, 19.

[72]*Daily Diary*, No. 32 SFTS (RAF), 8 October 1942.

[73]"First Letter Home," *The Moth Monthly*, February 1943, 19.

[74]Egan, *The Worst Hard Time*, 54.

[75]Ronald Rees, *New and Naked Land: Making the Prairies Home* (Saskatoon, SK: Western Producer Prairie Books, 1988), 95–106.

[76]Franklin Le Van Baumer, "Romanticism," in *Dictionary of the History of Ideas*, 4 vols., ed. Philip P. Wiener (New York: Scribner's, 1973), 4:202.

[77]See Charles Taylor, *Hegel and Modern Society* (Cambridge: Cambridge University Press, 1979), 1–3 and *Sources of the Self: The Making of the Modern Identity* (Cambridge, MA: Harvard University Press, 1989), 380.

[78]William Wordsworth, "Lines Written in Early Spring," in William Wordsworth, *Selected Poems*, ed. Nicholas Roe (London: Folio, 2002), 58.

[79]William Wordsworth, "The Ruined Cottage," Part 1, in William Wordsworth, *Selected Poems*, 7.

[80]Jean-Jacques Rousseau (1712–78) articulated what would become a fundamental axiom of European romanticism: "Flat country, however beautiful it might be, has never seemed beautiful to me. I must have torrents, rocks, pine trees, black forests, mountains, steep paths to climb and descend, precipices around all to make me feel fear." See his *Oeuvres complètes de J.-J. Rousseau*, ed. Bernard Gagnebin, Marcel Raymond, et al. (Paris: Gallimard, 1959–95), I, 172, in Maurice Cranston, *Jean-Jacques: The Early Life and Work of Jean-Jacques Rousseau 1712–1754* (Chicago: University of Chicago Press, 1982), 344–45.

[81]In 1884, August Renoir spoke of his admiration for irregularity and its importance in his art. See C. E. Gauss, *The Aesthetic Theories of French Artists, 1855 to the Present* (Baltimore: Johns Hopkins University Press, 1949), 36–37.

[82]Saskatchewan had witnessed several prior attempts to transform its landscape and harsh climate into something more amenable to British sensibilities. The Barr colonists and the residents of Cannington Manor were rudely awakened from their romantic slumbers by conditions scarcely imaginable to benighted dreamers. See Rees, *New and Naked Land*, 80–85.

[83]Lehr, et al., "The Making of the Prairie Landscape," 14.

[84]Emily Dickinson, poem # 1398, in Roger Lundin, *Emily Dickinson and the Art of Belief*, 2nd ed. (Grand Rapids, MI: Eerdmans, 2004), 228. Captain Charles Tweedale, who immigrated to Saskatchewan in 1903, later reported his keen disappointment. "[M]ost of us pictured our homesteads as picturesque parkland with grassy, gently-rolling slopes interspersed by clumps of trees, a sparkling stream or possibly a silvery lake thrown in, the whole estate alive with game of all kinds." See his "The Barr Colony," *Maclean's*, 15 May 1938, in Berton, *The Promised Land*, 108.

[85]Rees, *New and Naked Land*, 156. Prairie geography may have even been mentally hazardous. John Conolly, the great asylum propagandist, reported that the celebrated Robert Hall attributed his temporary insanity "to a change of residence from a picturesque and interesting part of the country to a cheerless plain, of which the dullness, flatness, and invariable monotony saddened his heart." See John Conolly, *The Construction and Government of Lunatic Asylums and Hospitals for the Insane* (London: Churchill, 1847), 9.

[86]Vernon Peters to Vera, 18 December 1941.

[87]See "Course No. 65 Notes," *The Moth Monthly*, November 1942, 23 and "Course No. 68 Notes," *The Moth Monthly*, February 1943, 21.

[88]See Michael C. Foster, "Cold Weather—Warm Welcome," *Airforce* 13, no. 4 (January–March 1990), 12.

[89]Vernon Peters, in an 18 December 1941 letter to his wife, Vera, mentioned that the village of Caron only had 150 residents. The once-thriving town, founded in 1906, saw its population slowly dwindle due to major fires, the drought and Depression of the 1930s, smaller families, and improved access to major centres like Moose Jaw and Regina. By 1978, it had been reduced to an organized hamlet. See "Caronport, Saskatchewan, Rural Municipality of Caron # 162: Statistical Profile" (Moose Jaw, SK: Regional Economic Development Authority, 2008), 2.

[90]The phrase "dirty-faced buildings" appears in Egan, *The Worst Hard Time*, 167.

[91]"First Letter Home," *The Moth Monthly*, February 1943, 19.

[92]Ibid.

[93]Ibid. Winston Churchill had a similar, romantically-disappointing, experience in the late nineteenth century: "The banks of the Nile, except by contrast with the desert, display an abundance of barrenness. Their characteristic is monotony. Their attraction is their sadness. Yet there is one hour [sunset] when all is changed." See Winston S. Churchill, *The River War: The Reconquest of the Soudan*, 2nd ed. (New York: Longmans, Green, 1902), 3.

[94]*Daily Diary*, No. 32 SFTS (RAF), 8 October 1942.

[95]Ibid.

[96]Egan, *The Worst Hard Time*, 40.

CHAPTER 6

Serving Caron

Quique sui memores alios fecere merendo.[1]
—Virgil

An impressive variety of services complemented Caron's formal instructional activities. Those rendered by the YMCA, the Salvation Army, the Canadian Committee, and the padres are especially noteworthy. Additional support for the primary teaching mandate arose from Caron's motor transport, works and buildings, medical, and maintenance units. After its civilization in mid-1942, many of Caron's auxiliary operations were assumed by BBFTS civilians, more than seventy of whom were female. Ten airmen and officers offered the supreme service to the war effort: they lost their lives while attached to Caron. And although many of Caron's flying instructors toiled in relative obscurity, several received official commendations for their exemplary work.

On 10 September 1939, the very day that Canada entered the Second World War, the National Council of YMCAs sent a telegram to the prime minister offering its services. Shortly thereafter, three other national service organizations—the Canadian Legion, the Knights of Columbus, and the Salvation Army—made similar offers. By the end of the following month, DND's Directorate of Auxiliary

Services announced that all four organizations would share in the delivery of recreational services at its airbases and army camps. The directorate intended to supervise with a light hand, giving each group autonomy in its programming.

In late April of the following year, DND and the YMCA National Council signed a formal agreement in which the latter pledged to provide the necessary facilities, personnel, and operating funds for its assigned sites. It would keep meticulous financial records and derive no net income from its war services.[2] Prices for its goods would be competitive with local prices so as not to adversely affect existing businesses. Any profit generated would be turned over to DND for the benefit of service personnel and their dependants.

In the fall of 1940, James Gardiner, minister of national war services, called all seven major welfare organizations together. In addition to the four already providing auxiliary services, this larger group included the Canadian Red Cross, the Navy League of Canada, and the YWCA. During the meeting, the minister expressed concern that their competing fundraising campaigns were causing confusion among the public. In late December, Privy Council issued an order requiring all members of the group to participate in a joint fundraising campaign. Monies raised would be allocated in proportion to each group's prior expenditures. The joint campaign raised nearly seven million dollars in the first year.[3]

In 1941, the Canadian government ordered the suspension of all fundraising by the group, except for the Red Cross.[4] It offered, instead, to directly fund their operations and place them under the oversight of a National War Services Funds Advisory Board. The primary concern of the government seemed to be that any further fundraising would divert money away from its own Victory Loan campaigns.[5] Each group would henceforth be required to submit an annual budget, which would be funded directly by a grant. Allocations for 1942–43 are shown in Table 6.1.[6]

Table 6.1

National war services allocations, 1942–43

Recipient Organization	**Allocation**
Navy League of Canada	$140,000
YWCA War Services	$183,000
Knights of Columbus	$998,626
Salvation Army Red Shield War Services	$1,231,849
Canadian Legion War Services	$1,569,891
YMCA War Services	$2,375,788
Total	**$6,499,154**

In fall 1940, the RAF began transferring its primary training schools to Canada. By that time, it had already determined that the YMCA would be offered an exclusive contract to provide dry (non-alcoholic) canteens and other recreational facilities at its establishments in Canada.[7] Both parties agreed that the RAF would provide the necessary buildings, maintenance, furnishings, and utilities. In return, the YMCA would offer its services for no net profit.[8] Any surplus would be turned over to the commanding officer for the benefit of the local airbase.[9] The YMCA eventually served at all twenty-eight RAF establishments in Canada.[10]

In October 1941, the YMCA approved Arthur Etter as a site supervisor.[11] Prior to his appointment, Etter had been a GIS instructor in Winnipeg. He arrived in Caron in early December after a short stint with the YMCA at No. 2 Manning Depot in Brandon, MB. He immediately began preparations for opening Caron's canteen (building no. 10). F/L Brickendale, auxiliary services officer from No. 4 Training Command, a canteen manager, and several assistants aided Etter.[12] On 20 December, the facility opened.[13]

The canteen hosted most of the entertainment at Caron for the first few months.[14] Vernon Peters recalled the first movie screenings:

> Soon after Christmas, a cinema projector arrived and we stuck it up on a beer-barrel, rigged up a plain ordinary common, or garden, bed sheet to serve for a screen, and filled the canteen twice weekly for a show. Very

> posh, too. At the back two wide trestle tables were supports for two rows of wooden armchairs to accommodate the elite, while the hoi-polloi, or as you would have it, the "erks" congregated on chairs, brought with them from the cookhouse and taken back afterwards (or else!), or on the floor, munching peanuts and oranges and strewing the floor with the wrappings of O'Henrys and Wrigleys. It mattered little that we had seen all the films before, nor that the film never ran for five minutes without a break [breakage]. There was always music to fill the gaps. Such music, too! At that time we had only one record. "Elmer's Tune" was on one side, and on the other "Chattanooga Choo-Choo," but we got more fun out of those two tunes, repeated so often that everyone knew them by heart.[15]

The canteen featured a piano, radio, table games, darts, and a full line of goods for sale. It also housed a rather respectable library, thanks to generous donations from Moose Jaw's mayor and city librarian.[16] It also provided free stationery and envelopes, compliments of the YMCA. Etter tirelessly organized impromptu concerts, sing-alongs, quiz competitions, spelling bees, and tournaments of various sorts.

In the first issue of the *Moth Monthly*, the station magazine, Etter indicated that preparations were underway for an airmen lounge in the canteen. Chesterfields, chesterfield chairs, and wicker chairs had been ordered. These would complement the lamps, rugs, and writing tables already in place. The airmen could look forward to having a place to sit, rest, and read. The lounge would be stocked with magazines, newspapers, cablegram forms, travel information, and "practically any reasonable thing you could ask for." To allay concerns about excessive noise, Etter reassured his readers that most organized activities would be transferred to the nearby recreation building. He expected that the additional facility would soon host small games tournaments, quizzes (without interruptions), novelty games nights, concerts with guest artists, gramophone concerts, travelogues, and dances.[17]

Etter further reported that during January 1942, the Caron canteen received 10,107 visits; 15,000 stamps were sold; 345 magazines and newspapers were distributed; 4,000 pieces of free writing paper were utilized; 5,000 pieces of mail were posted; and 1,520 men attended movies screened in the unfinished station hospital.[18] Etter had even arranged a private dance for his airmen at the YWCA gymnasium in Moose Jaw.[19]

YMCA services were officially withdrawn from Caron when its contract with the RAF lapsed with the civilian takeover in May 1942.[20] Almost fifty years later, a former student pilot recalled that Art Etter never lost his cool in those chaotic early days. In his view, Etter deserved a medal.[21] This spirit of cooperation shone as he worked with the incoming auxiliary services staff. His successor, Jack Nelson of the Salvation Army, reported that Etter's smiling face and cheery disposition made the first few weeks a great deal easier for the new staff.[22] Etter found himself in the same boat as many of the others who were shocked by the change in management. He too was being transferred to who knows where. Like Vernon Peters, Etter wished that they all could just stay in Caron. He concluded his farewell note thus: "Fellows, it has been a lot of fun to run a canteen for you and try to make you feel at home so far from your own homes. It has brought a tear to our eye and a lump to our throat more than once to see how much you have enjoyed what we tried to do for you."[23]

Captain John (Jack) Nelson, of the Salvation Army's Red Shield War Services, served at No. 18 EFTS in Boundary Bay prior to its closure.[24] Although there was some confusion as to when the Salvation Army should relocate, by early June, Captain Nelson was at Caron taking over from Art Etter.[25] Nelson served at Caron until the late fall when he departed for the UK (see Figure 6.1).[26] Captain Nick Belkovitch who had been at No. 3 AOS in nearby Regina replaced him.[27] By the beginning of 1943, Belkovitch had been replaced by Captain Fred Hewitt, who served until No. 33 EFTS (RAF) disbanded at the end of the year.

The Salvation Army had a stellar reputation for services rendered during the Anglo-Boer and First World Wars. Like the other auxiliary service organizations, it laboured to help service personnel overcome the boredom, loneliness, and dehumanizing conditions of war. Its supervisors and volunteers served unstintingly. In many cases, they operated just behind the front lines, busily setting up movie screenings and offering refreshments, stationery, and magazines to war-weary troops. When called upon, Salvation Army workers cheerfully assisted with medical care and even helped bury the dead.[28]

Figure 6.1. Captain Jack Nelson, fall 1942, Caron. Source: Author's collection.

Jack Nelson and Fred Hewitt continued where Art Etter and his staff left off.[29] They supervised the canteen and kept detailed financial records. They oversaw the thrice-weekly movie screenings and scrambled to adjust when movies failed to arrive. Since Caron lacked an education or recreation officer after civilianization, the auxiliary services supervisors often led in these areas. Typically, they conducted their work through joint service-civilian committees. For instance,

Captain Hewitt sat on a committee dedicated to personnel welfare; he also formed an entertainment committee to help organize activities.

The auxiliary services staff encouraged a wide variety of educational activities at Caron. Captain Hewitt took up Art Etter's concern that RAF servicemen learn more about Canada. The editor and staff of the *Tailspin*, the successor to the *Moth Monthly*, also embraced this challenge. They sought to communicate that Canada is not entirely composed of "baldheaded prairie."[30] Caron's most significant educational endeavours, apart from the flying and ground schools, were conducted in partnership with the Canadian Committee.

In the summer of 1942, Michael Huxley (formerly of the British Foreign Office) made a tour of RAF airbases in Canada. A ten-thousand-pound donation to promote better cultural relations between Canada and the UK prompted his visit to a dozen or more airbases as well as RCAF headquarters, the UKALM, and a variety of other governmental offices. His report recommended, among other things, the establishment of an organization to promote the interpretation of Canada to RAF personnel. A group of five leading Canadians, chaired by J. T. Thorson, president of the exchequer court of Canada, established a trust to administer the donated funds. The trust immediately hired a full-time executive secretary, Walter B. Herbert, and set up offices in Ottawa. The Canadian Committee officially commenced its activities in mid-November 1942.[31]

The committee immediately undertook a survey of the leisure-time opportunities at RAF stations across Canada. Their research revealed that while there were substantial libraries at most stations, "there were astonishingly few books about Canada."[32] In response, and at the urging of the COs at these stations, the committee identified books and pamphlets that could remedy the deficiency. In late March 1943, Captain Hewitt informed Walter Herbert that Caron had received its shipment of Canadiana books.[33] By fall 1943, the committee had purchased and delivered 1,500 books and over 1,000 pamphlets to RAF stations across Canada.[34]

The survey revealed much the same about Canadian periodicals: they were largely absent from RAF stations. The committee arranged for the periodicals listed in Table 6.2 to be delivered to the various mess halls at each RAF station in Canada.[35] In correspondence with Captain Hewitt, Walter Herbert remarked: "You will be interested in knowing that the list of magazines being received regularly at your station shows that 33 EFTS is the best supplied RAF station in Canada in this respect."[36]

Table 6.2

Periodical subscriptions donated by the Canadian Committee

Periodical
The Beaver
MacLean's
Queen's Quarterly
National Home Monthly
Canadian Forum
New World
Dalhousie Review
Canadian Nature
Canadian Geographical Journal
Rod & Gun in Canada
Review of Music and Art
Maritime Art
Food for Thought
Saturday Night

The Canadian Committee also established a program to circulate documentary films and other visual arts among the RAF stations. In cooperation with the National Film Board of Canada, the National Film Society, various levels of government, and several private corporations, films focused on Canadian subjects were identified and acquired.[37] By August, at least four such films had been screened at Caron.[38] Captain Hewitt also took advantage of an art program sponsored by the committee. On 9 April, he formally requested an allotment of Canadiana photographs.[39] The committee duly sent along a collection of enlarged photographs of picturesque Canadian scenes. As part of its arts program, the committee also forwarded high-quality reproductions of Canadian oil paintings to interested RAF stations.[40]

A further initiative of the Canadian Committee did not go over well at Caron or elsewhere. Its so-called Canada clubs were intended to provide a forum for those who might wish to settle in Canada after the war.[41] Although many other clubs flourished, Canada clubs never took off. Perhaps a tincture of disloyalty attached to those who openly expressed interest in post-war resettlement? Or perhaps the quite natural longing for home made such considerations offensive and premature, to say the least? Notwithstanding the lack of interest in Canada clubs, Captain Hewitt reported that lectures on the mounted police and Indians would be universally welcomed at Caron.[42]

By the end of March, Walter Herbert informed Captain Hewitt that Professor Grant MacEwan of the University of Saskatchewan had agreed to deliver a lecture at Caron on 15 April. The officers and NCOs messes would jointly host a reception after the meeting. Captain Hewitt expected between seventy-five and one hundred to attend.[43] By all accounts, the lecture succeeded, even though only fifty-five attended. Captain Hewitt blamed night flying for occupying twenty-five or so who were interested.

The lively interest shown during the lengthy question period heartened Hewitt.[44] A highly-complimentary *Tailspin* article noted that Professor MacEwan's lecture traced the history of the west from first settlement to the final quarter of the nineteenth century.[45] The RAF personnel were particularly impressed by the fortitude of the early settlers. Speaking on behalf of those in attendance, the article declaimed: "We feel justly proud that these men and women who came from the comparative security of Britain to this wild land of wandering savages and lonely prairies to found a new nation, were of a stock common to ourselves, and we feel a certain reflected glory from their achievements."[46]

A report from a visiting staff member of the Canadian Committee noted that the Canadiana book collection at Caron sat unused. Although Captain Hewitt proudly reported that he had read all the volumes himself, apparently very few others had gained access to the collection. The visitor noted: "I found our volumes locked away in a glass case looking very virginal and quite unsullied by the hand of the Common Erk [airman]. I arranged . . . that they be instantly released for general consumption."[47] Captain Hewitt had given a somewhat different account in a June 1943 newsletter in which he reported that "an additional section is being added to the Library to accommodate a selection of 'Canadiana' literature." He added, tellingly, "[t]hese books are of exceptional value and will be loaned only on personal application."[48] Perhaps it is not surprising that few applied for the privilege of perusing Hewitt's private collection.

At the end of the war, the charitable organizations were rightly praised for their "magnificent and sustained cooperation" in maintaining high morale among the armed forces. The YMCA received deeply appreciative letters from Colin Gibson, Canada's minister of national defence for air, L. D. D. McKean of the UKALM, and Sir Archibald Sinclair of the UK Air Ministry. For his part, Sir Archibald commended the "magnificent service" of the YMCA at the RAF schools in Canada. He expressed gratitude for its cheerful spirit and that "although the prices were kept very low, the profits were able to provide first class amenities for the members of the Royal Air Force." He concluded: "I should like to add an expression of my own deep sense of gratitude for your splendid work. We are full of admiration for it."[49]

The spiritual support of the padres and chaplains at Caron complemented the work of the auxiliary service organizations and the Canadian Committee. The padres who served at Caron were supervised by No. 4 Training Command's staff chaplains. Initially, religious services were held at Caron on a weekly basis and conducted by a resident Church of England padre; after civilianization, bi-weekly visits from a Protestant chaplain or Roman Catholic padre became the norm. Volunteers cobbled together sacred services as best they could during the weeks when the padre was absent. A small room at the rear of the balcony in the recreation hall (building no. 22) served as a worship space; its spartan furnishings included an oak altar and rail.[50]

Vernon Peters inadvertently became quite active in the spiritual life at Caron. He found himself reading the lesson at Sunday services when they were first held in the canteen.[51] Thereafter, responsibility for the entire service often came his way when the padre was absent, or, after civilianization, when the padre only visited every second week. Peters admitted that his church attendance became much more regular at Caron. His congenial manner and willing spirit led to many occasions when he filled in for the absent padre. On rare occasions, he expressed exasperation at always being picked on to carry the load.[52]

In late October 1942, the padre officially put Peters in charge of the church service on those weeks when he had to be elsewhere. In letters to his wife, Peters described his order of service. He typically began by playing several gramophone recordings of sacred music. This would be followed by readings from the Church of England prayer book. Some of his supplementary readings were not particularly sacred and he knew it: on more than a few occasions, he resorted to inspirational readings from the *Readers' Digest*.[53]

In addition to the auxiliary and spiritual services offered at Caron, at least one commercial enterprise plied its wares near the airbase. Of special interest is the Caron Airport Café, which crouched just across from the main entrance. This small, one-storey building had been transported to the site by John Chow, a restaurateur from Moose Jaw. In addition to the Caron Café, Chow operated Lampton House, a rooming establishment on Manitoba Street in Moose Jaw.[54]

Figure 6.2. Caron Airport Café, ca. 1943. Source: Archibald Library Archives, 80042 J 006. Used with permission.

Although it also advertised laundry, mending, and taxi services, the café's inexpensive cuisine won it local renown. In December 1941, Vernon Peters, who had just settled at Caron, wrote that he had recently enjoyed a forty-cent steak and chip dinner at the establishment.[55] Several years later, he recalled that on payday the entire headquarters staff made a beeline for "Smokey Joe's" where, if one could ignore the surroundings, "a truly wizard steak-an'-chip-coffee-apple pie, and a small Phillymolly" could be had for next to nothing.[56]

It was not uncommon for entrepreneurs like Chow to erect refreshment booths, cafés, or even dance halls in the vicinity of military facilities. However, since many of these enterprises violated the RCAF's strict zoning regulations, they were often ordered to shut down or relocate. Dispossessed owners occasionally sought damages in civil court. On at least two occasions, Privy Council ruled that proprietors were not entitled to compensation if officially displaced.[57] Apparently, the Caron Airport Café's location did not run afoul of the RCAF's flightway restrictions.

It did, however, receive another devastating blow. At some point prior to the spring of 1943, the CO at Caron officially declared it out-of-bounds.[58] He had already taken a similar action against the Odd Fellows Hall in Moose Jaw.[59] Prohibitions of this sort were typically imposed because the facility posed a moral (i.e., sexual) danger to air force personnel.[60] Local rumour had it that the café offered prostitution services. James Richardson, a student pilot at Caron, referred to the café as a "knocking shop," British slang for a place of illicit sex.[61] The CO's decision meant the end of the café. In Vernon Peter's words, Smokey Joe "unhappily departed."

After civilianization, most support functions at Caron were turned over to the BBFTS. For instance, civilian mechanics and drivers now operated the mechanical transport (MT) section (building no. 17). Its eight motor vehicles—two crash tenders, two refueling tenders (bowsers), a station wagon, a half-ton truck, a panel truck outfitted as an ambulance, and an air direction control car—were now under the care and control of the operating company. This improved matters since it seems that the RAF never sent qualified drivers to Caron.[62] Prior to civilianization, most MT drivers were ill-trained volunteers: none had any experience driving large vehicles on prairie roads.[63]

All airfields require directional lighting if they are to be used at night. The MT's air direction control car and trailer aided Caron's night flyers by setting out flare pots in a path that guided them safely to the ground. On "all-way" fields, like Boharm's, the flare path would be set across the grass along an axis aimed into the prevailing wind. If the aerodrome had hard surfaced runways, like Caron, the flare path indicated wind direction and which runway should be used. So long as night flyers were aloft, the direction control crew had to maintain the flare pots, re-orient them if the wind direction changed, and refill their kerosene reservoirs as needed.

The MT section also included a panel truck (a.k.a. the ambulance) equipped with basic medical equipment. When dispatched to Boharm, it stood by the airfield in case of an emergency. The MT section provided a driver for the ambulance and the airbase hospital, an orderly. On one occasion, Lou Piper, who came to Caron with the BBFTS group, volunteered as a driver even though he had never driven a vehicle of any type! As luck (or inexperience) would have it, he rolled the ambulance when he misjudged a corner.[64]

In May 1942, the civilian management company also took over the W&B section (building no. 15) and, with it, responsibility for maintaining Caron's buildings and aerodrome.[65] The equipment put at the disposal of this unit is itemized in Table 6.3. Although there were many routine maintenance tasks associated with the buildings at Caron, the bulk of the unit's efforts were directed at the airfield and runways.[66] In the warm weather, the grass turf needed constant attention. Hank McDowell, who worked for this section, seeded the original turf in late fall 1941. The following spring, he compacted the grass with the turf roller to keep its soil as firm as possible and help it resist the wear and tear of aircraft traffic. The small agricultural tractor pulled the compaction roller as well as the mower and sickle.

Table 6.3

Works & buildings equipment established at Caron

Number	Item
2	Cletrac [Cleveland Tractor] crawler tractors
2	Snow rollers
2	Snow drags
1	Agricultural tractor
1	Mower trailer to fit agricultural tractor
1	Sickle bar to fit agricultural tractor
1	Turf roller
1	Heavy duty, four-wheel-drive truck
1	One-way snow plough
1	Snow blower mounted on truck w/ aux. engine

Throughout the winter, W&B personnel were occupied with snow compaction and removal. By the time Caron opened, DoT had gained considerable experience in these matters.[67] Three-gang, corrugated snow-rollers and heavy snow-drags, which levelled the snow just ahead of the rollers, had been improved and standardized by the time. DoT had learned, for instance, that it is best to compact snow on western Canadian aerodromes rather than plough it aside, since the latter invites higher drifts the next time it snows.[68] In a May 1940 memorandum, R. R. Collard of the DW&B indicated that compacting the entire aerodrome (i.e., its runways and interior areas) increased the available flying time by some forty per cent.[69]

A report filed by Mr. McCready, W&B superintendent at Caron, chronicled the enormous effort that went into snow compaction during the winter of 1942–43.[70] That winter, the aerodrome saw an inordinate snowfall, accompanied by high winds and deep drifts. McCready reported that his W&B crew had been continuously active in dragging and compacting snow. All totaled, the two Cletrac tractors logged some 1,150 hours and the four-wheel-drive truck logged an additional 450 hours in dragging, ploughing, and hauling snow.

The BBFTS officially assumed all aircraft maintenance operations when it arrived in May 1942. From that point on, civilian mechanics like Lou Piper and Pete Rutherford performed all the routine maintenance tasks.[71] Although Piper and Rutherford had no formal training, they were deemed fully-qualified airframe mechanics within six months of their hiring. They were responsible for maintaining the aircraft's mechanical and structural systems as well as carrying out daily flight preparation tasks. On occasion, they assisted with recovery or salvage operations at crash sites. In total, some ninety-seven accidents were reported at Caron. Of these, seven were deadly, producing ten fatalities. Table 6.4 analyzes Caron's accidents in terms of their raw numbers and incidence per hours flown.[72]

Table 6.4

Flying accidents, by quarter and hours flown, Caron, 1942–43

Quarter Ending	Hours Flown	Total Accidents	Accidents per 1000 Hours	Hours Flown per Accident
31 March 42	7,896	6	0.76	1,316
30 June 42	13,090	6	0.46	2,181
30 Sept. 42	18,295	7	0.38	2,613
31 Dec. 42	21,540	1	0.05	21,540
31 March 43	18,278	16	0.87	1,142
30 June 43	29,829	19	0.63	1,570
30 Sept. 43	28,980	23	0.80	1,260
31 Dec. 43	23,757	19	0.80	1,250

The mechanics typically rose early to prepare the aircraft for first flight. They were responsible to have the planes warmed up and dispersed along the flight line at the edge of the taxi strip when the instructors and student pilots arrived at 8:00 a.m. The Tiger Moths were difficult to start in the dark and bitter cold of the prairie winter. Since they were not equipped with a starter, their propellers had to be manually turned over by the mechanics. Once started, they had to be watched carefully since their engines tended to "rev up" as they warmed. After a few serious incidents, the mechanics began to warm up the aircraft in the hangars before taking them outside to the flight line.[73] Not unexpectedly, when this unauthorized practice came to light, their supervisors immediately curtailed it.

Due to the high winds at Caron, the lightweight Moths easily blew over once they landed. As a remedy, mechanics were sent out onto the aerodrome to catch them as they touched down. It is not hard to see why the mechanics were not thrilled to be out on an icy surface, in high winds, lunging at wing tips, hanging on for dear life, and all the while knowing that their craft was piloted by a novice! Once "caught," the Moth taxied to the safety of the hangar with a mechanic dangling from either or both wing tips.

Although much of what Prime Minister King said when he opened No. 18 EFTS in Boundary Bay is long forgotten, some seventy years later, Jessie Reagh still recalled his announcement that for the first time, women were employed at a Canadian airbase in trades other than clerical or domestic.[74] Leslie Martin later reiterated the prime minister's claim in a speech delivered in Moose Jaw. By the summer of 1942, more than fifty women were employed in a variety of traditional and nontraditional trades at Caron. Mr. Martin expected those numbers would only increase.[75] In the end, at least seventy women worked for the BBFTS at Caron.[76]

Figure 6.3. Female headquarters staff, deputy inspector general's visit, 19 August 1942. (l–r): Elizabeth Martin, Margaret Bowles, Claire Bailey, May Baker, Beverley Martin, Mary Mitchell, Susan Jackson, and May White. Source: Author's collection.

The prime minister knew that the RCAF faced significant changes that summer (1941) with respect to the enlistment and employment of women. Throughout the first half of the year, the RAF had been prodding the Canadian government to establish a women's division along the lines of its own Women's Auxiliary Air Force (WAAF). Unless and until the RCAF had a similar program, it would be difficult for the RAF to recruit and employ much-needed female workers at its bases in Canada. For political and public relations reasons, the RAF would not and could not move ahead in this matter until the RCAF established its own policy.[77]

Meanwhile back in Britain, WAAF personnel were serving as wireless telepathy slip-readers and operators, instrument mechanics, aero-fabric workers, spark plug testers, equipment assistants, cooks, teleprint operators, radio operators, and aircraft hands.[78] Under pressure from British officials, scores of Canadian women's groups, and the well-publicized success of the WAAF, the Canadian government finally announced on 25 June—a mere week before the prime minister's speech at Boundary Bay—that the RCAF would form its own female auxiliary service.[79]

By the time that Leslie Martin reminded his female staff of their trailblazing role in the summer of 1942, hundreds of Women's Division (WD) personnel were proceeding to RCAF stations across Canada. In most cases, accommodation, lounges, and canteens had to be constructed or remodeled to suit their needs. Caron, too, underwent significant renovations to accommodate its new civilian staff. Although many male officers found these changes disruptive, in the end, many acknowledged the significant contribution made by the WD. By the conclusion of the war, some 17,038 women had served in the RCAF.[80]

In addition to those who, like Jessie Reagh and Agnes Green, came from Boundary Bay, the BBFTS employed local women from Caron and the surrounding areas.[81] For instance, Lena Crosbie, who hailed from a nearby farm, worked in the airmen mess at Caron. She had previously worked as a cook's assistant for the Bird Construction Company while it assisted with the construction of the Caron airbase in 1941. In February 1943, Crosbie joined the WRNS, the female division of the Royal Navy. After training in the cooking trade, she served at naval stations in Ottawa and Victoria, BC.[82]

The greatest service rendered at Caron is memorialized in the municipal cemetery, located two miles northwest of the former airbase. A small, enclosed section along the western flank of the cemetery is the final resting place for the ten RAF servicemen killed in flying accidents while attached to No. 33 EFTS (RAF). Their graves are watched over by a tall cross as well as headstones bearing their names and the emblem of the RAF. Those listed in Table 6.5 have won a place of honour among their fallen comrades.

Table 6.5

Service personnel who succumbed to flying injuries, Caron, 1941–43

Name	Rank	Service No.	Deceased	Aircraft ID	Age	Hometown
Reginald G. Littlewood	P/O	106584	23 Dec. 41	Tiger Moth No. 5967	43	Holmer Green, Bucking-hamshire, England
Frederick H. Bouchard	SGT	914682	28 May 42	Tiger Moth No. 5955	n/a	Regents Park, London, England
Dalis G. Davies	P/O	48776	08 Sept. 42	Tiger Moth No. 4294	24	Whitland, Carmarthenshire, Wales
William V. Edmundson	LAC	1548854	06 Jan. 43	Tiger Moth No. 5959	19	Kells, Whitehaven, Cumberland, England
Raymond H. Nicholls	F/O	131530	28 April 43	Cornell No. FH874	20	Royton, Lancashire, England
Stephen O. Nethercot	LAC	1587243	28 April 43	Cornell No. FH874	20	Westbury-on-Trym, Bristol, England
Gordon A. Shearer	SGT	1451605	18 May 43	Cornell No. 10626	21	Spalding, Lincolnshire, England
Thomas K. J. Simpson	LAC	1566910	18 May 43	Cornell No. 10626	20	Greenock, Renfrewshire, Scotland
William D. Jarratt	F/L	128023	11 Oct. 43	Cornell No. FH890	25	Solihull, Warwickshire, England
Wilfred D. Nethercott	LAC	1587887	11 Oct. 43	Cornell No. FH890	19	Northam, Devon, England

P/O Reginald Littlewood was the first to be fatally injured while attached to No. 33 EFTS (RAF). The board of inquiry concluded that the primary cause of his accident on 23 December 1941 near Medicine Hat, AB was his "deliberate unauthorized low flying."[83] On 28 May 1942, SGT Frederick Bouchard became the first flying fatality in the immediate vicinity of the Caron aerodrome (near Tuxford). Although his pupil, LAC Vardigans, survived, Bouchard succumbed to his injuries in the Station Sick Quarters that same day. The board of inquiry concluded that the accident occurred as Bouchard demonstrated low flying. As best as could be determined, it seemed that the aircraft stalled as its pilot responded to unsettled weather conditions.[84]

On 8 September 1942, P/O Dalis Davies was fatally injured when he crashed his Tiger Moth about fifteen miles northwest of the Caron aerodrome near Rowletta. P/O Davies, a Rhodesian Air Force officer seconded to the RAF, had been undergoing training as a pilot when he was killed. Two days later, a board of inquiry, consisting of officers from RAF airbases in Swift Current, Moose Jaw, and Caron, began its investigation.

Figure 6.4. William Edmundson's fatal crash, 6 January 1943.

Source: Sylvia Lindridge collection. Used with permission.

LAC William Edmundson was killed in the final Tiger Moth accident at Caron on 6 January 1943 (see Figure 6.4). His instructor, P/O J. E. Whitehead, sustained multiple injuries, including severe frostbite, but survived. Gordon and Evangeline Deagle, who lived near the crash site, recalled that it took a long time to find the downed aircraft in the dark.[85] Several officers from No. 32 SFTS (RAF) in Moose Jaw joined F/O Unwin and P/O P. H. Herbert from Caron as members of the board of inquiry. Three weeks after the incident, the board concluded its deliberations and disbanded.[86]

Caron would record three more fatal accidents. Unlike the preceding four, which involved Tiger Moths, the next three accidents occurred in the new Cornells. Regrettably, all three Cornell accidents took the lives of both instructor and student pilot. On 28 April 1943, F/O Raymond Nicholls and his pupil, LAC Stephen Nethercot, were killed when their Cornell struck another Cornell some fourteen miles northwest of the airbase. They crashed in the shallow waters of Pelican Lake between Mortlach and Rowletta. The instructor and student pilot in the second aircraft managed to bail out and land without injury. Flying instructor "Jock" Brown later recalled wading waist-deep in the lake (with CFI Eric Bradley) looking for pieces of the downed aircraft.[87]

This accident presents several intriguing aspects. For one, the instructor in the second Cornell, Felix McKnight, faced a general court martial two months later. It may be that serious charges arose out of the investigation into this incident. The accident itself is suspicious. The fact that two Cornells from Caron crashed together in mid-air fourteen miles from the aerodrome may indicate that the occupants were carrying out unauthorized manoeuvres. Perhaps they were performing aerobatics or other competitive stunts when things went horribly wrong?[88]

On 18 May 1943, SGT Gordon Shearer and his student pilot, LAC Thomas Simpson, were killed when their Cornell crashed a few miles northeast of the aerodrome. The board of inquiry, presided over by S/L P. E. Barnes from No. 32 SFTS (RAF) in Moose Jaw, met shortly thereafter. "Jock" Brown believed that the board reached "unsatisfactory conclusions" in this matter since it failed to properly consider the aircraft's pre-existing wing-flutter, a condition which Brown himself had reported some time earlier.[89]

The final fatal accident at Caron occurred on 11 October 1943 when F/L William Jarratt, and his student pilot, LAC Wilfred Nethercott, were killed in a crash involving another Cornell from Caron. LAC Nethercott was undergoing a flying examination at the time. The occupants of the other Cornell escaped unscathed. Both aircraft were attempting a landing at the forced-landing airstrip northeast of Archydal.

Most of the funeral services for RAF flyers were held at the Caron Anglican Church. To take one instance, F/L Jarratt and LAC Nethercott were laid to rest in the municipal cemetery after a brief service at the church on 13 October 1943. Rev. S/L D. C. Mitchell, who served as padre at both Caron and Assiniboia, officiated with the assistance of the local pastor, Rev. John E. Jeary. Charles Clark, BBFTS's assistant manager, presided at the organ. At the graveside, F/L J. L. McRitchie conducted a full military parade. Many officers, NCOs, and student pilots were in attendance.[90]

At least six members of the RAF staff at No. 33 EFTS (RAF) were cited for meritorious service at Caron. Five were flying instructors. Two NCOs were officially commended. SGT Robert Brown's citation indicated that he had completed a total of 1,754 flying hours, most of them as an instructor. His devotion to duty and ability as an instructor were cited as exemplary.[91] FSGT Eric Craig received the AFM for his extremely able and conscientious instruction. At the time of his award, he had flown some 1,300 hours, including 423 hours in the past six months.[92]

The RAF commended WO Bernard Aldhous for his valuable services in the air on 1 January 1944. His citation lauded his great ability and devotion to duty as a flying instructor over the previous nineteen months. Of his 1,862 flying hours, some 1,691 had been devoted to instruction.[93] On the same day, F/L Henry Edge received the AFC. His citation noted his great competence and keenness as a flying instructor at Caron and his outstanding executive ability as squadron commander. At the time of his citation, F/L Edge had flown an impressive 3,020 hours, 2,170 of which had been for instructional purposes.[94]

Two other staff members at Caron were commended after it disbanded. F/L Hugh Featherby received the AFC on 5 May 1944. His citation indicated that of his 2,465 flying hours some 2,000 had been flown as an instructor. At the time of his award, Featherby had served for two years as a flying instructor in Canada. Throughout his instructional service he displayed sound judgement and a devotion to duty. He exhibited exceptional skill as a pilot and instructor and contributed greatly to the high standard of flying training at his unit.[95]

On 1 January 1946, SGT Kenneth Greenaway received the British Empire Medal (BEM) for his administrative services. His citation, which concludes this chapter, is also a fitting tribute to the many others who served under similar conditions and with equal dedication.

> This non-commissioned officer is a member of the regular Air Force, having been with this unit since its formation. He has been in charge of the Orderly Room staff, and by good discipline and alert and energetic manner has throughout handled his work with great competence. He has not spared himself in maintaining smooth co-operation with the civilian staff and it is due to his efforts that the orders of successive Administrative Officers have been intelligently and efficiently executed by a changing staff.[96]

Endnotes

[1]"Those who by service have won remembrance among men." Virgil, *The Aeneid*, book vi, line 664.

[2]Alan Hurst, *The Canadian YMCA in World War II* (Toronto: National War Services Committee of the National Council of YMCAs of Canada, 1948), 317–23, includes a copy of the agreement between DND and the YMCA.

[3]Hurst, *The Canadian YMCA*, 17.

[4]"PC 2199," 20 March 1942, authorized this new arrangement. See "Auxiliary Services, RCAF—Organization & Policy," in RG24, vol. 3467, LAC. A benefit dance at Caron on behalf of the Red Cross on 18 May 1942 raised $180.00. See *Daily Diary*, No. 33 EFTS (RAF), 18 May 1942.

[5]The Canadian government sponsored nine Victory Loan campaigns during the war, beginning in June 1941. In all, some twelve billion dollars were raised for the war effort. The civilians and RAF personnel at Caron participated wholeheartedly. The combined contribution of all Caron personnel to the fifth campaign amounted to $41,400. See *Daily Diary*, No. 33 EFTS (RAF), 6 November 1943.

[6]*Public Accounts of the Dominion of Canada for the Fiscal Year Ended March 31, 1943* (Ottawa: King's Printer, 1944), N–13.

[7]The UKALM would later defend its exclusive contract with the YMCA by noting that it had examined the four main auxiliary service organizations in Canada and had concluded that the YMCA's reputation, merits, and equipment made it the "most suitable for this purpose." Subsequent experience showed that the COs at each location universally affirmed the "very able and satisfactory manner in which the YMCA have undertaken this duty." See the memorandum from the liaison-officer-in-chief, UKALM, in "National War Services Committee, Executive Committee: Minutes, February 1942–April 1942," in MG28 I 95, vol. 106, LAC.

[8]The Empire Air Training Scheme Committee, which met under the authority of the UK secretary of state for air, looked favourably on this aspect of the proposed agreement with the Canadian YMCA. See "Notes of the 27th Meeting Held on Friday 7th February 1941," 2, in AIR 20/1379: "Empire Air Training Scheme Committee Minutes of Meetings, Jan. 1940—October 1945," UKNA.

[9]Memorandum from E. A. Deacon, RCAF director of auxiliary services, 27 November 1940. See "Auxiliary Services, RCAF—Organization & Policy," LAC. Also see a copy of the formal agreement in Hurst, *The Canadian YMCA*, 324–27.

[10]Hurst, *The Canadian YMCA*, 328.

[11]"National War Services Committee, Executive Committee: Minutes, February 1942–April 1942," in MG28 I 95, vol. 106, LAC.

[12]Harold A. Elliott would also serve alongside Art Etter at Caron until the end of January 1942 when he was posted to No. 34 EFTS (RAF) which was about to open in Assiniboia, SK. Elliott, who had been a teacher at Bradford, SK before joining the YMCA, had spent a month at No. 5 B&GS at Dafoe, SK before arriving in Caron. He would finish his YMCA service in May 1943

after serving at Assiniboia, No. 37 SFTS (RAF) at Calgary, and No. 32 EFTS (RAF) at Bowden, AB. See Hurst, *The Canadian YMCA*, 301. Additional information provided to the author by Ian Fleming, YMCA (Canada) archivist.

[13]*Daily Diary*, No. 33 EFTS (RAF), 20 December 1941. The *Moose Jaw Times-Herald* reported on 19 December that the YMCA canteen at Caron opened on 17 December 1941.

[14]*Moose Jaw Times-Herald*, 19 December 1941.

[15]Peters, "Looking Backward," 3, 5.

[16]Vernon Peters to Vera, 10 January 1942.

[17]*The Moth Monthly*, February 1942, 39.

[18]*Moose Jaw Times-Herald*, 20 February 1942. A later report in the *Moth Monthly* suggested that 13,903 customers had been served in the canteen during the month of January 1942. See the March 1942 issue, 42.

[19]*Moose Jaw Times-Herald*, 20 February 1942.

[20]The YMCA, which had withdrawn from the RAF EFTSs when they were civilianized, was eventually invited back to No. 31 EFTS (RAF) at De Winton, AB, No. 32 EFTS (RAF) at Bowden, AB, and No. 36 EFTS (RAF) at Pearce, AB. See "National War Services Committee, Executive Committee: Minutes, January 1943–May 1943," 8, in MG28 I 95, vol. 106, LAC.

[21]Foster, "Cold Weather—Warm Welcome," 12.

[22]Jack Nelson, "Red Shield War Services Department," *The Moth Monthly*, July 1942, 35.

[23]Art Etter, "The Y's Farewell," *The Moth Monthly*, June 1942, 35.

[24]Memorandum dated 30 December 1941, in "Auxiliary Services (Air): Organizations Under Agreement with Dept. of National Defence for Air—YMCA War Services," in RG24, vol. 3472, LAC.

[25]On 1 May 1942, William Dray, secretary of the Salvation Army's war services telegraphed S/L Lee of DND's Directorate of Auxiliary Services asking for authorization to transfer the Salvation Army's equipment and personnel to Caron. Not surprisingly, he indicated that the matter was urgent. See document dated 1 May 1942 in "Auxiliary Services (Air): Organizations Under Agreement with Dept. of National Defence for Air—YMCA War Services."

[26]*The Moth Monthly*, January 1943, 27. Vernon Peters noted in a 26 October 1942 letter to his wife that Jack Nelson was being transferred to England.

[27]*The Moth Monthly*, November 1942, 13. See also William Dray, letter dated 30 December 1941, in "Auxiliary Services (Air): Organizations Under Agreement with Dept. of National Defence for Air—Salvation Army," in RG24, vol. 3472, LAC.

[28]Robert Moyles, *The Blood and Fire in Canada: A History of the Salvation Army in the Dominion 1882–1976* (Toronto: Martin, 1977), 195–96.

[29]In addition to those mentioned in this paragraph, the Salvation Army provided the following services: bank accounts could be opened; money orders could be purchased; flowers could be telegraphed; personal items could be purchased, and watches could be repaired. Writing paper

and envelopes were supplied free of charge. It also kept up-to-date information on bus, plane, and train schedules and fares. Cablegrams and telegrams could be sent to all parts of the empire and the USA. See the *Moth Monthly*, February 1943, 22.

[30]*The Tailspin*, March 1943, 3.

[31]"The Canadian Committee: Origins," in MG28 I 179, vol. 1, LAC.

[32]The Canadian Committee, "Review of Activities, October 1943," in "RAF Stations, 1942–1945," 1, in MG28 I 179, vol. 46, LAC.

[33]The following titles were included in the initial shipment to Caron: *Canada Year Book; Canada*, by Stephen Leacock; *Canada*, by Lady Tweedsmuir; *Unknown Country; The Indians of Canada; Birds of Canada; History of the RCMP;* and *Hudson's Bay*. See letter dated 26 February 1943, in "R.A.F. Caron, Saskatchewan 1943," in MG28 I 179, vol. 47, LAC.

[34]The Canadian Committee, "Review of Activities, October 1943."

[35]Ibid., 2.

[36]Letter dated 26 February 1943, in "R.A.F. Caron, Saskatchewan 1943."

[37]The Canadian Committee, "Review of Activities, October 1943," 3.

[38]Letter dated 3 August 1943, in "R.A.F. Caron, Saskatchewan 1943."

[39]"R.A.F. Caron, Saskatchewan 1943."

[40]The Canadian Committee, "Review of Activities, October 1943," 3. Similar schemes were launched in the UK. One program, created by the National Gallery, planned to loan paintings to RAF messes for the duration of the war. It came to naught, however, when the RAF refused to assume liability for any damage caused to the paintings by its personnel. See Martin Francis, *The Flyer: British Culture and the Royal Air Force, 1939–1945* (New York: Oxford University Press, 2008), 122, 155.

[41]The Canadian Committee, "Review of Activities, October 1943," 4.

[42]Captain Hewitt to Walter Herbert, 11 March 1943, in "R.A.F. Caron, Saskatchewan 1943."

[43]Letters dated 23 and 30 March 1943, in "R.A.F. Caron, Saskatchewan 1943."

[44]Letter dated 19 April 1943, in "R.A.F. Caron, Saskatchewan 1943."

[45]Professor MacEwan wisely terminated his public address with the late nineteenth century. It would have been much more difficult to end on a high note if agriculture in the west had been discussed through the 1920s and 1930s!

[46]"Visit of Professor MacEwan, Saskatchewan University," *The Tailspin*, May 1943, 33.

[47]"RAF Stations, 1943," in MG28 I 179, vol. 46, LAC.

[48]"Auxiliary Services (Air): Organizations Under Agreement with Dept. of National Defence for Air—Salvation Army."

[49]Copies of these letters can be found in Hurst, *The Canadian YMCA*, 375–76, 378.

[50]Vernon Peters to Vera, 20 May 1942.

[51]Vernon Peters to Vera, 25 February 1942.

[52]Vernon Peters to Vera, 19 October 1942.

[53]Vernon Peters to Vera, 19 and 30 October 1942.

[54]*Henderson's Moose Jaw Directory 1941*, 145.

[55]Vernon Peters to Vera, 20 December 1941.

[56]Peters, "Looking Backward," 5.

[57]See "PC 3867," 28 November 1939, and "PC 3867" (amended), 17 January 1941, in "History of Construction Engineering," n.p., in AIR 74/20, DHH.

[58]Gordon Deagle who farmed nearby recalled that the café was ruled out-of-bounds by the RCAF. See Gordon and Evangeline Deagle, interview by Terence Sinclair, Oral History Project, Western Development Museum (SK), tape counter #099.

[59]Vernon Peters to Vera, 11 February 1942.

[60]During the war, solicitation activities moved from bawdy houses to restaurants and dance-halls, in other words, to places frequented by military personnel. The RCAF policy mandated that locations be declared out-of-bounds if more than one airman contracted a venereal disease because of a contact made at the establishment. See Jeffrey Keshen, "Morale and Morality on the Alberta Home Front," in *For King and Country: Alberta in the Second World War*, ed. Ken Tingley (Edmonton: The Provincial Museum of Alberta, 1995), 152.

[61]James C. Richardson, "An Amateur Aviator: Memories of World War Two," 1999, item no. X001–0493, RAF Museum, London.

[62]SGT "Jock" Brown, who arrived with the initial RAF contingent claimed that someone in the RAF forgot to send drivers for the MT section. See his letter to Gordon Elmer, 21 January 1981, 1–2.

[63]*The Moth Monthly*, February 1942, 29.

[64]The luckless orderly who accompanied Piper received the meritorious *Orderlies Boharm Endurance Medal* from his peers. According to their report, this was the second such incident with the ambulance. Their tongue-in-cheek recommendation suggested that either the airfield at Boharm or the bridge leading to the same should be bombed to "prevent us from having to take our lives in our hands each time to visit the verdant field." See the *Tailspin*, July 1943, 7.

[65]Appendix A to Secret Organization Order No. 65, May 5, 1942. A similar equipment establishment was sent to Boharm to maintain its turf. The five-bay building erected at Boharm was intended to house W&B equipment.

[66]The W&B section at Caron was responsible for a host of building maintenance activities including, but not limited to, boiler start-up and shut-down, tightening bolts in the superstructure of the hangars and drill hall, as well as testing and maintaining the water and sewage systems.

[67]The RAF inspector general made notes on the snow compaction techniques developed in Canada. In a 6 March 1941 report entitled, "Snow Menace on Aerodromes," he advised his UK colleagues to study the equipment and methods used in Canada as a way of addressing their own

problems with snowy aerodromes in the UK. See his report in AIR 8/481: "Airfield Construction, 1941–1943," 3, UKNA.

[68]DoT recognized that complete snow removal was necessary at its principal eastern airports, which had tight schedules and much heavier, high-speed aircraft. See *Report of the Dept. of Transport for the Fiscal Year from April 1, 1939 to March 31, 1940* (Ottawa: King's Printer, 1940), 23.

[69]"Works & Buildings, RCAF. Construction of Works & Bldgs—Policy Governing," in RG24, vol. 4777, LAC.

[70]"Works & Buildings, RCAF: Aerodrome Maintenance & Aerodrome Maintenance Equipment—Policy Governing," in RG24, vol. 4781, LAC.

[71]A list of the BBFTS airframe mechanics (engineers) who served at Caron is included in Appendix B.

[72]"Quarterly Analysis of Flying Accidents." The data in this table is compiled from the quarterly reports in this file.

[73]Lou Piper recalled that one mechanic received a serious wrist or hand injury from a propeller. Spencer Dunmore reports that an RAF mechanic at Caron by the name of Arthur Eddon had a mishap with a Tiger Moth he was attempting to start. The engine mistakenly fired and the propeller slashed through his overalls. Miraculously, it missed him. See Dunmore, *Wings for Victory*, 296.

[74]Jessie (Reagh) Belcher, telephone interview by the author.

[75]*The Moth Monthly*, September 1942, 42–43. In a telling anecdote, Leslie Martin indicated that he hired his first female assistant, Miss Audrey Strong, after he lost three male secretaries to active service. With Miss Strong's assistance, Martin hired an additional fourteen women by the time No. 18 EFTS opened in April 1941. See "No. 18 EFTS Leads Air Schools; Uses Women to Fill Positions," *Ladner (British Columbia) Optimist*, 20 November 1941.

[76]For a list of those women known to have worked at Caron, see Appendix C.

[77]The chronic shortage of skilled and semi-skilled workers and the obvious relief that women could provide for these deficiencies made the British quite impatient with the Canadian government's reluctance in this matter. See "Notes of the 31st Meeting Held on Friday 28th March, 1941," 4.

[78]"Women at Work with RAF—Replacing Men in 25 Trades," *London Times*, 12 March 1941, in "Employment of Canadian and British Women in Semi-Skilled Ground Duties with RAF Training Schools in Canada," in RG25, vol. 2709, LAC.

[79]Entry dated 25 June 1941 in "Employment of Canadian and for British Women." "PC 4798," 2 July 1941, officially granted permission to the RCAF to enlist women. See Carolyn Gossage, *Greatcoats and Glamour Boots: Canadian Women at War (1939–1945)* (Toronto: Dundurn, 1991), 35.

[80]Mary Ziegler, *We Serve That Men May Fly: The Story of the Women's Division Royal Canadian Air Force*, 2nd ed. (Hamilton, ON: RCAF WD Association, 1974), 159.

[81]See Appendix C.

[82]Lena Smith, telephone interview by the author, Caronport and Whiterock, BC, 16 June 2011.

[83]"Quarterly Analysis of Flying Accidents."

[84]*Daily Diary*, No. 33 EFTS (RAF), 27 May 1942.

[85]Gordon and Evangeline Deagle, interview by Terence Sinclair, Oral History Project, Western Development Museum (SK), tape counter #053.

[86]*Daily Diary*, No. 33 EFTS (RAF), 27 January 1943.

[87]"Jock" Brown, letter to Gordon Elmer, 14 February 1981, 3.

[88]A 1982 interview with Gordon and Evangeline Deagle, who farmed nearby, raised another tantalizing possibility as to the type of misbehaviour that perhaps led to these fatalities. The Deagles reported that it was quite common for training aircraft to be used for hunting or chasing coyotes. The intriguing aspect of their offhand remark was that this type of activity was known to occur near Rowletta/Lake Valley, exactly where the Nicholls and Nethercot aircraft went down. An allegation of this sort would surely warrant a general court martial if a fatality occurred. See Gordon and Evangeline Deagle, interview by Terence Sinclair, Oral History Project, Western Development Museum (SK), tape counter #049.

[89]"Jock" Brown, letter to Gordon Elmer, 14 February 1981, 3.

[90]*Daily Diary*, No. 33 EFTS (RAF), 13 October 1943.

[91]*London Gazette*, 2 June 1943 and AFRO 1459/43, 30 July 1943. See also "Honours and Awards: RAF, RAAF, RNZAF Personnel in Canada, http://rcafassociation.ca/heritage/1914-1945/raf-raaf-rnzaf-personnel-in-canada/. A picture of SGT Brown and a brief congratulatory note appeared in the July 1943 issue of the *Tailspin*, 11.

[92]*London Gazette*, 2 June 1943 and AFRO 1459/43, 30 July 1943. See also "Honours and Awards: RAF, RAAF, RNZAF Personnel in Canada." A picture of FSGT Craig and a brief congratulatory note appeared in the July 1943 issue of the *Tailspin*, 11.

[93]*London Gazette*, 1 January 1943 and AFRO 113/44, 21 January 1944. See also "Honours and Awards: RAF, RAAF, RNZAF Personnel in Canada."

[94]Ibid.

[95]*London Gazette*, 5 May 1944 and AFRO 1380/44, 30 June 1944. See also "Honours and Awards: RAF, RAAF, RNZAF Personnel in Canada."

[96]*London Gazette*, 1 January 1946 and AFRO 82/46, 25 January 1946. See also "Honours and Awards: RAF, RAAF, RNZAF Personnel in Canada."

CHAPTER 7

Entertaining Caron

Where there is one Englishman there will be a garden.
Where there are two Englishmen there will be a club.[1]
—A. W. Smith

The recreational activities at Caron revolved around the messes, canteen, drill hall, sports fields, and recreation hall. Since most of these facilities were not ready when the RAF personnel arrived, the NCO mess and YMCA canteen were pressed into double duty. In addition to functioning as an entertainment hub, the NCO mess found itself serving meals to all ranks and hosting a makeshift medical clinic.[2] For its part, the canteen expanded its usual services to include movie screenings, gramophone concerts, and even choir rehearsals.

In the midst of the early hubbub, Art Etter, the YMCA supervisor, formed an entertainment committee.[3] It immediately began preparations for a stage show set to coincide with the opening of the theatre (recreation hall) in April.[4] Production and direction duties fell to the ever-willing Vernon Peters.[5] In late January, F. F. Le B. Crankshaw, a seasoned stage show producer in the UK, arrived in Caron.[6] In addition to his chaplaincy duties, Padre Crankshaw took an immediate interest in the theatre building and requested that its stage be enlarged.[7] With training command's approval, he personally designed, constructed, and decorated the new stage.[8] Art Etter later remarked that the padre's work made the theatre at Caron one of the finest in the land.[9]

S/L K. L. Warrington came to Caron a month after Padre Crankshaw. His well-known variety show, *Contact*, had recently played in the Blackpool Opera House for over a year.[10] Vernon Peters gladly relinquished his plans for opening night in deference to S/L Warrington. The version of Warrington's *Contact* staged at Caron on 22 April consisted of acts by RAF and Moose Jaw artists, including a male chorus, a monologue by Vernon Peters, duets, solos, an illusionist, band pieces, comedy sketches, tap and ballet dances, and impersonations. Guest officers and their wives from No. 32 SFTS (RAF) in Moose Jaw joined with a small number of invited guests from the surrounding area. *The Moth Monthly* lavished praise. The audience no less so: it insisted on thirty minutes of encores.[11]

Caron hosted a great variety of stage shows and concerts. The Moose Jaw orchestral society, a Ukrainian concert party, and the Moose Jaw boys' choir performed on various occasions.[12] In December 1942, the theatre hosted the Mortlach players, an amateur troupe from a small town ten miles west of the airbase. The following fall, an eager crowd took in *Command Performance*, a show written and produced by two sergeants attached to No. 4 Training Command in Calgary. The performance was recorded live before a large and appreciative audience.[13]

In early 1943, the student pilots of course no. 70 presented a stage show, which featured an opening chorus, several comedy sketches, a magic act, impersonations of their instructors as well as a bit of "serious" music, aptly performed. But their "Bevy of Beauty," all-male chorus line stole the show. The precision leg work, costumes, and well-suited music brought the house down. F/L Douglas Adcock, who rose to congratulate the student pilots on their performance, noted that they had prepared their show despite having to make up flying time lost to bad weather.

Several professional touring groups performed at Caron in the spring and summer of 1943. In early May, an Entertainments National Services Association (ENSA) troupe, headquartered in London's Drury Lane Theatre, arrived. It featured professional actors and high-ranking stage and concert performers dedicated to bringing top-quality entertainment to British service personnel wherever they might be. The singing, dancing, comedic, and acrobatic acts were polished and professional. On 20 August, the same ENSA cast returned to Caron for a second show.[14] In an embarrassment of riches, Caron hosted yet another entertainment troupe five days later. The No. 1 RCAF Entertainment Group brought its popular *Blackouts of 1943* to Caron. This show would eventually be performed before seventy-thousand service personnel in Canada and overseas.[15] The *Daily Diary* called it the best show yet.[16]

Live instrumental music also played an important part in the after-hours life at Caron. By the end of the first month (January 1942), instruments had arrived, and the entertainment committee had appointed LAC Stan Hillier as bandmaster. The first major performance by the station orchestra occurred during the grand opening of the drill hall (building no. 11) in early March. Many smaller groups also performed at Caron. Pete Rutherford and his pal, Lou Piper, both of whom came east from Boundary Bay, formed the nucleus of a dance band. They performed on many occasions, most notably, the New Year's Eve benefit concert and dance organized on behalf of the aid-to-Russia fund, a charitable project launched by Clementine Churchill, wife of the British prime minister.[17] In May 1943, the transfer of two members finally dissolved the band.[18]

Figure 7.1. New Year's Eve dance, 1942–43, led by Pete Rutherford and his band. Source: Sylvia Lindridge collection. Used with permission.

From the beginning, interested parties hosted gramophone concerts at Caron. In late January 1942, the canteen sponsored the first such event. For the occasion, A. J. Wickens, a well-known lawyer from Moose Jaw, generously loaned his gramophone, amplifier, and records from his substantial personal collection. Later, he would permanently install the equipment in the theatre building.[19] On occasions when live music could not be secured, the gramophone provided the soundtrack for station dances.[20] More commonly, it offered up weekly music appreciation concerts. A review of these concerts by Vernon Peters indicated that works by Strauss, Gilbert and Sullivan, Miss Gracie Fields, and Harry Lauder as well as heavier pieces by Beethoven, Brahms, Mussorgsky, and Grieg had been aired on recent Friday evenings.[21] In mid-October 1942, Peters wrote his wife indicating that he had recently been called at the last minute to host the appreciation concert. He recounted how once he had announced a selection from the stage he had to hasten to the projection room in the balcony to play the records. He thusly shuttled back and forth throughout the program.[22]

Not everyone appreciated the dominance of classical music at Caron.[23] An April 1943 article in the *Tailspin* complained that the "long-haired" repertoire needed to be supplemented with other types of music designed for entertainment and relaxation. Surely, the "likes-what-I-likes" crowd should be permitted to enjoy themselves too. The author opined that the hegemony of high-brow music threatened to "develop into a closed circle exclusively reserved for a select group of musical connoisseurs." As a partial remedy, the article called for a series of fireside chats (rather than patronizing lectures), which would patiently teach the finer points of classical music.[24]

The debate at Caron over highbrow music nicely illustrates the tension between the entertainment proclivities of aircrew and the cultural expectations of pilots. The romance of aviation lived on. The public expected pilots to be well-read, gentlemanly, and in possession of a sensibility suited to those who soared above the clouds. Many were disappointed to learn that their "knights of the air" had much more prosaic or even philistine interests in popular music, pin-up art, and pulp fiction. Although the romantic ideals were still evident among the officers, aircrew often preferred "the populist, the cheesy, and the escapist."[25]

Figure 7.2. The romance of the pilot. Unidentified student pilot, Caron. Source: Author's collection.

Dances were prominent in the social life at Caron. The entertainment committee arranged for young ladies from Moose Jaw to be transported to Caron for such occasions.[26] Padre Crankshaw, who led in these matters in the early days, enjoyed the full cooperation of the YWCA in Moose Jaw, which recruited and vetted young ladies for this patriotic duty. Those chosen to go to Caron could expect to be back in the city by midnight since the dances ended promptly at 23:30 with the singing of "God Save the King."[27]

Caron hosted its first all-station dance on 30 April 1942. The ubiquitous Vernon Peters served as master of ceremonies on this thrilling occasion.[28] Due to a shortage of young ladies, Peters skillfully interjected "excuse me" dances, which permitted an unaccompanied male to cut in on partners. Members of the sergeants mess graciously provided waiter services. In response to the padre's supplication, the CO authorized a wet bar for this singular occasion; the padre saw to it that the men handled the privilege responsibly.[29]

Within a month of the first dance, news came that Caron would be civilianized. Station dances continued under BBFTS management. A dance held in October 1942 seems typical. Al Wright and his band from Moose Jaw provided the music. FSGT Geoffrey Baskwill assumed the emcee duties. Plenty of young ladies from Moose Jaw were on hand. The evening came to its apogee with a variety of dance competitions. "God Save the King" rang out promptly at 23:30; everything ended abruptly when the young ladies were escorted home.[30]

The dancing deportment of the Canadian girls took some by surprise. A recent arrival from the UK reported that his naïve notion that the gentleman should take the lead had been violently overturned by the treatment he received from his first partner. She apparently grabbed him and threw him into "convulsive shudders and spasmodic jerks." His neck took a beating as he whirled about in a general confusion. His next dance partner did much the same but this time during what should have been a slow foxtrot. He belatedly decided not to make Canadian girls dance "English style." As a public service, he solemnly warned his readers to watch out.[31]

Movies also played a central role in the entertainment life at Caron. From their first projections onto a bedsheet in the canteen through their brief stint in the unfinished hospital to their final home in the theatre, Caron's movie screenings nicely illustrate the ingenuity it took on the part of the auxiliary services supervisors to keep things going. YMCA and Salvation Army supervisors were famous for the pains they took to make sure that the show would go on. By early January 1942, two movies a week were available at Caron. By the end of the month, there were three showings each week (Monday, Wednesday, and Saturday).

Significant distribution problems plagued the auxiliary services' movie screenings at the beginning of the war. In response, the agencies formed movie pools or circuits in the various regions of Canada and overseas. Nevertheless, the scheduling problems were daunting: so much depended on the weather, train schedules, and the efficiency of the local supervisor. The technical problems were not insignificant either. Power fluctuations, quite common at the time, wreaked havoc on the projectors.[32] Further, the acetate film became brittle with use, age, temperature variances, and rugged conditions. Vernon Peters had good reason to complain about the frequent breakages at Caron.

Some of the RAF personnel complained that they had seen most of the movies. Although later in the war, the American film companies, which produced and distributed virtually all the feature films shown at Caron, released movies in 16 mm at the same time as their theatrical release (in 35 mm), early on, they released them in the smaller format only after they had been out for a year.[33] The movies shown at Caron in March 1942, which are listed in Table 7.1, bear this out. In at least two cases, *Singapore Woman* and *Million Dollar Baby*, viewers in Caron saw movies that had been released only nine months prior. In general however, most of Caron's movies had been released long before the original RAF cohort embarked for Canada. An avid movie-goer in Britain could have already seen most of them.

Table 7.1

Feature films shown at Caron, March 1942[34]

Date Shown	Title	Theatrical Release
2 March	*Sante Fe Trail*	28 Dec. 1940
4 March	*Green Hell*	26 Jan. 1940
7 March	*Lillian Russell*	24 May 1940
9 March	*City for Conquest*	21 Sept. 1940
11 March	*Parole Fixer*	2 Feb. 1940
14 March	*Slave Ship*	16 June 1937
16 March	*Singapore Woman*	17 May 1941
21 March	*In Old Chicago*	6 Jan. 1938
23 March	*Million Dollar Baby*	31 May 1941
30 March	*South of Suez*	16 Nov. 1940

Beginning in May 1942, travel films featuring "the more appealing sections of Canada" were screened on Sunday evenings at Caron.[35] In late August of that same year, a GIS instructor sponsored a special screening of *Target for Tonight*.[36] Within a few months of its London debut in July 1941, this movie had been shown across the UK, the United States, Canada, and Sweden. It chronicled the planning and execution of a night bombing raid over Freihausen, Germany and featured actors drawn from the RAF. At a time of troubling setbacks, the UK government hoped that it would bolster public morale by showing how a new phase of the air war would take the conflict from the skies and cities of England into the German heartland.[37]

Many of the recreational activities discussed heretofore required little of those who took them in. There were, in addition to these large-scale events, many recreational activities at Caron that operated on a voluntary basis and thus called for much greater personal engagement. By the time of the Second World War, voluntary activity and the self-help principle were firmly established in Anglo-Canadian culture. When it came to recreation, everyone should expect to chip in. Art Etter, the first auxiliary supervisor at Caron, commended those who had already discovered that "entertainment on this camp will be best if everyone digs in and does his part."[38] This spirit seemed especially alive in the first few months. To their credit, Vernon Peters and Padre Crankshaw were preternaturally active in organizing the recreational activities that were to be continuing features of life at Caron.[39]

One of the first voluntary groups at Caron came together to produce a monthly magazine. Within a few weeks, the first issue of the *Moth Monthly* appeared. The following month, the sponsoring committee organized itself into various functional responsibilities. The editor, P/O H. R. Howard, served as chairman, SGT T. F. Healy as vice chairman, P/O E. A. Cameron as secretary, and P/O J. Currie as treasurer. Three other committee members rounded out the group, including Padre Crankshaw who served until he was transferred to Prince Edward Island in June 1942.[40] After civilianization, P/O Howard took up the added duties of business manager. That summer the executive committee shrank to only three members, although two new members were added in early fall. Later in the year, several others, including Miss Joan Bailey and the indefatigable Vernon Peters, joined the committee.[41]

Readers of the Caron magazines could expect a message from the padre, an update from the auxiliary services supervisor, as well as reports from the various cohorts of student pilots making their way through the school. Social events were covered as were the fortunes and misfortunes of the sports teams. The medical officer often submitted a piece on the goings on at the hospital. Most issues contained humorous pieces about life on the base or the escapades of novice pilots. From time to time, articles appeared with information on noteworthy places in Canada and the UK.

From the start, the *Moth Monthly* received impressive support from businesses in Moose Jaw. About half of the twenty-nine firms that advertised in the first issue continued their patronage until the magazine folded in December 1943. Appendix D lists the top thirty advertisers. They are listed in descending order by the total number of advertising pages purchased. Their participation rate, that is, the percentage of the twenty-two issues in which their advertising appeared, is also noted. The total number of pages dedicated to advertising peaked at just under twenty in September 1942.

Only three businesses from the nearby village of Caron placed advertisements in the Caron magazines. A. L. Reeves drew attention to his automobile garage for a six-month stretch in early 1942, H. B. Lowe advertised his insurance business for four months, and Switzer's Saloon invited the *Moth Monthly's* readers to its eating establishment for two months. The rather sporadic and short-lived participation of Caron businesses corroborates the fact that No. 33 EFTS (RAF) had little to do with the nearby village.[42]

Within the first month of operations, Art Etter assessed the level of interest in a Rover Scout club at Caron.[43] He called on former or active Rovers to step forward if they were interested in continuing its activities at Caron. Although both Vernon Peters and Padre Crankshaw had been Rover Scouts in the UK, the club apparently had some difficulty getting going. In May 1942, the *Moth Monthly* informed its readers that the formal affiliation papers were now complete and in the hands of the padre.[44] By September, things seemed to be finally under way. Vernon Peters reported that weekly meetings were being held and that Jack Nelson of the Salvation Army and Padre R. H. Vernon Vivian, both of whom had scouting experience, were prominent in the club.[45]

Several other hobby clubs formed at Caron. A model aeroplane club emerged during the first month. The group intended not only to produce replicas for display but to compete in terms of which model could fly the furthest, the fastest, and stay in the air the longest.[46] The CFI kindly offered a heated room in one of the hangars.[47] There also seems to have been interest in model boat, model railway, model rifle, and photographic clubs.[48] In contrast to these modest and fleeting ventures, the riding club garnered a great deal of interest.

In the spring of 1942, Charles McDowell offered his barn to the riding club. Although discussions were held as early as April, the club only commenced using his barn in August.[49] That same month, Leslie Martin informed Vernon Peters that he had been appointed to the club's executive committee. Peters, initially taken aback since he had never ridden a horse, soon surmised that he must have been chosen to represent the absolute novices who would join. Peters quickly reconnoitered the club's equine stock. One horse, *Spirit of the West*, a high-spirited, "untamed prairie kicker" caught his attention.[50] By comparison, the other horses seemed docile.[51]

The inaugural public meeting of the club took place on the evening of 8 September. About fifty were in attendance. Leslie Martin informed the assembly that they were fortunate to have the services of stable master H. R. MacDonald who came from a family in the Argentine well-known for its horsemanship. Mr. Harry Chipperfield, an old cavalry riding instructor, had also offered his services.[52] He knew how to handle horses and could teach just about anyone a trick or two. In his brief address, Chipperfield promised that he could teach anyone to ride. He looked forward to introducing jumping to the more experienced riders, competing against the Moose Jaw riding school, and offering excursions into the countryside around Caron.

Vernon Peters rose to announce the policies agreed to by the oversight committee. Rides would be offered to all members. Memberships would be open to all staff (to date, no decision had been reached about student pilots). Dues were provisionally set at one dollar per month but would, in the end, depend on the extent of volunteer labour. Riding sessions were available twice a day but must be booked in advance through Miss Audrey Strong.[53]

The club's horses had been gathered from hither and yon. Some hailed from Grayson's ranch in Archive, SK and others from Greenley's ranch near Climax, SK. *Tip* was a longtime resident of the McDowell farm, being none other than the horse Charles' son, Hank, rode to school as a boy.[54] One of the horses had been purchased for the club by P/O Unwin.[55] The following were ready for active service: *Lady Diana, Toby, Tip, Pride of the West, Johnny, Elizabeth, Puss,* and *Smoky*. Sometime in early 1943, *Toby* returned to his farm "to help with the war effort." *Roany* replaced him.[56]

The next week Vernon Peters exercised his privilege as a member by venturing forth on the high-spirited *Pride of the West*.[57] Three weeks later, this unruly horse threw him and sprained his elbow.[58] From then on, Peters enjoyed riding the much older and docile *Tip*. On one occasion, the two of them went on an eight-mile ride.[59] Peters would enjoy many long rides that first fall, including one in the snow. By the end of October, the club had approximately forty members. However, that old nemesis, staff transience, soon decimated the club's oversight committee. Stable master MacDonald had been transferred and the club chair, Harry Trueman, had to vacate his post due to the press of other duties. Mr. Martin agreed to step in temporarily until these positions could be filled. P/O Unwin and Miss Mary Smith also agreed to serve in an interim capacity.[60]

Figure 7.3. Vernon Peters riding *Lady Diana*, 11 October 1942.
Source: R1545.1.136, PASK. Used with permission.

Mr. Chipperfield organized several group excursions before operations were suspended for the winter. The horses overwintered in McDowell's barn, tended by a hired groomsman.[61] With time on his hands that winter, Vernon Peters composed a poem modelled on Rudyard Kipling's "If." It appeared in the January 1943 issue of the *Moth Monthly*.[62]

If you can stick the sound of ribald laughter
That greets you when you call the tail a mane;
If you can post from here to Ever-after
And eat your dinner sitting, just the same;
If you can ride to hounds and be their Master
And not, like me, just curse the common pup
If neither Pride nor gentle Tip gets past yer
If Lady Diana's never "shot you up";

If you can cope with Toby's whims and fancies
If Johnny's just another horse to you;
If you can keep a steady pace and not take chances,
That cause Jock to curse you black and blue;
If you can tell your unbelieving mess-mates
That sixty minutes on a horse is fun,
That you held on—that there was nothing to it,
Except the darned confounded thing would run!

If you can bear to hear the truth you've spoken
Twisted by wags to make the groundlings roar;
If, knowing all the nags you've ever broken,
You still come back again and ask for more;
In fact, old man, if riding is a pleasure
You'd better join the club, we'll fix you up,
And do it now—repent ye at your leisure—
There's better men than you who won't give up.

The March 1943 issue of the *Tailspin* featured an article by Vernon Peters on the upcoming riding season. Mr. Martin still served as interim chair. Peters had apparently added the role of interim treasurer to his secretarial duties. Miss Strong still handled the bookings and Mr. Chipperfield now served as both stable and ring master. Seven of the eight original horses were still available (*Elizabeth* was missing from the new roster). Due to a few complaints the previous year, Peters advised the members to stay off the roads as much as possible and stay on the beaten paths to avoid crop damage. The monthly fee remained at one dollar. Members could expect a full range of classes for beginners, intermediates, and jumping under the guidance of Mr. Chipperfield.[63]

In mid-June 1943, Vernon Peters was promoted and transferred to No. 36 SFTS (RAF) near Penhold, AB. Within a month, he received disturbing news that the riding club at Caron would be broken up. The horses were already being sold off. *Roany*, who had recently joined the stable, had been sold for twenty-five dollars, a mere pittance. Some of the officers at No. 32 SFTS (RAF) near Moose Jaw had apparently profited from the club's breakup; it exercised Peters that they had scooped up "some bargains for a quick sale."[64] The next month, he informed his wife that the sole remaining horse, *Lady Diana*, had been raffled off—apparently one of the sergeants won her.[65] Peters later lamented that the Caron stable had been broken up for want of someone to carry out the secretarial duties.[66] No doubt this troubled him since he had been the one who had vacated the post, albeit, unwillingly.

By July 1943, even the *Tailspin* had to confess that the doldrums had descended on the riding club. It blamed the recent rash of transfers, including the departure of many of Caron's civilians to No. 24 EFTS near Vancouver. But, despite its obvious depletion, the club fared well in a competition in Moose Jaw that summer, taking a second, third, and fourth place. Miss Mary Smith distinguished herself on *Puss* in the competition.[67]

From the outset, sporting competitions played a vital role in the recreational scene at Caron. Personnel competed in no less than sixteen sports. Competitions were held between units on the airbase as well as against teams from Moose Jaw and other RAF stations in southern Saskatchewan. In the absence of a recreational officer after civilianization, the auxiliary services supervisor and his committee did their best to coordinate and encourage these activities.

The RAF officers and airmen at Caron were determined to try ice hockey. Within weeks of their arrival, they prepared a small sheet of outdoor ice.[68] In early February, they packed up two hockey teams and headed to the Moose Jaw Arena Rink. An antic-laden battle between the officers and the airmen ensued, much to the delight of the spectators. The officers' team, which featured five Canadians who could skate, dominated the early play. But, in keeping with the British tradition of fair play, some of the experienced players from the officers' team went over to the airmen's side to even things up. It seemed to work: neither team dominated the second half. What the players may have lacked in skill and experience, they made up for in entertainment value. Fans were amused by the gentlemanly manners of players who stopped to apologize after inadvertent collisions.[69]

Personnel from Caron attended senior men's hockey games in Moose Jaw that first winter.[70] The behaviour of the fans, particularly their contempt for opposing players and referees, took some getting used to. An editorial in the *Moth Monthly* advised British spectators to be prepared for the "fervid partisans" who constantly bellowed that the referee "wholeheartedly favours the visiting team."[71] Observers noted that the British spectators were much more generous in their cheering. They were more likely to encourage a clumsy competitor than to yell "take him out of the game!" as the Canadians were wont to do. In general, the Brits appreciated the good-natured efforts of amateurs and exhibited a more wholesome sportsmanship.[72] Vernon Peters witnessed his first senior men's hockey game in mid-January. His account of the contest between the Moose Jaw Millers and the Flin Flon Bombers from Manitoba is a comedic gem.[73]

It is easy to misconstrue the more genteel approach of the British to sporting events. It is perhaps best to follow Cathy Ross and John Clark's suggestion that British attitudes towards sport are clearly differentiated along class lines. Sporting events favoured by the upper classes do in fact elicit more gentlemanly behaviours from participants and spectators alike. Among the working classes, however, things are quite different. A 1935 survey described the fanaticism of working-class men who followed the fortunes of their favourite football (soccer) teams. It noted that much like their Canadian cousins "they enter into the spirit of the game and shout remarks of praise and disparagement at the players and referees." Boxing, which had a very strong appeal to working men, excited blood-thirsty and vitriolic passions, and a completely unhinged anti-Semitism if a Jewish boxer happened to enter the ring.[74]

A large contingent from Caron made its way to the Arena Rink the following November fully expecting to witness the first senior men's hockey game of the season. Upon arrival, they were disappointed to learn that Moose Jaw would be unable to field a team due to a war-time shortage of players. In its place, two teams of youngsters took to the ice before approximately 1,000 fans. The match was closely contested until the second period when a fight broke out between a Moose Jaw player and a much smaller Sea Cadets opponent from Regina. Well into the mismatched fistfight, sixty Sea Cadets streamed over the perimeter boards in the direction of the altercation. The Moose Jaw pugilist abandoned his victim and waded into the onrushing mob, punching anyone he could. When matters settled down, the referee banished the original combatants to the penalty box where the fight briefly reignited. In the end, the Moose Jaw Canucks scored a late goal and won 4–3.[75]

On 5 December 1942, the outdoor ice rink at Caron officially opened.[76] It featured waist-high pine boards around its 540-foot perimeter as well as an enclosed changing/warming room. The following year, outdoor lights were installed.[77] The rink had been erected by local volunteers under the supervision of Bill McCready, head of the W&B unit at Caron. Financial contributions from the BBFTS as well as No. 4 Training Command helped fund the project.[78] As per RCAF policy, Caron received a five-hundred-dollar allowance for its skating rink; the remaining funds were raised privately.[79]

Despite the best efforts of the supervising committee, the relentless snowfall of the 1942–43 winter constantly interfered with the rink. Anticipating better days ahead, the committee advised would-be skaters to mind the rules posted in the canteen, the changing/warming room, and the ladies' lounge. The committee promised to post signs if there would be skating on any given day. They also implored skaters to do what they could to assist, including helping with snow clearing and ice scraping.[80] The outdoor rink only saw one winter of service due to the shutdown of No. 33 EFTS (RAF) at the end of 1943.

By February of the first winter, many UK personnel were hankering after their favourite (British) sports. The editor of the *Moth Monthly* sought a suitable location for a new soccer field.[81] Another article indicated that two soccer pitches and one rugby pitch would be needed soon.[82] Not knowing that suitable weather could still be months away, many openly pined for lawn bowling, soccer, cricket, swimming, tennis, and boating—even if the latter meant simply putting a canoe into the Moose Jaw Creek.[83]

On 4 March 1942, the drill and sports hall officially opened. This highly-anticipated event drew a large crowd from all ranks. Throughout the evening, the hall's cavernous space was put to good use: its tennis, badminton, and basketball courts were in continuous operation. The station band sounded a fanfare when CO Worger-Slade and administrative officer Warrington made their entrance. In his remarks, the CO expressed his pleasure at seeing such a large group. He informed the partisan crowd that he expected that No. 33 EFTS (RAF) would soon acquire trophies in competition with No. 32 SFTS (RAF) and No. 34 EFTS (RAF). Upon retiring from the platform, the CO, padre, and other senior officers joined in an impromptu basketball game.

P/O H. J. Lewis, Caron's first and only sports officer, orchestrated the grand opening of the facility. (Lewis would be transferred to No. 32 SFTS (RAF) at civilianization.) In an interview with the *Moose Jaw Times-Herald*, he noted that they were in desperate need of sports equipment. He hoped that a benefit dance at the Temple Gardens in Moose Jaw would alleviate their deficiency. Notwithstanding, everyone looked forward to inter-station competitions. The reporter noted that the men at Caron had already coined a name for their opponents from Assiniboia (the "Abyssiniboians") and had designed a new walk for them—the prairie hop.[84]

In late April (1942), FSGT R. J. Penney announced that an intramural soccer league had been formed at Caron. He hoped that they could field nine or ten teams. He also announced that two teams would represent Caron in the newly-formed Southern Saskatchewan Service Soccer League (SSSSL).[85] A site due west of the GIS building had been selected as the main pitch and a practice field had been laid out south of the drill hall. P/O Mitchinson had been appointed to control gophers at both fields.[86]

Initially, it seemed that only Moose Jaw (No. 32 SFTS), Caron (No. 33 EFTS), Mossbank (No. 2 B&GS), and Assiniboia (No. 34 EFTS) would enter teams in the SSSSL. In response, both Moose Jaw and Caron decided to enter two teams to make the league more interesting. Further adjustments had to be made when Assiniboia backed out and both Weyburn (No. 41 SFTS) and Estevan (No. 38 SFTS) were eager to join.[87] The first matches were held in early

May. In the first game, the Caron Nomads defeated the Casuals from Moose Jaw by a score of 1–0.[88] Later that month, the Nomads defeated Moose Jaw's second team, the Corinthians. In June, Captain Nelson of the Salvation Army reported that the Nomads were atop the SSSSL standings.[89]

In the aftermath of civilianization, Caron could no longer field two teams even after it resorted to drawing players from its transient student population. In the end, the teams from Estevan and Weyburn finished atop the SSSSL.[90] The Caron entry in the league the following year fared poorly.[91] The *Tailspin* complained that Caron had little chance against the larger SFTSs, some of which had a thousand RAF personnel from which to select.[92] At best, Caron could only draw from some ninety RAF staff and perhaps two hundred student pilots.[93]

On 23 April 1942, a small contingent of boxers left Caron for Swift Current, SK to take on a team from No. 39 SFTS (RAF). The *Daily Diary* noted that although they had little time to prepare, the boxing team possessed some "useful material."[94] A large crowd took in the competition at the Swift Current Arena. Although four boxers from Caron won trophies in their weight divisions, the team narrowly missed the overall award, falling 14–12 to the home squad.[95] Although some talked about a rematch, there is no record of any further boxing competition at Caron.

As the British personnel struggled through their first prairie winter, they looked forward to springtime cricket.[96] However, despite the initial enthusiasm, very little cricket seems to have been played at Caron. In one notable exception, an ad hoc group set out from Caron on 10 July 1943 to face the Royal Canadian Mounted Police at their training depot in Regina. The Caron players acknowledged that they were rusty, not having played for several years. They did, however, manage to preserve their dignity and the good name of their school even though they lost 71–68.[97]

By early fall 1942, teams from Caron were entered in five-pin and ten-pin bowling leagues in Moose Jaw.[98] Despite some early victories, the Caron ten-pin team struggled. At the end of January 1943, they were last in the ten-team field.[99] In the fall, the Caron team once again entered the Moose Jaw commercial league. They continued to play into the new year (1944), even though No. 33 EFTS (RAF) had been effectively disbanded by that time. Remarkably, by mid-January, the Caron bowlers were atop the league.[100] However, over the remainder of the season, the team lost most of its games.[101]

Intramural sports thrived at Caron. Athletes typically competed alongside members of their unit. For instance, teams from the GIS, police service (guards), flying instructors, and civilians are known to have challenged each other in softball, table tennis, soccer, badminton, and basketball.[102] Even the ladies' lounge fielded table tennis and badminton teams, sports deemed suitable for their gender.[103] The organizing committee planned to aggregate points won in a variety of intramural sports and award a trophy to the overall winner.[104]

With the opening of the drill and sports hall in March 1942, basketball figured prominently in the intramural sports scene at Caron. It was not until the following fall, however, that players from Caron competed against teams in the Moose Jaw city league.[105] In one of their first matches, they faced the undefeated city police and lost by a score of 35–22. By early December, Caron had moved out of last place and into second place behind the mighty police team. The stellar play of Joe Mayowsky changed the fortunes of the Caron basketball team. Unfortunately, and despite their league success, the fourth-place team upset Caron in the playoffs.[106]

Badminton also figured in the recreational life at Caron. In late May 1942, the locals were already enjoying it.[107] That September, Vernon Peters informed his wife that he too played the game.[108] However, it was not until later that fall that organized badminton appears in the record. By December, the Caron club's twenty members were ready for the season.[109] They had already hosted an intramural tournament and hoped to sponsor additional competitions, including one against No. 32 SFTS (RAF) in the new year.[110]

Caron was invited to send a relay team to the No. 32 SFTS (RAF) track and field sports day on 23 September 1942. The day turned out to be "relentlessly wintry;" the temperature only reached 37°F.[111] Although foot races could still be held on the cinder track, the field events had to be postponed due to wet and frigid conditions. The relay team from Caron defeated Moose Jaw and took home the silver cup. Moose Jaw's *Daily Diary* noted that Caron prevailed in the relay only because Moose Jaw's main man, LAC Harrison, had been worn out by earlier events.[112] Indeed, the record shows that Harrison had competed in the half-mile, mile, and three-mile races.[113] His fatigue may well have been the decisive factor in Caron's favour.

Very little is known about indoor tennis, golf, and gymnastics at Caron even though they are mentioned in the record.[114] Ice skating seems to have been quite popular, both at the Moose Jaw Arena Rink and at the outdoor rink on the airbase. Skaters from Caron were observed on outdoor ponds in the surrounding district. Even the commercial bus which ferried personnel back and forth to Moose Jaw carried several pairs of ice skates for anyone who wished to borrow them.[115]

By July 1942, intramural competition was well underway in softball. Although some of the British personnel doubted its manliness since only Canadian girls seemed to play it, they caught on quickly.[116] By summer's end, a softball team from Caron had entered the provincial playoffs. Unfortunately, they were trounced 10–0 by a team from No. 2 B&GS in Mossbank. Since it was a two-game, total-point series, Caron wisely defaulted on the second game and thus conceded to their opponents.[117] The following spring Caron entered a team into the Moose Jaw softball league and contemplated an entry into the southern Saskatchewan softball league.[118]

It was not until the summer of 1943 that swimmers from Caron entered local swimming competitions. On 14 August, teams from No. 33 EFTS (RAF), No. 32 SFTS (RAF) and No. 2 B&GS squared off against each other in swimming races.[119] Two weeks later they would again be locked in combat with local swimmers as part of a Moose Jaw aquatic club event. Everyone expected that LAC Leonard de la Bretoniere, the speedy Netherlander who had dominated the inter-station meet on 14 August, would triumph once again.

Endnotes

[1]A. W. Smith, "Plain or Fancy Gardener," *The Atlantic Monthly*, July 1936, n.p.

[2]*The Moth Monthly*, March 1942, 28–29. It is likely that alcoholic beverages were only temporarily sold in the canteen, that is, only until the officer and NCO messes were complete.

[3]A similar committee would continue under the Salvation Army supervisor when he took over No. 33 EFTS (RAF) in early June 1942. By August of that same year, a sports and entertainment committee had been established. GIS instructor, Hugh Barclay, volunteered to chair the committee and look after the cinema. See the *Moth Monthly*, August 1942, 36.

[4]The entertainment committee also formed a choir and dance orchestra that first month. See the *Moose Jaw Times-Herald*, 20 February 1942.

[5]Vernon Peters to Vera, 18 January 1942.

[6]Vernon Peters to Vera, 24 January 1942.

[7]On 13 March, training command authorized the project. See *Daily Diary*, No. 33 EFTS (RAF), 13 March 1942.

[8]*The Moth Monthly*, May 1942, 23, 36. See also *Daily Diary*, No. 33 EFTS (RAF), 11 April 1942. Vernon Peters mentioned the special curtain tracks in a 2 April 1942 letter to his wife, Vera.

[9]*The Moth Monthly*, May 1942, 36.

[10]*Contact* apparently broke a record by raising nearly $221,000 for the RAF benevolent fund in a single matinee. See *Daily Diary*, No. 33 EFTS (RAF), 21 April 1942.

[11]*The Moth Monthly*, May 1942, 37.

[12]*The Moth Monthly*, June 1942, 27. See also *Daily Diary*, No. 33 EFTS (RAF), 9 May 1942, and the Salvation Army Canadian War Services newsletter, dated June 1943 in "Auxiliary Services (Air): Organizations Under Agreement with Dept. of National Defence for Air—YMCA War Services."

[13]*Daily Diary*, No. 33 EFTS (RAF), 6 October 1943.

[14]*The Tailspin*, September 1943, 15.

[15]Laurel Halladay, "'It Made Them Forget About the War for a Minute': Canadian Army, Navy and Air Force Entertainment Units During the Second World War," *Canadian Military History* 11, no. 4 (Autumn 2002): 27.

[16]*Daily Diary*, No. 33 EFTS (RAF), 25 August 1943.

[17]Sir Martin Gilbert, *From the Coming of War to Alamein and Stalingrad 1939–1942*, vol. 1 of *The Second World War 1939–1945* (London: Folio, 2011), 281.

[18]*The Tailspin*, May 1943, 15.

[19]*Moose Jaw Times-Herald*, 20 February 1942.

[20]A social evening held in the sergeants mess on 11 October 1942 ended with a dance to recorded music. Some one hundred guests from outside the airbase were in attendance. See the *Moth Monthly*, November 1942, 17.

[21]*The Moth Monthly,* October 1942, 39.

[22]Vernon Peters to Vera, 19 October 1942.

[23]Perhaps the short-lived swing music appreciation night every second Tuesday in the fall of 1942 was indicative of this dissatisfaction. See the *Moth Monthly,* November 1942, 9.

[24]*The Tailspin,* April 1943, 30.

[25]Francis, *The Flyer,* 154–55. For a discussion of the rise and fall of the romance of the pilot, see Jonathan F. Vance, *High Flight: Aviation and the Canadian Imagination* (Toronto: Penguin Canada, 2002), 57–58, 70–71, 97–105, and 268–78.

[26]*The Moth Monthly,* March 1942, 42.

[27]*The Moth Monthly,* November 1942, 21. Hank McDowell, who operated the snow plough at Caron, recalled being awakened after midnight in the middle of a severe snow storm and being told to look for a missing busload of young ladies returning to Moose Jaw. The road to Moose Jaw was in rough shape and the snow plough barely made it through. At the edge of the city, McDowell came upon their abandoned bus. Apparently, the young ladies left it when it got stuck and walked to a nearby farmhouse. By the time McDowell arrived, taxis had been summoned, and the ladies had been safely conveyed home.

[28]*Daily Diary,* No. 33 EFTS (RAF), 30 April 1942.

[29]*The Moth Monthly,* May 1942, 23.

[30]*The Moth Monthly,* November 1942, 21.

[31]*The Tailspin,* May 1943, 20–21.

[32]Hurst, *The Canadian YMCA,* 50–53.

[33]Hurst, *The Canadian YMCA,* 49. Caron, like most auxiliary services centres, used 16 mm film projectors.

[34]Data in this table is taken from the *Moth Monthly,* March 1942, 43 and the Internet Movie Database, http://www.imdb.com.

[35]*The Moth Monthly,* May 1942, 36.

[36]*Daily Diary,* No. 33 EFTS (RAF), 23 August 1942.

[37]*Target for Tonight,* 1941, http://www.youtube.com.

[38]*The Moth Monthly,* February 1942, 37.

[39]Vernon Peters to Vera, 20 May 1942.

[40]*The Moth Monthly,* July 1942, 3 and Vernon Peters to Vera, 16 June 1943.

[41]*The Moth Monthly,* December 1942, 1.

[42]Ryan Richdale notes that the BCATP is often lauded for its positive impact on local communities. The situation with respect to relation of the village of Caron and No. 33 EFTS (RAF) is not so sanguine. Although local residents were employed at the airbase, little commercial activity came to the village. This was largely due to the good transportation links to nearby Moose Jaw and

its amenities. BCATP or RAF installations near big towns or small cities were generally a boon to the local economy. See Ryan Richdale, "West Coast Aerodromes: The Impact of the British Commonwealth Air Training Plan on Delta and Abbotsford, British Columbia" (master's thesis, University of Victoria, 2012), esp. 12–13.

[43]Rover Scout clubs consisted of young adults, typically those too old to be boy scouts, who wished to continue its service activities and comradery.

[44]*The Moth Monthly*, May 1942, 35.

[45]*The Moth Monthly*, October 1942, 37.

[46]*The Moth Monthly*, February 1942, 7.

[47]Ibid., 30.

[48]*Daily Diary*, No. 33 EFTS (RAF), 1 April 1943. See also "The Salvation Army Canadian War Services Red Shield Newsletter," June 1943, 3, in "Auxiliary Services (Air): Organizations Under Agreement with Dept. of National Defence for Air—Salvation Army."

[49]*The Moth Monthly*, May 1942, 3. See also *Daily Diary*, No. 33 EFTS (RAF), 21 August 1942.

[50]Vernon Peters to Vera, 9 November 1942.

[51]Vernon Peters to Vera, 25 August 1942.

[52]Vernon Peters to Vera, 6 October 1942.

[53]*The Moth Monthly*, October 1942, 7, 9.

[54]Hank McDowell, interviews by the author, Moose Jaw, SK, 4 June, 7 June, 20 August 2010.

[55]*The Moth Monthly*, October 1942, 9.

[56]*The Tailspin*, June 1943, 12.

[57]Vernon Peters to Vera, 15 September 1942.

[58]Vernon Peters to Vera, 9 November 1942.

[59]Vernon Peters to Vera, 19 October 1942.

[60]*The Moth Monthly*, January 1943, 25.

[61]*The Tailspin*, March 1943, 9.

[62]*The Moth Monthly*, January 1943, 9.

[63]*The Tailspin*, March 1943, 9.

[64]Vernon Peters to Vera, 22 July 1943.

[65]Vernon Peters to Vera, 9 August 1943.

[66]Vernon Peters to Vera, 22 October 1943.

[67]*The Tailspin*, August 1943, 7.

[68]*The Moth Monthly*, February 1942, 7. See also Vernon Peters to Vera, 3 February 1942.

[69]*The Moth Monthly*, March 1942, 39.

[70]Ibid., 11.

[71]*The Moth Monthly*, February 1942, 8.

[72]In 1943, the Royal Canadian Artillery issued *A Guide for Guys Like You: A Gunner's Guide to Great Britain*, which highlighted the subtle cultural differences between Canadians and the British. It intended to eliminate some of the friction between the two groups while the Canadians were stationed in England. The different approaches to sports and sporting events occupied an entire section. The pamphlet is reprinted in Jonathan F. Vance, *Maple Leaf Empire: Canada, Britain, and Two World Wars* (Don Mills, ON: Oxford University Press, 2012), 223–32.

[73]Vernon Peters to Vera, 22 January 1942.

[74]Cathy Ross and John Clark, *London: The Illustrated History* (London: Penguin, 2011), 269.

[75]*The Moth Monthly*, December 1942, 19. Caron entered a hockey team in the Moose Jaw commercial hockey league in the winter of 1942–43. Little is known of their fortunes other than that they were soundly defeated by a team from No. 32 SFTS (RAF) in their first game. See *Moose Jaw Times-Herald*, 19 December 1942.

[76]*Daily Diary*, No. 33 EFTS (RAF), 5 December 1942.

[77]*Daily Diary*, No. 33 EFTS (RAF), 22 November 1943.

[78]*The Moth Monthly*, January 1943, 27.

[79]"History of Construction Engineering," part 4, 18.

[80]*The Moth Monthly*, January 1943, 27.

[81]*The Moth Monthly*, March 1942, 11.

[82]Ibid., 39.

[83]Ibid., 11.

[84]*Moose Jaw Times-Herald*, 6 March 1942.

[85]*The Moth Monthly*, May 1942, 9.

[86]Ibid., 3.

[87]*The Prairie Flyer*, October 1942, 29.

[88]*The Moth Monthly*, June 1942, 29.

[89]*The Moth Monthly*, July 1942, 35.

[90]*The Prairie Flyer*, November 1942, 31.

[91]*The Tailspin*, August 1943, 15.

[92]Ibid., 15.

[93]This estimate of the number of RAF personnel at Caron is taken from a report submitted to the Canadian Committee on 22 September 1943. See "RAF Stations, 1943."

[94]*Daily Diary*, No. 33 EFTS (RAF), 23 April 1943.

[95]*Daily Diary*, No. 33 EFTS (RAF), 29 June 1942.

[96]*The Moth Monthly*, March 1942, 11.

[97]*The Tailspin*, August 1943, 21.

[98]*Daily Diary*, No. 33 EFTS (RAF), 30 September 1942.

[99]*Moose Jaw Times-Herald*, 27 January 1943.

[100]*Moose Jaw Times-Herald*, 11 January 1944.

[101]*Moose Jaw Times-Herald*, 15 February 1944.

[102]*Daily Diary*, No. 33 EFTS (RAF), 31 August 1942. See also the *Moth Monthly*, August 1942, 14.

[103]*The Moth Monthly*, August 1942, 14.

[104]Ibid., 14.

[105]Although No. 32 SFTS (RAF) had been invited to place a team in the Moose Jaw city league, it was unable to drum up enough interest in a basketball team, much to the consternation of their sports officer. See the *Prairie Flyer*, November 1942, 31.

[106]*Moose Jaw Times-Herald*, 25 February 1943 and 4 March 1943.

[107]*The Moth Monthly*, June 1942, 11.

[108]Vernon Peters to Vera, 2 September 1942.

[109]*The Moth Monthly*, December 1942, 33.

[110]*The Moth Monthly*, January 1943, 33.

[111]*Daily Diary*, No. 33 EFTS (RAF), 23 September 1942.

[112]Ibid.

[113]*The Prairie Flyer*, November 1942, 29.

[114]*The Moth Monthly*, June 1942, 11. See also the *Tailspin*, June 1943, 27.

[115]*The Moth Monthly*, December 1942, 33.

[116]*The Moth Monthly*, August 1942, 14. The March 1942 issue of the *Moth Monthly* included a lengthy itemization of the rules of softball and baseball.

[117]*Moose Jaw Times-Herald*, 3 September 1942.

[118]*Moose Jaw Times-Herald*, 15 April 1943. See also the "Salvation Army Canadian War Services Red Shield Newsletter," June 1943, in "Auxiliary Services (Air): Organizations Under Agreement with Dept. of National Defence for Air—Salvation Army."

[119]*Moose Jaw Times-Herald*, 13 August 1943.

CHAPTER 8

Concluding Caron

It is a characteristic of the prairies that things hide in plain view.[1]
— Candace Savage

Due to the overwhelming success of the combined air training plan, BCATP and RAF officials discontinued operations at Caron after a mere twenty-four months. Immediately after closure, a small staff from Moose Jaw began preparations for Caron's new life as a relief field (R.1) for No. 32 SFTS (RAF).[2] Over the following eight months, No. 32's Oxford II aircraft practiced takeoffs and landings in virtual seclusion; only a skeleton staff remained on site.[3] Fortunately, there were only a handful of incidents and no serious injuries.[4] Sadly though, little remained of Caron's vibrant heyday.

A further contraction of the air training plan prompted the closure of No. 32 and its R.1 at Caron on 17 October 1944.[5] Understandably, rumours of another round of closures created anxiety in cities and towns across the country. The citizens of Moose Jaw were relieved to learn that their city would likely host the western Canadian headquarters of the RCAF. By mid-November, however, the RCAF had confirmed that its western headquarters, No. 2 Air Command, would operate out of Winnipeg, MB. Despite this disappointment,

J. Gordon Ross, member of Parliament for Moose Jaw, informed his constituents on 16 November that their former airbase had been selected to host a Reserve Equipment Maintenance Unit (REMU), which would be responsible for the on-going maintenance and repair of surplus training aircraft.[6]

REMUs, or their equivalent, are necessary since aircraft, unlike automobiles, require constant maintenance and operation when they are not in service.[7] According to DND's plan, the REMU at Moose Jaw would be supported by Reserve Equipment Maintenance Satellites (REMSs) operating out of former airbases in Caron, Assiniboia, Mossbank, and Weyburn. A small staff at each REMS would rotate aircraft in and out of the central REMU depot in Moose Jaw. No. 203 REMS (Caron) was officially established on 2 December 1944.[8] It operated under this authority until the following September when it too was disbanded.[9]

The Canadian government had been planning for post-war conditions long before the cessation of hostilities. On 30 June 1944, the *Surplus Crown Assets Act* came into force. The act established a Crown Assets Allocation Committee (CAAC) to advise the government on matters related to the disposal of surplus war assets.[10] Since the act did not give specific policy directives, the CAAC had to elaborate its own disposal priorities. It determined that surplus goods would be offered first to the various federal departments. If these agencies had no need of them, they would be offered, in turn, to provincial governments, municipal bodies, and public-service organizations.[11] DoT would receive special priority in the matter of surplus aerodromes since some of these facilities would likely be added to an expanding civil aviation network after the war.[12] If none of these agencies or organizations expressed interest, surplus items would be sold on the open market through War Assets Corporation (WAC), an entity also established by the act.

After the war, millions of surplus items falling into hundreds of categories came into the possession of WAC. Its inventory included decommissioned ships, real estate, millions of clothing items, and all manner of tools, kitchen utensils, automobiles, and other machines. By policy, it withheld and stored selected items to protect commercial enterprises dealing in such items from plummeting prices. It tried to neutralize profiteering by selling directly to the public.[13] By the end of 1948, when the torrid pace finally let up, WAC had generated sales of $450 million.[14]

On 10 August 1945, DND declared the assets at Caron surplus to its needs. In a letter to the CAAC, it recommended that its property be offered to DoT for its consideration. The letter also noted that the air force had received several inquiries regarding Caron's buildings.[15] Ten days later, the property and buildings were formally transferred to DoT.[16] By early December, DoT had determined that it did not need Caron's facilities. In a letter dated 10 December, it formally returned the buildings, property, and utilities to the CAAC for their further determination.[17] Once again, queries regarding the purchase of one or more buildings were noted in the record. On 20 December, the CAAC declared Caron's entire establishment (i.e., all its buildings) surplus to the federal government's needs. The entire lot was turned over to WAC for disposal in accordance with its priorities. The CAAC noted that the province of Saskatchewan had expressed interest in the site and should be given priority.[18]

Figure 8.1. The former No. 33 EFTS (RAF), ca. 1946. Source: Archibald Library Archives, 84039 M 002. Used with permission.

In early May 1945, the provincial government in Regina established the Saskatchewan Reconstruction Corporation (SRC), intending therewith to procure building materials for veterans' housing projects.[19] The SRC's interest in the province's airbases centred on their massive lumber stores, a commodity sorely needed, given the looming housing crisis.[20] Estimates submitted to the Dept. of Veterans Affairs suggested that between fifty and a hundred thousand housing units would be needed in the first year after the war and some seven hundred thousand in the first postwar decade.[21]

In early April 1945, the Saskatchewan minister responsible for reconstruction and rehabilitation announced that his government would actively pursue the province's surplus airbases since their accommodation facilities could be put to immediate use by returning veterans. Lumber salvaged from non-accommodation buildings would be used for housing projects in the province's urban centres.[22] A facility at the former No. 2 ITS in Regina had already been converted to veterans' housing.[23]

In a letter dated 19 November 1945, federal reconstruction officials notified their Saskatchewan counterpart that the buildings at Caron were now available to the provincial government, its municipalities, and school boards at eight per cent of the original cost.[24] Since the Saskatchewan government intended to purchase all available air force buildings in the province, it requested a bulk-purchase rate of six per cent of cost. On 20 February 1946, the SRC issued a purchase order for twenty-seven buildings at Caron in the amount of $30,720, a figure which represented six per cent of the original cost ($512,277).[25] Two days later, WAC agreed to the sale subject to the following conditions:

- The SRC must purchase all buildings once they are available;
- If the SRC elects not to purchase the land, it must move all buildings and restore the property to its original condition;
- If the SRC wished to purchase the land, the sale would be subject to the approval of Privy Council; and
- The buildings must be used for housing, institutional, or educational purposes.[26]

The SRC acquiesced in these conditions. The few buildings excluded from the sale were either already sold or would be released to the SRC when they became available.

Although the official record is scant, it appears that a proposal to locate a public institution at Caron, possibly a vocational school, had been set before the provincial cabinet. Rumours to this effect circulated in the Caron district. However, in addition to the province, several other parties were interested in keeping the former Caron airbase intact.[27] A group of businessmen from Regina had proposed to purchase the decommissioned airbase and lease it to several smaller organizations.[28] In early 1946, the leader of another private organization made a pitch for the former airbase.

Figure 8.2. Sinclair Whittaker, 1941.

Source: Archibald Library Archives, 80042 J 007. Used with permission.

Sinclair Whittaker of Briercrest, SK pushed forward the interests of his upstart group. Whittaker, who owned a small chain of general stores in south-central Saskatchewan, also chaired the board of directors of the Briercrest Bible Institute (BBI). Like many others in the region, Whittaker had moved west from Ontario and settled in Briercrest in 1910 where he put his retail experience to use. From 1929–34, he served as a member of the provincial legislative assembly. After losing his bid for re-election, Whittaker helped found BBI in 1935.[29]

Despite the economic depression, BBI expanded rapidly from its initial intake of eleven students. By the early 1940s, it occupied all the available buildings in the village of Briercrest. Not only did its growth run up against an accommodation shortage but the village's water supply also proved inadequate. The persistence of these deficiencies prompted Whittaker to consider the possibility of acquiring a surplus airbase after the war.[30] A facility of this sort would provide a great deal of accommodation space as well as complete water and sewage systems—rarities in the rural areas of the province in those days. As an alternative, Whittaker suggested that airbase buildings could be moved to Briercrest to help alleviate the housing shortage.[31] However, further unsuccessful attempts to locate suitable water supplies made relocation imperative, especially given the expected surge in enrolment after the war.[32]

In early 1946, Whittaker made several trips to Ottawa inquiring into the status of the Caron airbase. This site interested him because it was one of the smaller airbases (an EFTS rather than a SFTS) and relatively close to BBI's support base. On his second trip to Ottawa, Whittaker spoke directly with a WAC official who told him in no uncertain terms that it was highly unlikely that a private group would be able to acquire the Caron airbase. The WAC official showed Whittaker a sheaf of index cards containing formal requests for the buildings at Caron. And to make Whittaker's chances even more remote, these interested parties had CAAC priority. Despite the disappointing news, Whittaker learned that if the Saskatchewan government exercised its priority, it would be free to sell the airbase to BBI.[33]

Whittaker returned home and through a friend in the provincial government arranged an interview with E. E. Eisenhauer, deputy minister of reconstruction and rehabilitation. During the conversation, Whittaker announced that BBI had a range of educational and social service programs in mind for the former airbase, including a home for orphans.[34] (Even though he chaired BBI's governing board, these plans were likely Whittaker's alone at this point. The board would only later give approval to some of his visionary projections.[35]) During a subsequent meeting with the premier, Tommy Douglas, Whittaker learned that the provincial government planned to use Caron for its own educational enterprise.[36] Notwithstanding, the provincial cabinet formally accepted Whittaker's petition. To reduce costs, BBI only purchased eighteen of the twenty-seven principal buildings at Caron.[37] (Details regarding the final disposition of Caron's buildings can be found in Appendix E.)

The SRC determined that it would offer the buildings to BBI at a higher price than the six per cent of cost it had been charged. As Appendix E indicates, most of the buildings were marked up to approximately ten per cent of cost. It should be noted, however, that the costs of major improvements to the buildings were not passed along to the SRC nor to the final purchaser. The SRC later reported a $17,374 profit from the sale of Caron's buildings, a gain of over fifty per cent on its investment.[38]

By late May, the SRC received word that the Veteran's Land Act Administration would not exercise its priority on the land at Caron.[39] This decision released the Caron property to WAC who offered it to the SRC for $8,280. The SRC board agreed to WAC's terms and purchased the 680 acres attached to the former airbase.[40] Over the course of the following year, BBI and Charles McDowell received official title to their portions of the land. BBI purchased its 480 acres for $4,700; McDowell had his original two-hundred acres returned to him for $3,580.[41]

By fall 1946, Philip Yates could again egress southward on the recommissioned dirt road. However, one of the drainage manholes along the northern edge of the runway system sat squarely in the middle of the reopened road. Even after it had been removed by Hank McDowell, traffic still eased around the low spot left in its absence. And even though the manhole and its depression are now long gone, the dirt road still bends to avoid a long-departed hazard at the edge of a phantom runway.

The BCATP reached peak output in October 1943. That month, it graduated 5,157 aircrew, including 2,046 pilots.[42] Even though it had recently shifted towards navigator training, the combined air training scheme still produced far too many pilots. Consequently, pilot training had to be scaled back. RAF schools would be the first to close. Just as No. 33 EFTS (RAF) wound down in January 1944, the combined air training plan reached its maximum number of flying schools (97) and ancillary units (184). Over the course of five years, its 359 units and schools had occupied approximately 350 sites at one time or another.[43]

For its part, the RCAF had ballooned from a mere 3,100 service personnel in 1939 to 215,173.[44] At peak, over 70,000 air force personnel served in the air training program alone. They were aided by nearly 20,000 service personnel from the UK, Australia, and New Zealand as well as 12,000 civilians.[45] However, this stunning, seventy-five-fold increase in personnel paled in comparison to the increase in air defence spending. Compared with the year before the war, in fiscal 1944–45, Canada's air defence expenditures had risen 113-fold.[46]

Of the 1,837 student pilots who graduated from Caron, it is likely that some 250 washed out at the SFTS stage of their training.[47] It is probable, furthermore, that fifty per cent of the 1,600 or so who did earn their wings eventually flew operations with Bomber Command. It is reasonable, thus, to suppose that 1,000 aircrew from Caron (depending on how many, like Abraham Lawrence, were re-mustered into other trades) were at some point airborne over enemy territory. And given the fifty per cent mortality rate in Bomber Command, where most aircrew served, it is likely that some 500 of Caron's alumni lost their lives during the war.

The BCATP cost $2.118 billion, a sum roughly equivalent to Canada's total federal expenditures over the four years preceding the war.[48] When the air training plan officially concluded in March 1945, Canada's financial contribution stood at $1.192 billion, the UK's at $924.9 million, Australia's at $65.1 million, and New Zealand's at $48.0 million. By that time, a mutual aid agreement with Australia and New Zealand had already cancelled approximately $28 million of their obligations to Canada. In the year following the war, the Canadian government cancelled the UK's $425 million BCATP debt.[49] As per the arrangement, Canada took possession of all BCATP and RAF assets and eventually realized an estimated $112.5 million from their sale by WAC.[50] As shown in Table 8.1, Canada's total contribution to the BCATP amounted to $1.505 billion or about seventy-one per cent of the total.

Table 8.1

Total BCATP expenditures by participating country

	Expenditures (1939-1945)		Adjusted Expenditures (as of 1946)	% of Adjusted Expenditures
UK	$924,967,468[51]	UK	$499,967,468	23.6
Australia	$65,181,068	Australia	$65,181,068	3.0
New Zealand	$48,025,393	New Zealand	$48,025,393	2.3
Canada	$1,192,955,109	Canada[52]	$1,505,455,109	71.1
Total	**$2,231,129,038**	**Total**	**$2,118,629,038**	**100**

The facilities at Caron cost approximately $1.05 million (see Table 8.2). Included in this figure is almost two hundred thousand dollars of expenses incurred by projects not included in the original contracts. WAC's sale of Caron's assets (land and buildings) to the SRC only recovered 5.3 per cent ($59,017) of these expenditures. After all known accounts were settled, the airbase at Caron cost just over one million dollars.

Table 8.2[53]

Total public expenditures at Caron, 1941–47

Description	Amount
Buildings (as per original contract)	$512,277
Aerodrome development costs	$402,220
Additions and other improvements	$197,840
Total war-time costs	**$1,112,337**
Post-war recovered land costs	($8,280)
Post-war recovered building costs	($50,737)
Total recovered costs	**($59,017)**
Total net cost	**$1,053,320**

The RAF airbase at Caron stands out in several ways. It hosted the first civilian-operated RAF facility in the country. Along with its sister airbase in Boundary Bay, it first employed females in non-traditional trades. For a while in the summer of 1942, no EFTS in Canada trained more elementary pilots, nor offered its training to four, sixty-pupil cohorts. Its civilian manager, Leslie Martin, operated two EFTSs at the same time and did so on two occasions. No one else managed four airbases over the course of the war. And finally, Caron's civilian operating company led the movement to economize by remitting all profits back to the government. In the end, it returned over three-quarters of a million dollars to federal coffers.

There are also many reasons to laud the combined air training plan. It should be celebrated, for instance, for its absorption of the UK's entire EFTS and SFTS training apparatus after 1941.[54] By January 1944, it had graduated 38,775 EFTS pupils at a cost of just over $900 per pupil.[55] It also should be cheered for training 131,553 aircrew, a staggering 40,000 of whom graduated in 1944 even as it wound down![56] It should be praised for its 50,000 pilots who accounted for fifty per cent of all pilots put at the disposal of the RAF and nearly four times as many as were trained in the UK during the war.[57]

Those who were closest to the BCATP, however, were most awed by its organizational triumph. It managed to unlock what Vernon Peters called Canada's hidden energy reserve. And as Peters predicted in early 1942, these airborne resources did indeed overwhelm the enemy's pretensions.[58] Charles Power, who served as minister of national defence for air during the war, called it "the most grandiose single enterprise upon which Canada had ever embarked."[59] Leslie Roberts, who witnessed it up close as a civil aviation official, rightly called it "the greatest single achievement of the Canadian people since our provinces came together in the Confederation that is Canada."[60]

For his part, A/V/M F. Vernon Heakes, AOC of Western Air Command (RCAF), admired the far-sighted acumen of those who had "planned broadly and sufficiently to meet any set of conditions that might arise."[61] This great undertaking had been rapidly and efficiently executed even as it expanded. In contrast to the gentlemanly pace at which aerodromes had been developed in the inter-war period, the acceleration and early completion of the BCATP as well as the simultaneous absorption of the RAF schools must be, as the Air Ministry itself declaimed, "rightly regarded as a great achievement."[62]

Archibald Sinclair, UK secretary of state for air, acknowledged Canada as the program's "managing partner and director." In a letter to Canada's minister of national defence for air, he noted that the training plan "will always stand out as one of the best conceived and most efficiently executed measures for winning the war."[63] Sinclair's colleague, Anthony Eden, secretary of state for foreign affairs, also commended the RCAF for its "well-planned execution." He confessed that at the start no one had any notion that the plan would influence the "whole course of the war." He further noted that even "if Canada had done nothing else in this war, her predominant share in the Commonwealth air training scheme would insure her an enduring place in the roll of fame."[64] And Maurice Dean, wartime head of the UK Air Staff Secretariat, praised the air training scheme as "one of the most brilliant pieces of imaginative organization ever conceived."[65]

For those on the ground, the experience at Caron and the lessons learned went well beyond the formal curriculum and encounters with the austere environment. Except for an incident during the early days of transition to civilian management, personal relations were unusually cordial. S/L Eric Bradley, who served at both civilian- and RAF-operated airbases, noted the outstanding spirit of cooperation between the various staffs at Caron. He praised the operating company for this happy state of affairs.[66] This spirit continued through the final weeks as the dispersal and apportioning of its shared equipment took place.[67] The *Daily Diary* entry for 31 January 1944 also noted "the smooth running of the disbandment of this Unit." The cooperative spirit, which had "always been a feature of this Unit was maintained up to the final closing."

S/L Bradley was not the only one to endure less than cordial relations in other settings. Although we only have the official record left by the RCAF, there is little doubt that the relation between the BBFTS and the RCAF had been deeply strained prior to the former's move to Caron. A nasty dispute had arisen between the parties when the RCAF imposed a blackout on the west coast of BC after Pearl Harbor. Animosity from these tensions spilled over into the rapid departure of the BBFTS from Boundary Bay. The general confusion regarding the administrative structure of the combined air training plan did little to alleviate the tension.

Thus, there is little in the history of the BBFTS that suggests that its relations with the RAF, RCAF, or No. 4 Training Command would be good-natured at Caron. No doubt the new independence given to civilian managers helped smooth out the chain of command issues which had festered previous disputes. An additional, soothing influence can be attributed to the decision of the BBFTS to turn over its entire profit to the government. This meant that there would have been little or no friction over compensation, expenses, or lost profits. The removal of these pecuniary motives no doubt reduced the number of occasions when conflict could arise.

This spirit of cooperation not only infused senior-level relations; student pilots and others who spent time at Caron made a point of mentioning it. It should be noted that even the most junior personnel had experience at other bases. Most would have been through an ITW and a grading course in the UK. Thus, virtually all would have had short-term postings at other facilities, including a stint at the personnel depot in Moncton. So, even though they were novice pilots, their view of relations at Caron carries some weight. A report from course no. 69 noted the "air of friendliness and comradeship prevalent throughout the station."[68] Their peers in course no. 75 similarly wrote that they found Caron to be "a very friendly place—a happy station."[69] And Captain Fred Hewitt of the Salvation Army, who served at Caron throughout most of 1943, informed those new to the airbase that they would find it "a homey spot, nothing soft, but mighty congenial."[70]

When SGT "Jock" Brown reflected on his experience at Caron some forty years later, he vividly recalled that they had been a "very close knit bunch of men, each was the other's brother, irrespective of rank or trade." He attributed this usual closeness to the fact that all ranks were compelled to share the same housing, messing, and recreational facilities at the start. He also recalled that, despite the initial consternation, the partnership between the RAF flying instructors and the BBFTS civilians was "highly successful, everyone pitching in on the common cause."[71] J. H. McRitchie, who served as the officer-in-charge during the final days of No. 33 EFTS (RAF), also believed that the comradery had not arisen spontaneously. "[W]e did not experience any difficulties because we did not let them arise. Our association with the Civil Management was most cordial and any problems from either side were ironed out immediately and regular RAF/Civil meetings were held."[72]

But perhaps the most poignant tribute to the life at Caron comes from Vernon Peters who had to prepare to leave on several occasions. After Caron was civilianized, he was transferred to No. 33 ANS (RAF) near Hamilton. He considered himself fortunate to be transferred back to Caron as soon as he arrived in Hamilton. On his return, he noted that some of his former colleagues who were now posted to Hamilton expressed envy when he was sent back. In a letter to his wife, Peters praised Caron for the quality of its food as well as the happy atmosphere of the place.[73]

His superiors eventually transferred Peters to No. 36 SFTS (RAF). He regretted the move. He had hoped to finish his two-year Canadian posting at Caron.[74] The Caronites, as he affectionately called them, were a "grand crowd." By July 1943, he had been informed that his cherished riding club was in some difficulty and would likely disband due to a lack of leadership.[75] As he contemplated these matters, he informed his wife that "[t]he chaps at Caron were all great fellows. I'd spend the next four years in a desert with them."[76] Little had changed from when he had commented a year previous that his attachment to Caron was "quite inexplicable."[77]

Shortly after he departed, Peters wrote Leslie Martin, the general manager at Caron. In his letter, Peters thanked Martin for his efforts on his behalf. In response, Martin wrote that he was proud of No. 33 EFTS "and the splendid record that has been established here through the whole-hearted cooperation of the RAF and Civilian Personnel." He continued: "In spite of the location of the Station, I do feel that it is one of the happiest Stations in the Training Scheme and this achievement can only be attributed to the team work and the support I personally received from each individual."[78]

Peters and Martin were by no means the only ones to experience Caron in ways contrary to their initial shock. W. Griffiths conceded that "[i]n spite of all the horrid things I've said about the Station . . . When it comes to parting from it, then my mind is not so clear."[79] The following year, the student pilots of course no. 70 suggested that "[i]t's going to be tough, real hard, to pull out of Caron . . . we've been treated wonderful here. I hope they don't send us far away."[80] Of course, it must be acknowledged that comradery is a natural effect of close companionship and mutual labour. Nonetheless, it is notable that Caron seems to have spun its web of attachment in unexpected ways, in ways that defied the obvious challenges of the setting and the perils of shared authority.

This study has shown that the cooperative spirit common to the war effort is on full display and supremely evident in the domestic and organizational biography of No. 33 EFTS (RAF). The air training plan relied on the good graces of no less than four sovereign states (five, if the United States is included), multiple air services, federal and provincial agencies, civilian managers, and legions of everyday citizens. Given the complexity of these interactions, it is remarkable that the record at Caron is virtually unblemished.

Canada came of age in the air training plan. The struggle of the King government to assert Canadian autonomy against real or imagined British imperialism found a decisive rite of passage in it. After the fall of France, even King's prickly Quebec caucus came to see that the BCATP offered the best way to support the

Allied cause without direct entanglement in British foreign policy or prolonged trench warfare. Once the RCAF became the *de facto* managing partner of the scheme, Canada poured out its energies and dissipated any lingering fear of the machinations of the old empire. The relative ease with which the RAF transferred its training schools to Canada shows just how successful the plan had been in quelling old worries and demonstrating Canada's maturity.

The experience of the Boundary Bay Flying Training School nicely recapitulates this broader movement towards national maturity. It had chafed under RCAF supervision at Sea Island and Boundary Bay for the simple reason that the authority structure could not fully utilize the energies of an efficient and entrepreneurial civilian company. However, once these issues were resolved in favour of the management company and a new cooperative partnership established at Caron, things went very well indeed. Like the country itself, the BBFTS exhibited a new vitality once it had been elevated to the level of its former master.

Endnotes

[1]Candace Savage, *A Geography of Blood: Unearthing Memory from a Prairie Landscape* (Vancouver: Greystone, 2012), 68.

[2]*Daily Diary*, No. 32 SFTS (RAF), 3 February 1944. Later that same month, a portion of the small residential staff at Caron returned to Moose Jaw when it was determined that night flying operations would not be carried out at the new R.1. See *Daily Diary*, No. 32 SFTS (RAF), 22 February 1944.

[3]*Daily Diary*, No. 32 SFTS (RAF), March 1944.

[4]*Daily Diary*, No. 32 SFTS (RAF), 18 May 1944, 17 August 1944, and 25 August 1944.

[5]Organization Order No. 453 officially disbanded No. 32 SFTS (RAF) as of this date. See *Daily Diary*, No. 32 SFTS (RAF), 17 October 1944. In May 1944, DND considered the former No. 33 EFTS (RAF) site at Caron as a possible location for an aircraft holding unit or a pre-aircrew training school since it could support 240 trainees. These potential uses for the facility disappeared from DND's planning chart by early November 1944. See "Disposition Chart: Units to Close During 1944," 3rd ed., 15 May 1944, 2 in "BCATP Schools: Re-Organization of," in RG24, vol. 3213, LAC.

[6]REMUs replaced Aircraft Holding Units. According to A/M Robert Leckie, the problem with the latter was that they simply stored aircraft and did not provide for their ongoing maintenance needs. Further, they did not distinguish between aircraft that were held and maintained as reserves and those that were simply surplus. In his view, REMUs and their allied REMSs were much more efficient in these matters. See Robert Leckie, "Progress Report No. 60," 19 December 1944, in "Supervisory Board—BCATP. Minutes of Meetings," in RG 24, vol. 5233, LAC.

[7]*Moose Jaw Times-Herald*, 17 November 1944.

[8]Robert Leckie, CAS(C), "Report on RCAF Establishments, 1 Sept. 1939—26 March 1947," in "Organization & Establishment: Approval of Establishments, Policy Governing," in RG24, vol. 3213, LAC.

[9]Ibid.

[10]J. de N. Kennedy, "War Assets Corporation," chapter 34 of *Controls, Service and Finance Branches, and Units Associated with the Dept.*, vol. 2 of *History of the Dept. of Munitions and Supply, Canada in the Second World War* (Ottawa: King's Printer, 1950), 474.

[11]"Standard Procedure: Crown Assets Allocation Committee," 28 April 1944, in RG28, vol. 134, LAC.

[12]The Dept. of Veterans Affairs was also given priority over surplus land and buildings as a severe housing shortage was anticipated for thousands of returning veterans.

[13]War Assets Corporation, *Annual Report July 12, 1944 to March 31, 1945* (Montreal: War Assets Corporation, 1945), 3.

[14]Kennedy, "War Assets Corporation," 477.

[15]Letter dated 10 August 1945, in DoT, "file 5168-913."

[16]Robert Leckie, CAS(C), "Report on RCAF Establishments, 1 Sept. 1939—26 March 1947." The transfer of the Caron property to DoT from the CAAC was formalized by "PC 7643," 3 October 1945. See copy, dated 20 August 1945, in DoT, "file 5168-913."

[17]Document dated 10 December 1945 in DoT, "file 5168-913."

[18]Document dated 20 December 1945 in DoT, "file 5168-913."

[19]*Annual Report of the Saskatchewan Reconstruction Corporation of the Province of Saskatchewan, Year Ending March 31, 1947* (Regina: McConica, 1947), 1–2.

[20]The Saskatchewan government provided several immediate solutions to the severe housing shortage after the war, many of which relied on building materials or entire facilities acquired from former airbases. In some places, such as at Regina, Saskatoon, Swift Current, North Battleford, and Prince Albert, apartments were developed in buildings still located on their original airbase sites. In other cases, such as at Saskatoon, Moose Jaw, and Humboldt, entire buildings were moved into the city from a nearby airbase. In other cases, such as in Regina, new apartments were constructed out of salvaged airbase materials. See "Report of the Reconstruction Division," in *Annual Report of the Saskatchewan Reconstruction Corporation of the Province of Saskatchewan, Year Ending March 31, 1947*, 11–12.

[21]Wartime Information Board, "Housing and Community Planning," 20 June 1944, in Dept. of Veterans Affairs, file 5401-01-1, vol. 1, LAC. For a wide-ranging analysis of the wartime and post-wartime housing shortage in Canada see Jeffrey A. Keshen, *Saints, Sinners, and Soldiers: Canada's Second World War* (Vancouver: University of British Columbia Press, 2004), 75–93.

[22]By 31 March 1947, the Saskatchewan Housing Reconstruction Corporation had completed 550 housing units. Most of the buildings materials for these units had been salvaged from airbase buildings. See *Annual Report of the Saskatchewan Reconstruction Housing Corporation of the Province of Saskatchewan, Year Ended March 31, 1947*, 2.

[23]*Moose Jaw Times-Herald*, 3 April 1945.

[24]"Caron Airport," in R-221: Saskatchewan Reconstruction Corporation, box 7, PASK.

[25]Several buildings were not included (nos. 19, 26, 27) since they had not been declared surplus yet. The hospital (building no. 9) and one-chair dental clinic (building no. 21) had already been sold to the town of Lucky Lake and Frank Wilson of Caron, respectively. The original cost figures appear to include the cost of the original construction but not the substantial improvements made to several buildings including the airmen quarters (building no. 6), the airmen mess (building no. 8), and Hangar No. 2, which included a new addition that nearly doubled its total cost.

[26]G. H. S. Dinsmore to J. H. Sturdy, 22 February 1946, in "Agreement," in R-221: Saskatchewan Reconstruction Corporation, box 7, PASK. See also "Caron Airport."

[27]Document dated 18 April 1946 in "Caron Airport."

[28]Hildebrand, *In His Loving Service*, 87–89.

[29]Tributes to Sinclair Alexander Whittaker, Legislative Assembly of Saskatchewan, 29 November 1974.

[30]Hildebrand, *In His Loving Service*, 86.

[31]BBI, *The Echo*, 3, no. 15 (March 1945): n.p.

[32]Nelson and Winifred Jeffery, interview by the author, Moose Jaw, SK, 13 August 2010. See also Bernard Palmer and Marjorie Palmer, *Miracle on the Prairies* (Chicago: Moody, [1960]), 55.

[33]Palmer and Palmer, *Miracle on the Prairies*, 56–57.

[34]A document published later that summer indicated that BBI (or at least Sinclair Whittaker) envisioned a high school, elementary school, business college, medical training facility, aviation school, and a Christian college at Caron. See "The Challenge of God to a Great Advance," *The Evangelical Christian* 42, no. 8 (August 1946): 392.

[35]The BBI Board of Directors approved the purchase of the former Caron airbase on 9 April 1946. See BBI Board of Directors' minutes, Archibald Library Archives, Caronport, SK.

[36]Palmer and Palmer, *Miracle on the Prairies*, 60. People in the Caron district were concerned about the fate of the former airbase. Gordon Deagle, in a 1982 interview, recalled that the notion was bandied about that the facility would be turned into a public school of some sort. Some were disappointed when BBI purchased the site. BBI, much like the airbase before it, would not directly benefit the local area in ways that a public institution perhaps would have. See Gordon and Evangeline Deagle, interview by Terence Sinclair, Oral History Project, Western Development Museum (SK), tape counter #230.

[37]Gordon Elmer, in a brief, unpublished history of No. 33 EFTS (RAF), suggests that Hangar No. 2 was sold separately because it was too expensive for BBI.

[38]"Caron Airport, Statement of Disposition of Buildings as at September 30, 1946," in "Airports," in R-221: Saskatchewan Reconstruction Corporation, box 7, PASK. According to the calculations in Appendix E, the SRC garnered a net profit of $17,683.09.

[39]Letter dated 23 May 1946, in "Caron Airport."

[40]Minute No. 73, in 29 June 1946 minutes, in "Minutes of the Board," in R-221: Saskatchewan Reconstruction Corporation, box 6: "Audit Reports, Inventories, etc.," PASK. See also WAC sales order HO 2-2716, 19 August 1946, in "Sales Orders, Aug. 1–Aug. 30, 1946," in R-221: Saskatchewan Reconstruction Corporation, box 13: "Sales Orders, August 1, 1946–Sept. 30, 1946," PASK.

[41]"Reports for E. E. Eisenhauer," in R-221: Saskatchewan Reconstruction Corporation, box 1, PASK.

[42]Leckie, *Final Report*, 50.

[43]Leckie, *Final Report*, 8–9. A/M Leckie reported that 231 sites, exclusive of relief airfields, were used by the BCATP. To arrive at a more comprehensive figure, *including* R.1s and R.2s, I estimate that there were some 120 additional sites. Since each SFTS originally called for two relief fields and the larger (and later) EFTSs for one, an additional 120 sites seems reasonable given that there were approximately the same number of SFTS and EFTS aerodromes.

[44]This figure represents the peak strength of the RCAF; the total number who served during the war was 249,622. See Brereton Greenhous et al., *The Crucible of War*, vol. 3 of *The Official History of the Royal Canadian Air Force* (Toronto: University of Toronto Press, 1994), 864.

[45]Charles Power, minister of national defence for air, "Termination of the British Commonwealth Air Training Plan," press release (No. 4579), 17 Nov. 1944, in AIR 20/1378: "Empire Air Training Scheme Committee, Papers Relating to Training in Canada, 1944–46," UKNA.

[46]The Dominion of Canada had air services expenditures of $11,062,000 in fiscal 1938–39. This amount rose to $1,258,944,000 in fiscal 1944–45, a 113-fold increase. During this same period, overall federal expenditures rose tenfold. Spending on the air services as a percentage of federal spending, also rose by a factor of ten, from around two per cent in 1938–39 to twenty-four per cent in 1944–45. See *Historical Statistics of Canada*, ed. Malcolm C. Urquhart (Toronto: University of Toronto Press, 1965), 202.

[47]The CAS(C) reported that the overall wastage rate at BCATP SFTSs was 13.7 per cent. See "Progress Report No. 64 by the Chief of the Air Staff to the Members of the Supervisory Board, BCATP," Monday, April 16th, 1945, in AIR 20/1378: "Empire Air Training Scheme Committee, Papers Relating to Training in Canada, 1944–46," UKNA.

[48]The total cost given by Minister Gibson ($2.231 billion) has been adjusted as per the discussion in this paragraph. See Colin Gibson, minister of national defence for air, in *Dominion of Canada Official Report of Debates House of Commons*, 28 March 1946, vol. 1, 357. For statistics on Canada's federal budget in the pre-war years see *Historical Statistics of Canada*, 202.

[49]Hatch, *Aerodrome of Democracy*, 197.

[50]Since BCATP expenditures were approximately twenty-five percent of the total defence expenditures during the war, it seems fitting to credit twenty-five per cent of WAC receipts to the plan's net cost. That is, $112.5 million of the $450 million taken in by WAC should be credited against BCATP expenses. Since the BCATP no longer existed after 1945, funds could not be returned to its account; they were remitted instead to the Receiver General of Canada. Nonetheless, these funds were returned to public coffers and are therefore considered to have reduced the cost of the BCATP by the stated amount.

[51]This sum includes $445,761,150 furnished "in kind" (chiefly, equipment, aero-engines, and supplies) by the UK as well as $479,206,318 provided in cash.

[52]Canada's adjusted BCATP expenditures (as of 1946) include a 1939–45 program cost of $1.192 billion, a $425 million UK debt cancellation expense, and a $112.5 million credit (est.) from WAC.

[53]By using its own (unspecified) costing procedures, the SRC determined that $1.146 million had been spent at Caron. See "Caron Airport." The amounts in this table are derived from Appendices A and E, as well as Table 3.1.

[54]*History of Flying Training*, Part II. See also "Official History of the Second World War, Works and Buildings: Unpublished sources," in WORK 46/7, UKNA.

[55]Cyrus MacMillan, parliamentary assistant to the minister of national defence for air, 16 March 1944, 19th Parliament, 5th session, https://www.lipad.ca/full/permalink/1336651.

[56]Leckie, *Final Report*, 50, 52.

[57]*History of Flying Training*, Part II, 147.

[58]Vernon Peters to Vera, 15 May 1942.

[59]Charles Power, *Roundel*, December 1949, 2, in Dunmore, *Wings for Victory*, 48.

[60]Roberts, *Canada's War in the Air*, 10.

[61]A/V/M Heakes, in "Parts of Canada Attend Closing Function at No. 24, Abbotsford," *Abbotsford, Sumas and Matsqui News*, 2 August 1944, 1, 6.

[62]Air Ministry, *Notes on the History of RAF Training 1939–44*, 130.

[63]Archibald Sinclair, letter dated 29 January 1944, in AIR 20/1378: "Empire Air Training Scheme Committee, Papers Relating to Training in Canada, 1944–46," UKNA.

[64]Speech by Anthony Eden, secretary of state for foreign affairs, 1 April 1943 in *Report of the Dept. of National Defence Canada for the Fiscal Year Ending March 31, 1943* (Ottawa: King's Printer, 1943), 17.

[65]Maurice Dean, *The Royal Air Force and Two World Wars* (London: Cassell, 1979), 77.

[66]"Any Day Now," *The Tailspin*, December 1943, 15.

[67]In a touching gesture, S/L Bradley and sixteen of his senior RAF staff engraved their signatures on a sterling silver presentation box given to BBFTS assistant manager, Charles Clark, as he prepared to transfer to No. 24 EFTS in Abbotsford, BC. Fittingly, it also bears the inscription: "token of happy days at 33 EFTS Caron." This box is in the author's possession.

[68]"Course No. 69—Their Sufferings and Idiosyncrasies," *The Moth Monthly*, January 1943, 8.

[69]"75 Course Notes," *The Tailspin*, May 1943, 30.

[70]Captain Fred B. Hewitt, Salvation Army auxiliary services officer, in the *Tailspin*, March 1943, 27.

[71]"Jock" Brown, letter to Gordon Elmer, 21 January 1981, 5, 9.

[72]J. H. McRitchie, letter to Gordon Elmer, 20 October 1981, 1, in "Correspondence 33 EFTS," Gordon Elmer Collection, Accession # 2015-132, box 16, PASK.

[73]Vernon Peters to Vera, 21 July 1942.

[74]Vernon Peters to Vera, 13 June 1943.

[75]Vernon Peters to Vera, 22 July 1943.

[76]Ibid.

[77]Vernon Peters to Vera, 21 July 1942.

[78]Leslie J. Martin to Vernon Peters, 22 June 1943, in Sylvia Lindridge's private collection.

[79]W. Griffiths, in the *Moth Monthly*, May 1942, 25.

[80]"Course No. 70," *The Tailspin*, March 1943, 26.

CHAPTER 9

Conceptualizing Caron

This too blurs the lines.[1]
— Rosa Brooks

Where is the former Caron airbase? Fifteen miles west of Moose Jaw along No. 1 Highway? On two parcels (W½ 28-17-28-W2 and E½ 29-17-28-W2) duly laid out in the Saskatchewan land registry? On an official map of the airfields in No. 4 Training Command? Yes, yes, and yes. These guides will surely lead to the village of Caronport and the site of the former No. 33 EFTS (RAF). However, as the preceding study has shown, one can also locate Caron's airbase in a broader context furnished by the prairie itself, the resources of an emerging dominion, and the exigencies of war. But there is more.

Something further remains to be said about how Caron is situated in its larger conceptual context, that is, with respect to the ideas available to those who acted in its biography. Of necessity, an inquiry of this type will take us well beyond Caron's domestic and organizational life. It invites us to contemplate ideas and practices extended several hundred years into the past. As it turns out, Caron's everyday life hints that the well-worn distinction between civilian and military affairs had already lost several critical conditions that made it plausible for so long. A new model of armed conflict is at hand.

It seems best to think of the conceptual changes in evidence at Caron as part of a dynamic new way of thinking about security needs, an account that no longer relies exclusively on traditional military actors and the monopolistic state. The argument which follows notes the congruence between the concepts deployed in what we will call the new security economy and those so energetically asserted by an influential religious group in nineteenth-century America. This startling, shared heritage exposes the assumptions and trajectory of the security economy nascently manifest at Caron.

European nation-states wasted little time in institutionalizing their supremacy after the Peace of Westphalia (1648).[2] Although centralizing processes had been under way for some time, states could now unabashedly assert their pre-eminence over everything within their borders. Their hard-won monopoly over jurisprudence, welfare, property regulation, and taxation naturally extended to armed force as well.[3] Henceforth, nation-states need no longer negotiate with nobles, militias, Holy Roman Emperors, or overreaching popes; neither internal nor external agents could legitimately stand athwart their interests.

A century later, Jean-Jacques Rousseau noted that wars were no longer fought between "one man and another" as they had been for the Romans who swore a personal oath against a named enemy. Rousseau rightly noted that modern wars were "between one State and another . . . individuals are enemies only by accident."[4] The dominance of the war-monopolizing state was so complete by Rousseau's time that his contemporary, David Hume, could ignore all other belligerents in his account of how national governments rose to prominence. In his short-sighted view, military force only entered the narrative of the state after its leader had consolidated his power and was left with the task of establishing subordinate institutions.[5] For Rousseau and Hume, nation-states enjoy what seemed like a natural monopoly over war-making; in fact, for many moderns, they are the only true military actors.

The same sovereign act of the modern nation-state that established armed forces also created its complement: the civilian. Both classes were instituted simply and solely by the sovereign will that called them into existence. Neither existed prior to or apart from the specific condition of their possibility, namely, the continuing pleasure of the sovereign. The civilian–military distinction that emerged under these conditions utterly depends on the ability of the post-Westphalian state to impose these categories on its people.[6] Any diminishment of its monopolistic power will, *ipso facto*, undermine the conditions that make this distinction possible and plausible.

At the end of the seventeenth century, Isaac Newton unintentionally furnished the conceptual resources necessary to undermine the absolutism of the Westphalian state. If, as he demonstrated, regularity and order can emerge through simple interactions operating under the benign influence of gravity, then, by analogy, perhaps political order could also arise without authoritarian imposition or control. No sooner had the nation-state's rivals been subordinated than Newton uncovered a more general ordering principle which threatened the hard-won superiority of the victors. Although Newton demurred from speculating on the broader implications of his account, the notion of a durable order emerging within a system of freely-interacting parts proved irresistible.[7]

Following Newton, many eighteenth-century thinkers came to believe that social interactions would produce beneficial outcomes if the heavy hand of political authority were removed entirely or to a suitable distance. Adam Smith is the best known of a host of thinkers who applied a systematic (Newtonian) analysis to the social world. Like Smith, many Anglo-American thinkers of the period argued that the state should not interject itself into the social sphere; it should merely supervise self-regulating actors. "Nothing like a Hobbesian sovereign, no social homunculus at the steering wheel, firmly in control of all social life, is needed . . . multiple roles, multiple institutions, perfectly distinct, and infinitely different from each other . . . add up not to chaos, but to order."[8]

Most of Newton's followers were Christians. They reasoned that God had designed and created a universal system such that its unregulated interactions would produce benevolent outcomes. In Alexander Pope's apt phrase, the whole was "one close system of Benevolence."[9] Some of Newton's later followers retained the purposiveness of the Christian system but argued that the necessary intentionality could be provided by a nondivine agency such as the state. Under God or the state's benign supervision, maximal individual freedom would yield maximal social benefits. Both variants of the applied Newtonian model concurred that the purposiveness of the whole—whether supplied by God or some other supervising agency—guaranteed that free interactions within the system would achieve an ordered good.

By the middle of the eighteenth century, many thinkers had adopted the language of system (or economy) to conceptualize the relation between independent agencies and their beneficial outcomes. Correspondingly, the term 'function' came into wide use for any good that a viable system must bring about: one or more of its agencies must carry out each requisite function. Where and by whom a given function is executed is a matter of indifference, given the system's tendency to produce it in one way or another.

Collective security is a necessary good, and thus, a function, of every viable social system. Since security goods are *functions of the whole* and not the exclusive province of any single actor (i.e., a military class), no agency can be permanently and exclusively tasked with their execution. The older view that there are proprietary military actors must yield, as indeed it has, to the functionalist contention that the security economy must be open to all agencies who can efficiently execute one or more of its essential functions.

In what follows, I argue that a functionalism (of this type) underwrites the evolving division of labour in the RAF, BCATP, and at Caron. This conceptualization also provides an analysis of the broader and more recent collapse of the civilian–military distinction. But before proceeding to examine Caron and more recent military affairs in this light, it is helpful to consider another important centre of traditional social agency that underwent a similar functionalist reconfiguration. In what immediately follows, I argue that nineteenth-century American evangelicals adopted a functionalist account of the religious world. The conceptual structure and trajectory of all functionalist systems is apparent in the career of this bellwether group. The remarkable parallels between evangelical practices, the division of labour in the air training plan at Caron, and the trajectory of current military affairs arises from their shared functionalism.

In the aftermath of the Revolutionary War, American evangelicals found their parishes under assault. The growing fluidity of the populace, increasing economic interdependence, and mounting populism called their longstanding notions of place, authority, and social agency into question. Nineteenth-century evangelicals responded to these pressures by abandoning certain tenets of their traditional parish-centric views.[10] Under the tutelage of what we've called systems or

Newtonian ideas, they reconceptualized the entire planet as a field over which a universal church operates. During the first few decades of the nineteenth century, they conjured up legions of independent (non-parish) agencies intent on executing the globalized purpose of this novel universal church. Although they rarely paused to reflect on their theoretical commitments, in practice, American evangelicals treated the universal church as circumscribing a set of necessary ministry functions, any one of which might be taken up by any agency committed to its execution.[11]

Early nineteenth-century parishes were buffeted by so-called para-church groups clamouring for pulpit time, financial support, and volunteers. Low-energy parish life paled in comparison to the entrepreneurial spirit animating the extra-parish groups dedicated to the triumph of the universal church. By the 1830s, even the major denominations had retooled themselves for this brave new economy. Their parishes would have a place in the evangelical scheme but only insofar as they reorganized themselves accordingly and recognized that they were equivalent to all other ministry agencies. And like other agencies, they would be judged by their ability to achieve the mandate of the universal system.

Nineteenth-century American evangelicalism clearly exhibited features common to all functionalist models. It defined an encompassing economy (universal church), identified the essential functions (ministries) that must be executed within said economy, and articulated the central purpose (the conversion of the world) which harmonized the energies of its free-wheeling agencies. Remarkably, but consistent with their underlying functionalist assumptions, American evangelicals did little to control the entry of agencies into the religious economy. All like-minded groups or persons were welcomed and treated respectfully—at least until their efficacy could be ascertained. No group—especially parishes or denominations—could claim proprietary rights over any ministry function.

Evangelical agencies exhibited another important feature of systems behaviour, namely, expansionism. When turned loose in the religious economy, most agencies initially took up a specific ministry function: tract or Bible distribution, foreign or domestic missionary work, or social relief directed at a select group, (e.g., sailors, immigrants, orphans). As these agencies matured, however, they expanded the range of their operations, took up new tasks, reached out to broader supporting constituencies, and positioned themselves as comprehensive centres of ministry activity. In other words, they aspired to carry out more functions. The Sunday school is a case in point.

Originally, Sunday schools had modest ambitions: they promoted literacy and moral deportment among children whose parents worked on Sundays.[12] By the early-nineteenth century, evangelical groups had absorbed them into their expanding suite of ministries. Parishes soon adopted them as well. Their success in bringing children and their parents into the churches meant that Sunday schools were soon charged with executing a broadening range of necessary functions. Just after the Civil War, a French delegation drew attention to the expansive role assumed by evangelical Sunday schools. Its report noted that the Sunday school is no longer just "an accessory agency in the normal economy of American education . . . Its aim is *to fill up by itself* the complex mission which elsewhere is in large measure assigned to the family, the school, and the church. All things unite to assign to this institution a grand part in the American life."[13]

The Sunday school's expansionism mirrored the behaviour of local churches as they adapted to the dynamic religious economy encircling them. By mid-century, many evangelical churches had birthed a wide range of internal programs, often borrowing unabashedly from their para-church competitors. Some of the larger churches hosted dozens of independent programs, which were primarily accountable to the mandate of the encompassing religious system and not to the local authorities. These parish-level adaptations were supported by the same functionalist assumptions as their para-church competitors, including the notions that the ministry field is open to all competitors, ministry functions can legitimately migrate within the economy, and local churches can enter the system but only as agents of the overall mandate.

Another important systems assumption operating within the competitive evangelical economy is what might be called the unproblematic transfer of function. The Sunday school's rapid expansion had a great deal to do with the perception that the nineteenth-century family had neglected its religious responsibilities. Some of the most laudatory accounts of the Sunday school were prefaced by condemnations of families who had been negligent in some aspect of their duty. By the end of the century, Henry Clay Trumbull could affirm, and without fear of contradiction, that God in his wisdom had established the Sunday school "to meet and supply an existing lack in the family."[14] For our purposes, it is critical to note that Trumbull's call for the transference of religious instruction to the Sunday school assumed that the family's failure somehow authorized the transfer of said function to some other agency. Like Trumbull, evangelicals typically evaluated families or parishes as any other function-executor and subjected them to the same remediation or displacement.

Evangelical systems behaviour is also apparent in the largely-overlooked effects of function-transfer on families and churches. The assimilation of these traditional institutions into the evangelical economy had been purchased at a price, namely, their traditional spheres of activity had been carved up into collections of functions. Because they were merely functions, their age-old duties were vulnerable to transfer to more efficacious agents. Both institutions, which had traditionally enjoyed permanent status, were now exposed to the re-distributional mechanisms of a religious economy. In evangelicalism, the systems model pressed its central tenet to the surface: there are no permanently differentiated spheres of action or privileged agencies.

All functionalist systems require a bounded territory in which to operate. However, any economy's territory is liable to subdivision or absorption into a more-inclusive economy which takes up its functions into a grander whole. The size of its operational sphere or territory is independent of the internal dynamics of the economy itself. Nevertheless, once a perimeter is provisionally demarcated, the economy and its agencies can only be appraised by their ability to execute its functions, that is, those tasks deemed necessary for its purpose.

All economies contain agencies or function-executors that are initially equivalent. However, if an agency proves unable to execute a given function, it must relinquish the same to a more efficacious agency. Functions must be free to migrate within their respective economies seeking, as it were, their most efficient agency. Formerly-privileged agencies such as families, churches, and even nation-states—who are also vulnerable in this model—can retain their place within their respective economies only insofar as they efficiently execute one or more of its necessary functions.

Mature economies naturally develop comprehensive or consolidated agencies, that is, those which have had their range of function-execution extended. But here too, their hold on any given function is tenuous and can persist only if they continue to execute it effectively. The initial equivalence of all agencies and the frictionless transferability of functions within economies means that it is likely that all agencies will be reduced, sooner or later, to their bare functions and eroded by aggressive competitors.

Although it is not until after the Second World War that something like a full-fledged security functionalism is apparent in western armed forces, the events at Caron clearly exhibit its basic tenets. In keeping with the indifference as to which agency executes the requisite functions, Anglo-Canadian air forces paid little heed to the fundamental distinguishability of civilian and service activities or personnel. In the period leading up to the First World War, UK air forces leaned heavily on so-called civilian knowledge, training, and technology. After the war, the RAF seamlessly transferred its elementary training to civilian-run organizations. For its part, the RCAF likewise relied on the interest and initiative of civilian firms and clubs for its elementary and ground school instruction. Perhaps most tellingly, in the interwar period, the RCAF found itself carrying out civilian tasks such as aerial surveying, mail delivery, mineral exploration, and insecticide spraying.

The cordial relations between the civilian and service parties within the BCATP were not just matters of cooperation and coordination: in many cases, their contributions were fully interchangeable. For example, either party could have carried out the full range of EFTS duties. Had the RCAF been more developed in 1939, it could have operated the BCATP's EFTSs. As it turned out, civilians were (somewhat) better positioned in the matter. The decision to task the flying clubs and their operating companies with these duties rested on classic functionalist grounds. Clearly, none of the parties believed that a hard-and-fast distinction between civilian and service could be, or had to be, observed.

This study has also shown that similar (functionalist, as it turns out) assumptions informed the Air Ministry as it considered how to staff its transferred air training program in Canada. It made its final determination in the matter only after it learned that neither UK nor Canadian civilian operating companies were available. Like the BCATP decision to staff its EFTSs with civilian operators, the decision of the Air Ministry to staff its transferred EFTSs with service personnel in no way assumed the categorical distinguishability of civilian and service spheres of operation.

This same substitutability of civilian and service agency is seen in the determination of the Canadian government to apportion its massive BCATP construction program between DoT and the RCAF. No fundamental principle informed this division of labour; the provision of aerodromes fell to DoT simply because of its experience with the Trans-Canada Airway. It is not obvious why the Ministry of Defence lodged the building design and erection responsibilities in the RCAF since it had virtually no experience in the matter. In any case, it is telling that immediately after the RCAF had been assigned the task, it recruited leading civilians to its DW&B staff. Whatever the reasons may have been for the division of labour, it is clearly not the case that the tasks assigned to the RCAF were in some proprietary sense military and thus had to be carried out under its auspices.

The debate about which group—RAF or BBFTS—should offer flying instruction at Caron is also illuminating. As we have seen, this dispute turned on which group could offer the best flying training. The RAF had a compelling advantage since some of its instructors were highly experienced and had flown operations in the Battle of Britain and elsewhere. Neither party assumed that only the air force could offer such training: the debate turned on which instructors were more suited in this situation. The RAF instructors had another advantage which may have been decisive, namely, that since the Air Ministry wished to maintain Caron's RAF identity, it needed to retain its own flying instructors. The fact that the debate occurred at all indicates that no one presumed that only the RAF could provide the necessary training.[15]

Just as at Caron, the Westphalian civilian-military distinction no longer parses the conceptual terrain occupied by contemporary security operators. When members of non-state, belligerent groups (e.g., the Taliban, Al-Qaeda, or Daesh), are confronted in Afghanistan, Pakistan, or Syria, they might well be facing American corporate employees operating under contract to the US Dept. of Defense or Central Intelligence Agency. Do these non-state belligerents face each other as traditional military combatants or as armed civilians? If there is no formal declaration of war, do the belligerent parties enjoy the protection of the traditional laws of warfare? Should their actions be reviewed in civilian or military courts?

The aftermath of non-state conflicts is no less conceptually taxing. If any of the groups mentioned above is defeated by US civilian contractors, uniformed US personnel may enter the district and begin to rebuild bridges, restore water supplies, open schools, erect and staff medical facilities, and even offer agricultural assistance. If the area is later deemed to be secure, the armed service personnel may withdraw so that non-state NGOs can take over their tasks. This complex assortment of actors, fluid divisions of labour, and apparent interchangeability of personnel confounds the traditional conceptual geography, especially its carefully demarcated spheres of military and civilian activity.[16]

This conceptual warping is not new.[17] In the early-twentieth century, it became apparent that civilians and combatants could no longer be categorically distinguished. Totalistic modes of warfare implied that so-called civilians played "an increasingly decisive role in determining the outcome of a war."[18] The variability of individual contributions to a war effort also meant that civilians could no longer be equated with the mass of passive peasants or townsfolk assumed in the Westphalian order. And because "directly-contributing" civilians could not be decisively separated from their inactive peers, the morale and indeed, the lives, of the entire population became an object of armed aggression.

In 1938, the International Law Association attempted to identify those who should be protected from enemy hostility. It concluded that a distinction must be drawn between immune and non-immune civilians, the latter of which included all those who directly aided the war effort through, for instance, work in munitions factories or in "aerodromes or aeroplane workshops."[19] The association concluded that civilian employees in such establishments were legitimate objects of enemy attack. Emily Camins notes that the implication seemed to be that once persons ceased employment in such establishments or even walked home in the evening, they would immediately enjoy immunity from hostilities.[20] It also seems to follow that the term 'civilian' no longer conferred protection on an entire class that could be set over against a militarily-active class. Immunity now attaches to non-hostile behaviours and not to classes per se.

Protocol I, a supplement to the 1949 Geneva Conventions, attempted to further strengthen the norms of immunity.[21] In it, immunity-bearing civilians were defined as those not taking a *direct* role in hostilities. Protected status would be immediately forfeited by direct participation in hostilities and immediately reinstated when such actions ceased.[22] In 2009, the International Committee of the Red Cross interpreted the crucial notion, "direct participation," to mean engagement in hostile acts. Here again, immunity comes and goes episodically; it does not derive from one's status as soldier or civilian per se.[23] Both combatants and non-combatants pass in and out of immunity protection as their circumstances and activities change. The ICRC subsequently undertook a painstaking analysis to determine when a potentially hostile act crossed the relevant harm, causal, and belligerency thresholds.[24]

Crafting the necessary distinctions and codes of international law erected on them has been made much more difficult by the emergence of non-state, armed belligerents. Conceptualizing the various groups and individuals engaged in armed conflicts within host states is challenging. The International Red Cross, which has been charged with formulating and proposing international law in these matters, has been forced to set aside the Westphalian-Rousseauian framework in its recognition that subnational groups are engaging in true warfare even though they are not affiliated with any state. Insofar as they participate in a "continuous combat function," members of these groups are now deemed to be official belligerents and subject to the protections and penalties of the laws of war.[25] Using this criterion, guerrillas or other irregular fighters pass in and out of protected status as they engage (or not) in continuous combat.

The civilian–military paradigm made sense in a world of set-piece battles fought by professional armies operating at the behest of unified nation-states. Military uniforms and ensigns made fully visible the categorical difference between the two great classes created by their respective states. However, the distinction no longer unpacks (without infinite qualification) contemporary conflicts and their various agencies. The shift from a protected-class to protected-person has given way to a protected-act account of immunity, which attaches protections to specific acts of civilians and combatants alike. Despite the subtlety of recent work on this issue, protected-act immunity will be limited in applicability since it requires a complex appraisal of specific acts and qualifying factors in the heat of battle.[26] Combatants can no longer be identified by their uniforms.

Functionalist assumptions underwrite the conjoint trajectories of immunity-protection and the civilian–military distinction. As in evangelicalism, functionalism in the security sector gradually erodes all independent spheres of proprietary action and the privileges assigned to their traditional agents. As security is conceptualized as a function of the whole society, the classes assumed by the civilian–military distinction no longer enjoy permanent status, nor the protections and privileges traditionally assigned to them. It is now the case that civilians and non-civilians alike are defined into and out of their status by specific acts just as evangelical agents retained their status only insofar as they successfully performed specific functions of the whole.

As functionalist assumptions gain ground, we should expect an increasingly active transfer of functions between agencies competing in the security economy. Like their evangelical forebears, we should expect a growing nonchalance over who is permitted to compete for security functions. A trend in this direction is everywhere apparent. Today, private contractors can be found at virtually all levels of military planning and operations. The raid to kill Osama bin Laden is typical. As Rosa Brooks reports, "a mix of civilian CIA and DoD employees, employees of private firms under contract to the intelligence community and the Defense Department, and active duty military personnel" planned and carried it out.[27]

Brooks also reports that the US military has greatly expanded the range of its operations. The Congressional Research Center recently concluded that up to one half of the DoD's programs would have been considered civilian in the past.[28] There is another complementary trend afoot as well. So-called civilian entities have entered the traditional military domain in large numbers. For example, the so-called cyber warfare being conducted by a variety of US agencies (including Homeland Security and the DoD) is supported by many highly-skilled civilian contractors. This mixture of agencies makes it difficult to determine if cyber warfare is warfare in any traditional sense. Should cyber "attacks" on critical civil assets by foreign-national civilians be considered acts of war simply because they are highly destructive? Or, are they simply civilian *crimes*? If they are enemy attacks, that is, acts of war, who are the combatants? Who are the civilians? Here again, it is impossible to shoehorn these complexities into the traditional categories.[29] The implicit functionalism in these cooperative endeavours quite naturally turns its attention away from classes of agents towards identifying functional necessities and the agents who can most successfully execute them.

Another fascinating intermixing of agency is occurring in the militarization of civilian police forces and the increasing policing duties assigned to traditional armed forces. Regarding the latter, *The Economist* reports that Brazilian armed forces were very active in policing matters in the lead-up to the 2016 Olympic Games as well as in the frontier areas of the country. "For the bulk of its forces [some 334,000 troops], Brazil has instead adopted . . . a 'constabulary mentality'—plugging the gaps left by domestic security bodies . . . The army's remit has expanded to mundane police work."[30] Correspondingly, civilian police forces in many countries have adopted tactics, equipment, and armament formerly identified with armed forces. In this complementary role expansionism, there is something of the Sunday school's attempt to "fill up by itself" the complex (security) mission given to the whole.

Functionalism also implies that the scope of the security economy is independent of its internal operations. Much like the nation-states demarcated by the Westphalian treaties varied greatly in size, but not in their internal sovereign privileges, so too the scope of a given security economy cannot be determined in advance but only after its threat-perimeter is established. If crop failure is a cause of civil unrest in Afghanistan and civil unrest breeds terrorists who are intent on harming Western countries, then providing agricultural assistance through military supply channels is within the ambit of the security economy. Since the boundaries of the security economy must encompass the most remote hostile possibility, they must expand and contract as these threats ebb and flow. Given that threat tentacles reach into far and sundry places, all hope for a tidy, a priori delimitation of the scope of the security economy and its necessary agencies recedes.

The organizational life at Caron manifests the vitality and trajectory of the security economy. The Westphalian era, with its presumptive state sovereignty and civilian-military distinguishability, has been largely superseded by functionalist or systems notions. The contemporary security economy, whose logic is clearly indebted to earlier functionalist theories and practices, relies on neither pre-defined military actors nor their sponsoring states. As at Caron, the systems account offers maximum flexibility to state, sub-state, and international bodies as they assign armed-force functions to a kaleidoscope of competing agencies.

Endnotes

[1]Rosa Brooks, *How Everything Became War and the Military Became Everything: Tales from the Pentagon* (New York: Simon & Schuster, 2016), 258.

[2]See Derek Croxton, "The Peace of Westphalia of 1648 and the Origins of Sovereignty," *International History Review* 21, no. 3 (1999): 569–91.

[3]Lawrence Stone, *The Family, Sex and Marriage in England 1500–1800* (London: Weidenfeld and Nicholson, 1977), 133.

[4]Jean-Jacques Rousseau, *Of the Social Contract or Principles of Political Right* [1762], I.4.ix, in *The Social Contract and other later political writings*, ed. Victor Gourevitch (Cambridge: Cambridge University Press, 1997), 46–47.

[5]David Hume, "Of the Origin of Government [1777]," in *Conservativism: An Anthology of Social and Political Thought from David Hume to the Present*, ed. Jerry Z. Muller (Princeton: Princeton University Press, 1997), 49.

[6]It is no coincidence that the contemporary meaning of the term 'civilian' (i.e., non-combatant) entered the English language in the mid-nineteenth century when armed forces were firmly under the control of nation-states. The *Shorter Oxford English Dictionary* indicates that the pre-nineteenth-century meaning of 'civilian' was "a student of, practitioner of, or expert in civil law." The first use of the term in its contemporary sense was applied to "a non-military employee of the East India Company," that is, a "person whose regular profession is non-military; one who is not in or of the army, navy, air force, or police." See the *Shorter Oxford English Dictionary on Historical Principles*, 5th ed., vol. 1, 416, s.v. "Civilian."

[7]See several important works by Margaret Jacob draw out the social and political implications of Newtonianism: "Newtonianism and the Origins of the Enlightenment: A Reassessment," *Eighteenth-Century Studies* 11, no. 1 (Fall 1977), 1–25 and *Scientific Culture and the Making of the Industrial West* (New York: Oxford University Press, 1997).

[8]Don Herzog, *Happy Slaves: A Critique of Consent Theory* (Chicago: University of Chicago Press, 1989), 169–70.

[9]Alexander Pope, *An Essay on Man*, IV.357, in *The Complete Poetical Works of Alexander Pope*, ed. Henry W. Boynton (Boston: Houghton, Mifflin, 1903), http://oll.libertyfund.org/titles/2278#Pope.

[10]David Bebbington offers what is now the standard analysis of evangelical belief: "There are the four qualities that have been the special marks of Evangelical religion: *conversionism*, the belief that lives need to be changed; *activism*, the expression of the gospel in effort; *biblicism*, a particular regard for the Bible; and what may be called *crucicentrism*, a stress on the sacrifice of Christ on the cross." See his *Evangelicalism in Modern Britain: A History from the 1730s to the 1980s* (Grand Rapids, MI: Baker, 1989), 2–3.

[11]The evangelical system is described in much greater detail in Joel L. From, "Antebellum Evangelicalism and the Diffusion of Providential Functionalism," *Christian Scholar's Review* 32,

no. 2 (Winter 2003): 177–201 and "The Moral Economy of Nineteenth-Century Evangelical Activism," *Christian Scholar's Review* 30, no. 1 (Fall 2000): 37–56.

[12]See Anne M. Boylan, *Sunday School: The Formation of An American Institution 1790–1880* (New Haven, CT: Yale University Press, 1988) and "Sunday Schools and Changing Evangelical Views of Children in the 1820s," *Church History* 48, no. 3 (September 1979). See also Thomas W. Laqueur, *Religion and Respectability: Sunday Schools and Working Class Culture, 1780–1850* (New Haven, CT: Yale University Press, 1976).

[13]"Report of the French Delegation," in Clarence Benson, *A Popular History of Christian Education* (Chicago: Moody, 1943), 185. Emphasis added.

[14]Henry Clay Trumbull, *The Sunday-School: Its Origin, Methods, and Auxiliaries* (Philadelphia: Wattles, 1888), 150.

[15]If this broad interchangeability is true of elementary flying training, it is worth asking if service-level training could have been conducted by civilians as well. Was it merely customary that service personnel conducted post-EFTS training (SFTSs, AOSs, OTUs, etc.)? Early in the war, service personnel had an advantage in that they typically had operational experience to offer their trainees. However, it is easy to imagine when this happenstance would not decisively favour service trainers. Could not civilian companies—in peacetime, perhaps—offer comparable instruction? Indeed, today civilian companies routinely offer advanced flying training to air forces.

[16]Samuel Huntington, in his classic study of military and civilian affairs, claims that "[t]he term 'civilian' . . . merely refers to what is nonmilitary." Regrettably, Huntington's tautology offers no insight into how either term is to be understood or demarcated and thus it cannot make sense of the complex interactions between the groups nor their overlapping range of application. See *The Soldier and the State: The Theory and Politics of Civil-Military Relations* (Cambridge, MA: Belknap, 1957), 89.

[17]Holger Hoock argues that one of the most troubling aspects of the American Revolution's internecine warfare had to do with the bewildering conceptual puzzles that arose over how to treat and classify prisoners of war who were members of irregular forces. As we noted, intra-state conflicts, because they are, by definition, within states, confound the military–civilian distinguishability erected on the state's power to impose these classes on its citizenry. If the state lacks this power, the distinction is in peril. See Holger Hoock, *Scars of Independence: America's Violent Birth* (New York: Crown, 2017), esp. 357.

[18]Toni Pfanner, "Editorial: Direct participation in hostilities," *International Review of the Red Cross* 90, no. 872 (31 December 2008), n.p.

[19]This definition challenges the notion that any of the personnel at Caron were civilians or at least immune civilians.

[20]Emily L. Camins, "The past as prologue: the development of the 'direct participation' exception to civilian immunity," *International Review of the Red Cross* 90, no. 872 (31 December 2008): 870.

[21]Although it cannot be part of this discussion, the category of protected persons as specified, for instance, in Article 3 of the 1949 Geneva IV Convention, included more than just civilians but also those within the armed services who were incapacitated and thus unable to take an active

part in hostilities. See Helen M. Kinsella, *The Image Before the Weapon: A Critical History of the Distinction Between Combatant and Civilian* (Ithaca, NY: Cornell University Press, 2011), 116.

[22]Camins, "The past as prologue," 878.

[23]International Committee of the Red Cross, "Interpretive Guidance on the Notion of Direct Participation in Hostilities under International Humanitarian Law," *International Review of the Red Cross* 90, no. 872 (31 December 2008), 1014. These interpretations were officially adopted by the ICRC on 26 February 2009.

[24]ICRC, "Interpretive Guidance," 1031.

[25]ICRC, "Interpretive Guidance," 1009.

[26]See Andreas Wenger and Simon J. A. Mason, "The Growing Importance of Civilians in Armed Conflict," *Center for Security Studies Analyses in Security Policy* 3, no. 45 (December 2008): 1–2.

[27]Brooks, *How Everything Became War*, 258.

[28]Brooks cites a Congressional Research Center report, which claimed that more than fifty per cent of the US Defense workforce in Afghanistan and Iraq were civilian contractors. See *How Everything Became War*, 258.

[29]Brooks, *How Everything Became War*, 131.

[30]"Enemies Wanted: Brazil's armed forces," *The Economist*, 8 July 2017, 30.

APPENDIX A

Buildings at Caron: Original and supplementary costs

Building	Building no.	Original cost	Supple. cost
Double landplane hangar	h1	$89,671	
One-half double landplane hangar with control tower	h2	$57,617	
1943 addition to h2	h2		$52,234
Headquarters & GIS (with heater room)	1	$28,716	
Steam heating installation			$3,851
Officers quarters	2	$18,571	
Steam heating installation			$3,282
Officers mess (with heater room)	3	$10,257	
NCO quarters	4	$29,573	
Steam heating installation			$3,991
NCO mess (with heater room)	5	$16,447	
Steam heating installation			$1,857
Airmen quarters	6	$43,450	
Steam heating installation			$4,995
Civilianization of building no. 6			$29,766
Airmen quarters	7	$43,450	
Steam heating installation			$4,995
Airmen mess (with heater room)	8	$25,000	
1943 addition to building no. 8			$8,635
Station sick quarters (with heater room)	9	$23,627	
Steam heating installation			$2,417

Building	Building no.	Original cost	Supple. cost
Canteen (with heater room)	10	$10,667	
Drill hall (with heater room)	11	$42,000	
Link Flight Training building	12	$7,645	
Tech. & quartermaster stores (no heater room)	13	$8,137	
Workshop (no heater room)	14	$6,386	
W&B section	15	$12,437	
Coal storage	16	$500	
MT 4-bay garage	17a	$1,800	
MT 8-bay garage	17b	$4,000	
MT 4-bay garage	17c	$1,800	
MT repair shop/office (no heater room)	17d	$5,900	
MT gasoline system			$780
Control tower (included in cost of h2)	18	$0.00	
25-yard range and shelter building	19	$6,870	
Guardhouse & post office (no heater room)	20	$5,900	
Dental clinic (one chair)	21	$2,875	
Recreation hall	22		$19,860
Warm air heating installation			$2,385
Cost adjustment for warm air heating			$17.70
Petroleum, oil & lubricants storage	23		$7,700
Oil and paint storage	24		$1,200
Fire hall	25		$10,443
Pump house	26		DoT expense
Water reservoir	27		DoT expense
Incinerator		$991	
Flagstaff		$490	
Hose reel houses (n = 6)			$300 (est.)
Chlorinator building, septic tank, screen house			DoT expense
Hot air handlers and steam boilers			$20,000[1]

Building	Building no.	Original cost	Supple. cost
Surfacing work in building area			$19,131.70
Excavation		$10,000	
Subtotal		**$514,777**	
Less (as per telegram, 21 August 1941)		-$1,000	
Less (substitution of cedar shingles as exterior cladding)		-$1,500	
Subtotals		**$512,277**	**$197,840.40**
Grand total (original plus supplementary costs)		**$710,117.40**	

Endnotes

[1]This figure estimates the cost of purchasing steam boilers for all the buildings that had steam heating systems as well as the cost of the hot air heating units in the hangars and drill hall.

APPENDIX B

Caron's civilian airframe mechanics (engineers)

Name	Home Town[1] (if known)
Abrams, Howard	Langley, BC
Ames, R.	
Angle, Lloyd	
Baird, J.	
Bayliss, F.	
Beadle, K.	
Becott, Kenneth	New Westminster, BC
Bennet, ?	
Bertalino, Joe	Vancouver, BC
Biddle, Herbert L.	Vancouver, BC
Bielens, Bernard G.	Regina, SK
Binion, E. E.	Ladner, BC
Bradbury, Leslie	Moose Jaw, SK
Brennen, Ralph H.	Aneroid, SK
Briegel, J. N.	Olds, AB
Broadbent, E. R.	Abbotsford, BC
Brown, Vernon R.	Regina, SK
Buchanan, G.	
Christenson, M.	
Clark C.	
Cook, F. C.	Moose Jaw, SK
Cox, D.	

Name	**Home Town**[1] (if known)
Crawford, C.	
Davies, M.	
Davis, J. C.	Moose Jaw, SK
Dawes, E.	Vancouver, BC
Doney, E. W.	Boharm, SK
Edridge, Bruce F.	Oyama, BC
Edwards, William	Vancouver Area
Elliott, M.	
Erickson, W.	
Esau, M.	Moose Jaw, SK
Fowler, S.	
Fox, J.	
Gable, Bernie	
Garratt, E.	
Gillingham, Ken	
Grant, Jim	
Hamilton, D.	
Hampton, Bert	Vancouver Area
Hardy, Walter V.	
Hare, Harry	Vancouver, BC
Hawkridge, Len	Vancouver, BC
Hewitt, Travis	
Hickling, Fred T.	Regina, SK
Holland, Douglas	
Howatt, Alec A.	Abbotsford, BC
Lace, B.	
Lacoque, R.	
Lacousiere, L.	
Lamb, R.	
Laurie, W. J.	Ladner, BC
Lennox, Robert	

Name	Home Town[1] (if known)
MacDonald, Al	
Main, E.	
Marsden, Ray	Moose Jaw, SK
Mayowsky, Joe	
McGee, John	Deloraine, MB?
McLaughlin, E.	
McNeil, ?	
Mireau, Lorne P.	Regina, SK
Moran, Pat	
Morgan, Bert	
Mosher, Ken	Kirkland, ON
Myers, Allan	Carlyle, SK
Nugent, M. J.	Vancouver, BC
Patterson, John L.	Moose Jaw, SK
Peters, C. G.	Vancouver, BC
Piper, Louis	Vancouver Area
Purves, George	Regina, SK
Ranger, Frank C.	Burquitlam, BC
Rollins, John C.	Moose Jaw, SK
Rutherford, Peter C.	Burnaby, BC
Sambrooke, W. E.	Abbotsford, BC
Sawchuk, P.	
Seitz, B.	
Sidhoo, Ajaib	Vancouver, BC
Sinclair, J. N.	Assiniboia, SK
Sirdinski, J.	
Smith, R. H.	West Vancouver, BC
Small, James	
Solloum, R.	
Sonmor, A.	
Stainsby, Jack	

Name	Home Town[1] (if known)
Staples, J.	
Stinger, Alf	Vancouver, BC
Stone, Francis	
Sylvester, G.	
Taylor, F.	
Taylor, Norman	
Telfer, O. Thomas	Moose Jaw, SK
Temple, Philp	
Thom, David	Moose Jaw, SK
Thomlinson, P.	
Trail, Vernon	
Walker, Jack	Vancouver, BC
Wallden, G.	
Warburton, J. F. L.	Vancouver, BC
Warner, T.	
Webb, D.	
Weir, I. H.	Invermere, BC
Woolard, Charles	
Wright, C. H.	Caron, SK
Young, V.	

Endnotes

[1]Some of those with a Moose Jaw address may have transferred with the BBFTS from Vancouver and thus were only temporary residents of the city.

APPENDIX C

Caron's female employees

Name	Home Town (if known)	Trade (if known)
Acorn, Lila*[1]	Spruce Home, SK	
Arthur, Miss Florence	Ladner, BC	General office clerk
Avery, Doris	Marquis, SK	Mechanical transport driver
Avison, Bernice*	Regina, SK	
Bailey, Miss Claire	Vancouver, BC	
Bailey, Miss Joan	Vancouver, BC	
Baker, Miss May	Ladner, BC	
Berg, Miss Helen	Central Butte, SK	
Berg, Miss Lucy	Central Butte, SK	
Bowles, Mrs. Margaret N.		Assistant wireless instructor
Brawdy, Vera L.	Tuxford, SK	
Brough, Miss Madeline J.	Vancouver, BC	
Brown, Joyce*	Meadow Lake, SK	
Burwell, Miss Dorothy		
Carlson, Mildred*	Dunkirk, SK	
Carnie, Mrs. Margorie		
Coombes, Mrs. Margaret	Deloraine, MB	Timekeeper
Coyer, Miss Olive		Timekeeper?
Crosbie, Miss Lena	Caron, SK	Cook's assistant
Dale, Miss Charlotte	Moose Jaw, SK	
Danilkewich, Jean*	Meadow Lake, SK	
Dittrich, Miss Sabina		

Edwards, Betty		
Elliott, Miss Lena	Moose Jaw, SK	
Finnigan, Miss Rose	Vancouver, BC	
Fulton, Miss Mary E.	Moose Jaw, SK	Waitress
Gable, Miss Theresa		
Gillies, Dorothy*	Mankota, SK	
Green, Miss Agnus E.	Vancouver, BC	Assistant head chef
Gustafson, Emma	Avonlea, SK	Timekeeper
Hansen, Miss Sally		
Jackson, Miss Gladys		
Jackson, Miss Susan T.	Toronto, ON	General office stenographer
Johnson, L.		
Jonas, Mrs. V.		
Kristjanson, Lois		Hangar assistant
Langdon, Miss Marguerita	Moose Jaw, SK	Nurse
Larocque, Grace*	Meadow Lake, SK	
Legge, Rita*	Moose Jaw, SK	
Long, Miss Isabelle	Limerick, SK	Timekeeper
Machan, Miss Vivien	Tuxford, SK	Flight office assistant
Martin, Elizabeth	Ladner, BC	Post office clerk
Martin, Miss Beverly E.	Vancouver, BC	General office clerk
McGee, Margaret	Deloraine, MB	Timekeeper
McPheat, Lila	Moose Jaw, SK	
Miller, Miss Irene		
Mitchell, Miss Mary	Vancouver, BC	
Montgomery, Miss Phyllis	Ladner, BC	
Mowat, Miss Dorothy E.	Ladner, BC	Canteen worker
Muckle, Mrs.		
Muckle, Miss Irene		
Olsen, June E.	Wymark, SK	Hangar assistant
Radcliff, Loraine		
Randa, Miss Helia		

Reagh, Miss Jessie	Ladner, BC	Waitress; Switchboard operator
Richards, Mrs. Violet	Valor, SK	
Robertson, Dorothy*	Mankota, SK	
Rorison, Jeanette	Moose Jaw, SK	
Sambrooke, Myra	Abbotsford, BC	Instrument clerk
Siddle, Mrs. Ada*	Riverhurst, SK	
Sinclair, Miss Una	Lac du Bonnet, MB	Officers mess waitress
Smith, Miss Mary	Boharm, SK	
Stang, Miss A.		
Stone, Miss Frances		Engineering staff
Strong, Audrey B.	Vancouver, BC	Secretary to BBFTS manager
Thomson, Alice		
Thomson, Hilda*	Moose Jaw, SK	
White, Miss May		Accountant's clerk
Wolfram, Miss Kay		
Zahara, Miss Ann J.		Canteen manager

Endnotes

[1]An asterisk indicates that this person is presumed to have been employed at Caron. Her name, along with a SK home address, appears among those who were later employed by the VATC at Abbotsford, BC. See *Sky: Memories of Abbotsford 1944*, 20–21.

APPENDIX D

Businesses advertising in Caron's station magazines

Name of Firm	Type	Location	Total Pages	Participation
No. 33 EFTS Canteen	Refreshments	Caron	17	77%
R. H. Williams & Sons	Dept. store	Regina	15	68%
Army & Navy	Dept. store	Moose Jaw	11	100%
Leonard Fysh	Drug store	Moose Jaw	11	100%
MJ Steam Laundry	Laundry	Moose Jaw	10.5	95%
Slater & York	Men's Clothier	Moose Jaw	10.5	95%
Joyner's	Dept. store	Moose Jaw	10	91%
The Rosery	Florist	Moose Jaw	10	91%
Central Motor Co.	Automobiles	Moose Jaw	8.7	82%
Timothy Eaton Co.	Dept. store	Moose Jaw	8.5	77%
Temple Gardens	Dance hall	Moose Jaw	8.5	77%
Times Pub. Co.	Printer	Moose Jaw	7.4	100%
E. R. Eaton	Furrier	Moose Jaw	5.5	100%
Grant Hall Hotel	Hotel	Moose Jaw	5.5	100%
Hotel Churchill	Hotel	Moose Jaw	5.5	100%
Johnston Dairies	Dairy products	Moose Jaw	5.5	100%
Plaxton's	Jeweler	Moose Jaw	5.5	100%
The Bidwell Studio	Photographer	Moose Jaw	5.5	100%
Ambassador Café	Restaurant	Moose Jaw	5.3	95%
Connaught Billiards	Billiard hall	Moose Jaw	5.3	95%
Co-op Groceteria	Groceries	Moose Jaw	5.3	95%
H. A. Davidson	Drug store	Moose Jaw	5.3	95%
Milk Bar	Refreshments	Moose Jaw	5.3	95%
Park Hotel	Hotel	Moose Jaw	5.3	95%

Name of Firm	Type	Location	Total Pages	Participation
Elite Café	Restaurant	Moose Jaw	4.8	86%
Whimster's Hardware	Hardware	Moose Jaw	4.5	82%
Brunswick Hotel	Hotel	Moose Jaw	8.4	95%
Elks	Service club	Moose Jaw	4.3	77%
J. E. Overs	Confectionery	Moose Jaw	4.3	77%
Red Indian	Service station	Moose Jaw	4.3	77%

APPENDIX E

Final disposition of Caron's buildings

Bldg no.	Facility	RCAF total cost	SRC cost	SRC resale price	Purchaser	Resale price as % of RCAF cost
h1	Hangar No. 1	$89,671	$5,380.26	$8,408.66	BBI	9.4
h2	Hangar No. 2	$109,851	$3,457.02	$5,000.00	Prairie Vegetable Oils, MJ	4.6
1	Headquarters & GIS	$32,567	$1,722.96	$2,872.00	Providence Hospital, MJ	8.8
2	Officers quarters	$21,853	$1,114.26	$1,857.00	Providence Hospital, MJ	8.5
3	Officers mess	$10,257	$615.42	$961.82	BBI	9.4
4	NCO quarters	$33,564	$1,774.38	$2,773.13	BBI	8.3
5	NCO mess	$18,304	$986.82	$1,542.27	BBI	8.4
6	Airmen quarters	$78,211	$2,607.00	$4,074.41	BBI	5.2
7	Airmen quarters	$48,445	$2,607.00	$4,074.41	BBI	8.4
8	Airmen mess	$33,635	$1,500.00	$2,344.31	BBI	7.0
9	Station sick quarters	$26,044	$1,890.16	$2,000.00	Lucky Lake Hospital	7.7
10	Canteen	$10,667	$637.62	$1,000.00	St. Agnes School, MJ	9.4
11	Drill hall	$42,000	$2,520.00	$3,938.44	BBI	9.4

12	Link Flight Training building	$7,645	$458.70	$800.00	Lucky Lake Hospital	10.5
13	Tech. & quartermaster Stores	$8,137	$488.22	$763.03	BBI	9.4
14	Workshop	$6,386	$383.16	$598.83	BBI	9.4
15	W&B section	$12,437	$746.22	$1,166.25	BBI	9.4
16	Coal storage	$500	$30.00	$46.89	BBI	9.4
17a	MT 4-bay garage	$1,800	$108.00			
17b	MT 8-bay garage	$4,000	$240.00			
17c	MT 4-bay garage	$1,800	$108.00	$1,265.93	BBI	9.4
17d	MT repair shop/office	$5,900	$354.00			
18	Control tower (for h2)	$0.00	$0.00	$0.00	BBI	0.0
19	25-yard range	$6,870	$0.00	$0.00	BBI	0.0
19a	25-yard range shelter	$0.00	$0.00	$150.00	Summerside School District	n/a
20	Guardhouse & post office	$5,900	$354.00	$550.00	Village of Caron	9.3
21	Dental clinic	$2,875	$172.50	$250.00	Frank E. Wilson, Caron	8.7
22	Recreation hall	$22,263	$1,191.60	$1,862.32	BBI	8.4
23	Petroleum, oil & lubricants storage	$7,700	$462.00	$500.00	Patron Oil Company, MJ	6.5

24	Oil and paint storage	$1,200	$72.00	$150.00	MJ Heating & Plumbing	12.5
25	Fire hall	$10,443	$626.58	$979.27	BBI	9.4
26, 27	Pump house/reservoir	DoT	$639.00	$639.00	BBI	n/a
	Incinerator	$991	$0.00	$0.00	BBI	0.0
	Flagstaff	$490	$0.00	$0.00	BBI	0.0
	MT gasoline system	$780	$0.00	$0.00	BBI	n/a
	Chlorinator building	DoT	$0.00	$0.00	BBI	n/a
	Hose reel houses	$300 (est.)	$0.00	$69.00	Various	n/a
	Small frame building	$0.00	$0.00	$100.00	Mrs. Hewlett, Caron	n/a
	Hot air handlers and steam boilers	$20,000 (est.)	$0.00	$0.00	BBI	0.0
	Surface work and excavation	$29,132	$0.00	$0.00	BBI	0.0
	Various credits	-$2500.60	-$193.00		n/a	n/a
	Totals	**$710,117.40**	**$33,053.88**	**$50,736.97**		

BIBLIOGRAPHY

PRIMARY SOURCES (Archival)

Aero Club of British Columbia—Pitt Meadows, BC

Martin, Leslie John. "Annual Report of the President of the Aero Club of BC." 16 May 1941.

"Minutes of a special meeting of the Directors of the Aero Club of BC held on Monday, June 3rd, 1940."

"Minutes of Directors meeting, Aero Club of BC (Vancouver) Branch, Wednesday, December 15, [1943]."

Sproule, W. K. "Annual Report of the President of the Aero Club of BC." May 1944.

Archibald Library Archives—Caronport, SK

Briercrest Bible Institute. Board of Directors' Minutes. Caronport, SK.

—. *The Echo* 4, no. 31 (October 1946).

Delta Museum and Archives—Delta, BC

RCAF. *Elementary Flying Training School Syllabus*. 22 January 1941. 4th ed. Accession 2005–037.

Directorate of History and Heritage—Ottawa, ON (DHH)

"Aeroplane Clubs." RCAF File 13/5. 181.009 (D 1037). DHH.

"Conferences, Conventions and Meetings—Air Council Meetings—28 November 1940–16 May 1941." In 96/124, box 6, file 2.

"History of Civil Flying Schools." In 180.009 (D3).

"History of Construction Engineering." In AIR 74/20.

"List of RCAF Constr projects underway 1 Sep 42 to 1 Jun 43." In 181.005 (D 80).

"Minutes of the Special Meeting of the Air Council." 21 February 1941. In "Conferences, Conventions and Meetings—Air Council Meetings—28 November 1940–16 May 1941." In 96/124, box 6, file 2.

"PC 3867." 28 November 1939. In "History of Construction Engineering." In AIR 74/20.

"PC 3867 (Amended)." 17 January 1941. In "History of Construction Engineering." In AIR 74/20.

"Policy—British Commonwealth Air Training Scheme." In vol. 1. RCAF file S-1-6.

"RCAF Binder—BCATP—Statistics—Aircrew Training Summary—Dec. 1941 to Jan. 1942." In 181.005 (D1790).

"Report of the Chief of the Air Staff [to the members of the BCATP Supervisory Board]." 5 August 1940. In 73/1558.

"United Kingdom Air Mission: Notes of a Meeting on 31st October with members of the Canadian War Cabinet." In 181.009 (D786).

Library and Archives Canada—Ottawa, ON (LAC)

"Accommodation—Policy Governing." In RG24, vol. 4782.

"Aircraft—Fairchild Cornell, Technical Aspects of." In RG24, vol. 5017.

"Airports and Airharbours [*sic*]. Construction and Maintenance—Aerodrome Development: RCAF Training Centres." In RG12, vol. 1836.

"Air Traffic—Operations Companies—Flying Schools and Clubs—Aero Club of British Columbia." In RG12, vol. 2268.

"Air Training Conference—May 1942—Training of Aircrew, United Nations—Statistics Of." In RG24, vol. 5388.

"Air Training Conference—May 1942—Conference Diary—Formal Minutes—Proceedings." In RG24, vol. 5389.

"Air Training: Elementary Flying Training Schools." In RG24, vol. 3389.

"Auxiliary Services (Air): Organizations Under Agreement with Dept. of National Defence for Air—Salvation Army." In RG24, vol. 3472.

"Auxiliary Services (Air): Organizations Under Agreement with Dept. of National Defence for Air—YMCA War Services." In RG24, vol. 3472.

"Auxiliary Services, RCAF—Organization & Policy." In RG24, vol. 3467.

"BCATP Schools: Re-Organization of." In RG24, vol. 3213.

"Boundary Bay Flying Training School Limited." In RG95, vol. 498.

"The Canadian Committee: Origins." In MG28 I 179, vol. 1.

The Canadian Committee. "Review of Activities, October 1943." In MG28 I 179, vol. 46: "RAF Stations, 1942–1945."

"[Caron, Saskatchewan—Dept. of Transportation, RCAF Aerodrome, EFTS]." In RG30, box 13808 [Winnipeg, MB].

"Conferences and Committees—Interdepartmental—Aerodrome and Projects Development Committee." In RG12, vols. 368–73.

Daily Diary [Operations Record Book]. No. 2 Air Command, Winnipeg, MB. In RG24, vol. 22501.

Daily Diary [Operations Record Book]. No. 4 Training Command, Calgary, AB. In RG24, vol. 22505.

Daily Diary [Operations Record Book]. No. 8 EFTS, Sea Island, BC. In RG24, vol. 22736.

Daily Diary [Operations Record Book]. No. 18 EFTS, Boundary Bay, BC. In RG24, vol. 22736.

Daily Diary [Operations Record Book]. No. 24 EFTS, Abbotsford, BC. In RG24, vol. 22739.

Daily Diary [Operations Record Book]. No. 32 SFTS (RAF), Moose Jaw, SK. In RG24, vol. 22751.

Daily Diary [Operations Record Book]. No. 33 EFTS (RAF), Caron, SK. In RG24, vol. 22740.

Dept. of National Defence Aerodrome Development Committee BCATP and Home War Establishment. Minutes dated 9 January 1941. In "Conferences and Committees—Interdepartmental—Aerodrome and Projects Development Committee." In RG12, vol. 368.

—. Minutes dated 13 May 1941. In "Conferences and Committees—Interdepartmental—Aerodrome and Projects Development Committee." In RG12, vol. 368.

—. Minutes dated 8 July 1941. In "Conferences and Committees—Interdepartmental—Aerodrome and Projects Development Committee." In RG12, vol. 369.

"Dept. of National Defence for Air—BCATP—RAF Schools." In RG2, vol. 28.

Dept. of Transport. "File 5168-913." vols. 1 & 2. In RG12, file 2345.

"Disposition Chart: Units to Close During 1944." 15 May 1944. 3rd ed. In "BCATP Schools: Re-Organization of." In RG24, vol. 3213.

"District: Westmount, Quebec, No. 155." *1901 Census of Canada*. Microfilm: T–6523.

"Employment of Canadian and British Women in Semi-Skilled Ground Duties with RAF Training Schools in Canada." In RG25, vol. 2709.

"Formal Contract. Smith Bros. & Wilson, Ltd., Regina, Sask." In RG28, vol. 402.

"General Policy Re: Works and Bldgs.—BCATP." In RG24, vol. 4778.

Leckie, Robert. "Progress Report No. 60." 19 December 1944. In "Supervisory Board—BCATP. Minutes of Meetings." In RG 24, vol. 5233.

—. "Report on RCAF Establishments, 1 Sept. 1939—26 March 1947." In RG24, vol. 3213: "Organization & Establishment: Approval of Establishments, Policy Governing."

"Martin, Leslie John." In RG150, vol. 5990.

"McKercher, Lieutenant Stewart." In RG150, vols. 6988–63.

"National War Services Committee, Executive Committee: Minutes, February 1942—April 1942." In MG28 I 95, vol. 106.

"National War Services Committee, Executive Committee: Minutes, January 1943—May 1943." In MG28 I 95, vol. 106.

"Organization & Establishment: Approval of Establishments, Policy Governing." In RG24, vol. 3213.

"Organization & Establishment—Elementary Flying Training Schools." In RG24, vol. 4955.

"PC 2199." 20 March 1942. In "Auxiliary Services, RCAF—Organization & Policy." In RG24, vol. 3467.

"PC 3710." 17 November 1939. In RG2, vol. 624.

"PC 7095." 10 September 1941. In RG2, vol. 1731.

"PC 7496." 25 September 1941. In RG2, vol. 1732.

"PC 8230." 24 October 1941. In RG2, vol. 1735.

"PC 8634." 7 November 1941. In RG2, vol. 1736.

"PC 9572." 9 December 1941. In RG2, vol. 1741.

"PC 11250." 16 December 1942. In RG2, vol. 1785.

"Quarterly Analysis of Flying Accidents—No. 4 Training Command, Calgary, Alta." In RG24, vol. 3280.

"RAF Caron, Saskatchewan 1943." In MG28 I 179, vol. 47.

"RAF Standard Syllabus: EFTS." In "Supervisory Board—BCATP. Minutes of Meetings." In RG24, vol. 5233.

"RAF Stations, 1942–1945." In MG28 I 179, vol. 46.

"RAF Stations, 1943." In MG28 I 179, vol. 46.

"Standard Form of Agreement for Operation of an Elementary Flying Training School at an Aerodrome Maintained by the Dept. of Transport." In "Supervisory Board—BCATP. Minutes of Meetings." In RG24, vol. 5231.

"Standard Procedure: Crown Assets Allocation Committee." In RG28, vol. 134.

"Supervisory Board—BCATP. Minutes of Meetings." In RG24, vol. 5231.

"Supervisory Board—BCATP. Minutes of Meetings." In RG24, vol. 5232.

"Supervisory Board—BCATP. Minutes of Meetings." In RG24, vol. 5233.

"Transfer of RAF Units for Training in Canada." In RG24, vol. 5173.

"Vancouver Air Training Company Limited." In RG95, vol. 984.

Wartime Information Board. "Housing and Community Planning." In Dept. of Veterans Affairs, file 5401-01-1, vol. 1.

"Works & Buildings, RCAF: Aerodrome Maintenance & Aerodrome Maintenance Equipment—Policy Governing." In RG24, vol. 4781.

"Works & Buildings, RCAF. Construction of Works & Bldgs—Policy Governing." In RG24, vol. 4777.

"Works & Buildings, RCAF. Drill Halls, Construction & Maintenance of—Policy Governing." In RG24, vol. 4764.

"Works & Buildings, RCAF. Financial Encumbrances—Policy Governing." In RG24, vol. 4770.

Provincial Archives of Saskatchewan—Regina, SK (PASK)

"Agreement." In R-221: Saskatchewan Reconstruction Corporation, box 7.

"Aug. 1—Aug. 30, 1946." In R-221: Saskatchewan Reconstruction Corporation, box 13: "Sales Orders, August 1, 1946—Sept. 30, 1946."

Brown, "Jock" (Robert James). Letter to Gordon Elmer, 21 January 1981. In "Correspondence 33 EFTS." Gordon Elmer Collection. Accession # 2015-132, box 16.

—. Letter to Gordon Elmer, 14 February 1981. In "Correspondence 33 EFTS." Gordon Elmer Collection. Accession # 2015-132, box 16.

"Caron Airport." In R-221: Saskatchewan Reconstruction Corporation, box 7.

"Caron Airport, Statement of Disposition of Buildings as at September 30, 1946." In R-221: Saskatchewan Reconstruction Corporation, box 7, file: "Airports."

Dominion Lands Surveyor Series. In R-183, file I. 322.

Macmillan, James A. "Letter to E. Deville, Chief Inspector of Surveys, Ottawa." Dominion Lands Surveyor Series. In R-183, file I. 322.

"Minutes of the Board." In R-221: Saskatchewan Reconstruction Corporation, box 6: "Audit Reports, Inventories, etc."

Peters, Vernon. Letters to Vera, 1941–1944. In R-1545.1.

"Reports for E. E. Eisenhauer." In R-221: Saskatchewan Reconstruction Corporation, box 1.

Township General Registers.

Royal Air Force Museum—London

Knox, George W. "Pilot's Logbook." Item no. X004-2396/001.

Richardson, James C. "An Amateur Aviator: Memories of World War Two." 1999. Item no. X001–0493.

United Kingdom National Archives—Kew, Richmond, Surrey (UKNA)

"Airfield Construction, 1941–1943." In AIR 8/481.

Air Ministry. "Air Training of RAF Pilots in Canada During the War." In AIR 2/3206.

—. "Canada—Transfer of Flying Training Schools." In AIR 20/1825.

—. "Code Names of Transferred Schools." In AIR 20/1370: "Empire Air Training Scheme: Training Schools."

—. "Memorandum on the Possibility of Increasing Training Capacity in Canada for the Royal Air Force." 2 September 1939. In AIR 2/3206: "Air Training of RAF Pilots in Canada During the War."

—. *Notes on the History of RAF Training, 1939–44*. In AIR 20/1347.

—. "Proposed Revision of Over-All Aircrew Training Requirements: Notes by AMT, RAF." In AIR 20/1378: "Empire Air Training Scheme Committee, Papers Relating to Training in Canada, 1944–46."

—. "Transfer of RAF Flying Training." In AIR 8/376.

Balfour, H. H. "Report to the [UK] Secretary of State." 10 September 1940. In AIR 19/469: "Empire Training Scheme. Report by the Under Secretary of State."

"Chief of Air Staff's Report to the Members of the BCATP Supervisory Board." 11 March 1940. In AIR 20/1374: "Empire Air Training Scheme Committee, 1940."

"Empire Air Training Scheme Committee, Papers Relating to Training in Canada, 1944–46." In AIR 20/1378.

"Enemy Attacks on Training Aircraft." In AIR 20/2956.

History of Flying Training, Part II. In AIR 32/14.

"Joint Air Training Plan + Discussions in Canada and USA." In AIR 19/339.

"Minutes of a Meeting held in A. M. P.'s Room at 1430 hours on September 10th, 1939, to discuss Flying Training Expansion." In AIR 2/3206: "Air Training of RAF Pilots in Canada During the War."

"Minutes of the 97th (Special) Meeting Held at 10:30 a.m. on Thursday, 4th November, 1943." In AIR 20/1379: "Empire Air Training Scheme Committee Minutes of Meetings, Jan. 1940—October 1945."

"Minutes of the Empire Air Training Scheme Committee." 8 May 1942. In AIR 20/1376: "Empire Air Training Scheme Committee 1942."

"Minutes of the Empire Air Training Scheme Committee." 17 July 1940. In AIR 20/1379: "Empire Air Training Scheme Committee Minutes 1940–1945."

"Notes of the 12th Meeting Held on Wednesday, 17th July, 1940." In AIR 20/1379: "Empire Air Training Scheme Committee Minutes of Meetings, Jan. 1940–October 1945."

"Notes of the 27th Meeting Held on Friday 7th February 1941." In AIR 20/1379: "Empire Air Training Scheme Committee Minutes of Meetings, Jan. 1940–October 1945."

"Notes of the 31st Meeting Held on Friday 28th March 1941." In AIR 20/1379: "Empire Air Training Scheme Committee Minutes of Meetings, Jan. 1940–October 1945."

"Official History of the Second World War, Works and Buildings: Unpublished sources." In WORK 46/7.

"Operations Record Book and Appendices, EFTS, Canada, 33–36." In AIR 29/624.

Power, Chubby [Charles Gavan]. "Termination of the British Commonwealth Air Training Plan." Press Release, No. 4579. 17 Nov. 1944. In AIR 20/1378: "Empire Air Training Scheme Committee, Papers Relating to Training in Canada, 1944–46."

"Progress Report No. 24 by the Chief of the Air Staff to the Members of the Supervisory Board, BCATP." Monday, December 15th, 1941. In AIR 20/1376: "Empire Air Training Scheme Committee, 1942."

"Progress Report No. 28 by the Chief of the Air Staff to the Members of the Supervisory Board, BCATP." Monday, April 20th, 1942. In AIR 20/1376: "Empire Air Training Scheme Committee, 1942."

"Progress Report No. 30 by the Chief of the Air Staff to the Members of the Supervisory Board, BCATP." Monday, June 15th, 1942. In AIR 20/1376: "Empire Air Training Scheme Committee, 1942."

"Progress Report No. 35 by the Chief of the Air Staff to the Members of the Supervisory Board, BCATP." Monday, November 16th, 1942. In AIR 20/1376: "Empire Air Training Scheme Committee, 1942."

"Progress Report No. 39 by the Chief of the Air Staff to the Members of the Supervisory Board, BCATP." Monday, March 15th, 1943. In AIR 20/1377: "Empire Air Training Scheme Committee, 1943."

"Progress Report No. 55 by the Chief of the Air Staff to the Members of the Supervisory Board, BCATP." Monday, July 17, 1944. In AIR 20/1408: "Empire Air Training Scheme Committee."

"Progress Report No. 64 by the Chief of the Air Staff to the Members of the Supervisory Board, BCATP." Monday, April 16th, 1945. In AIR 20/1378: "Empire Air Training Scheme Committee, Papers Relating to Training in Canada, 1944–46."

RCAF. "Secret Organization Order No. 65." May 5, 1942. In AIR 29/624.

"Report of the Chief of the Air Staff to the Members of the Supervisory Board, BCATP, Monday, June 10th, 1940." In AIR 20/1374: "Empire Air Training Scheme Committee, 1940.

"Report No. 17 by the Chief of the Air Staff to the Members of the Supervisory Board, BCATP." Monday, May 12th, 1941. In AIR 20/1375: "Empire Air Training Scheme Committee, Papers Related to Training in Canada, 1941."

"Report No. 18 by the Chief of the Air Staff to the Members of the Supervisory Board, BCATP." Monday, June 9th, 1941. In AIR 20/1375: "Empire Air Training Scheme Committee, Papers Related to Training in Canada, 1941."

Riverdale, Lord. "Mission to Canada in connection with the Dominion Air Training Scheme." In AIR 8/280: "Report of the Riverdale Mission to Canada on Dominion Air Training Scheme: Report and Memoranda, 1939–1940."

"Snow Menace on Aerodromes: Report by the [RAF] Inspector General." 6 March 1941. In AIR 8/481: "Airfield Construction, 1941–1943."

"Training of Short Service Officers (General Duties Branch) by the Canadian Government: Memorandum of Agreement." In AIR 2/3408: "Training In Canada of Pilots for the Royal Air Force."

"Training Progress, July–Dec. 1940." In AIR 19/175.

"Training Schools—Move from UK to Canada." In AIR 46/8.

"Training Schools Transfer from UK to Canada." In AIR 46/9.

Western Development Museum—Saskatoon, SK

Sinclair, Terence. Oral History Project. Western Development Museum (SK), 1982.

Author's Personal Archive

Dept. of Transport. 1941 Site Plan for No. 34 EFTS. Amended 1944.

"Ground [Instruction] School Schedule." No. 8 EFTS, July 1940.

Lawrence, Abraham Albert. *Aircraft Recognition Scrapbook.*

—. *Flying Logbook.*

The Moth Monthly. February 1942–February 1943.

Pape, Robert William. *Flying Logbook.*

Saskatchewan Certificate of Title, No. 167TT, 12 December 1927.

The Tailspin. March–September 1943; November–December 1943.

PRIMARY SOURCES (Published)

Agreement Relating to the Training of Pilots and Aircraft Crews in Canada and Their Subsequent Service between the United Kingdom, Canada, Australia and New Zealand. Signed at Ottawa, December 17, 1939. Ottawa: King's Printer, 1939.

Air Ministry [RAF]. *Air Crew Lecture Notes*. N.p., n.d.

—. *Elementary Flying Training: Cadets' Handbook*. London: Stationery Office, 1943.

Annual Report of the Dept. of Highways and Transportation of the Province of Saskatchewan for the Fiscal Year Ended April 30, 1940. Regina: McConica, 1940.

Annual Report of the Dept. of Telephones of the Province of Saskatchewan for the Financial Year Ended April 30, 1941. Regina: McConica, 1942.

Annual Report of the Saskatchewan Reconstruction Corporation of the Province of Saskatchewan, Year Ending March 31, 1947. Regina: McConica, 1947.

Dept. of the Interior. *Supplement to Homestead Maps of Manitoba, Saskatchewan and Northern and Southern Alberta*. Ottawa: Dept. of the Interior, 1916.

Dept. of Trade and Commerce. *Canada Year Book*. Ottawa: King's Printer, 1867–.

—. "The Influence of the War on Forestry." In *Canada Year Book, 1945*. Ottawa: King's Printer, 1945.

—. "Pre-War Civil Aviation and the Defence Program." In *Canada Year Book, 1941*. Ottawa: King's Printer, 1941.

Dept. of Transport. *Monthly Record: Meteorological Observations in Canada and Newfoundland, January, February, March, 1942*. Toronto: Dept. of Transport Meteorological Headquarters, 1942.

—. *Monthly Record: Meteorological Observations in Canada and Newfoundland, January 1943*. Toronto: Dept. of Transport Meteorological Headquarters, 1943.

Dominion of Canada. *Air Regulations 1938*. Ottawa: King's Printer, 1938.

Dominion of Canada Official Report of Debates House of Commons. Ottawa: King's Printer, 1939–1945.

Etter, Art. "The Y's Farewell." *The Moth Monthly*, June 1942.

Hind, Henry Youle. *Narrative of the Canadian Red River Exploring Expedition of 1857 and of the Assiniboine and Saskatchewan Exploring Expedition of 1858*. 2 vols. Edmonton, AB: Hurtig, 1971.

King, William Lyon Mackenzie. "Text of King Speech Concerning Training Airmen in Canada." *Hamilton Spectator*, 10 October 1939.

Leckie, Robert. *Final Report of the Chief of the Air Staff to the Members of the Advisory Board British Commonwealth Air Training Plan, Monday, April 16, 1945*. Ottawa: Dept. of National Defence, 1945.

—. "Notes on the Proposal to Establish a Flying Training School in Canada." In Robert Leckie, "A Background to History," *Roundel* 11 (December 1949): 14–15.

Nelson, Jack. "Red Shield War Services Department." *The Moth Monthly*, July 1942.

Peters, Vernon. "Looking Backward." *The Tailspin*, July 1943.

Powell, N. W. et al. *The Report of the Royal Commission on Dominion—Provincial Relations: Canada, 1867–1939*. Ottawa: Queen's Printer, 1954.

Public Accounts of the Dominion of Canada for the Fiscal Year Ended March 31, 1943. Ottawa: King's Printer, 1944.

Report of the Dept. of National Defence Canada for the Fiscal Year Ending March 31, 1940. Ottawa: King's Printer, 1940.

Report of the Dept. of National Defence Canada for the Fiscal Year Ending March 31, 1942. Ottawa: King's Printer, 1942.

Report of the Dept. of National Defence Canada for the Fiscal Year Ending March 31, 1943. Ottawa: King's Printer, 1943.

Report of the Dept. of Transport for the Fiscal Year from April 1, 1939 to March 31, 1940. Ottawa: King's Printer, 1940.

Report of the Minister of Agriculture for the Dominion of Canada for the Year Ended March 31, 1940. Ottawa: King's Printer, 1940.

Report of the Minister of Agriculture for the Dominion of Canada for the Year Ended March 31, 1941. Ottawa: King's Printer, 1941.

Report of the Minister of Agriculture for the Dominion of Canada for the Year Ended March 31, 1943. Ottawa: King's Printer, 1943.

War Assets Corporation. *Annual Report July 12, 1944 to March 31, 1945*. Montreal: War Assets Corporation, 1945.

SECONDARY SOURCES

Books, Chapters, and Articles

Air Ministry. *The Royal Airforce Builds for War: A History of Design and Construction in the RAF, 1935–1945*. Norwich: Stationery Office, 1997.

Bacon, Francis. *The New Organon*. Edited by Lisa Jardine and Michael Silverthorne. Cambridge: Cambridge University Press, 2000.

Barris, Ted. *Behind the Glory: Canada's Role in the Allied Air War*. Toronto: Allen, 2005.

Bashow, David L. *No Prouder Place: Canadians and the Bomber Command Experience 1939–1945*. St. Catharines, ON: Vanwell, 2005.

Bebbington, David. *Evangelicalism in Modern Britain: A History from the 1730s to the 1980s*. Grand Rapids, MI: Baker, 1989.

Berton, Pierre. *The Last Spike: The Great Railway 1881–1885*. Toronto: McClelland & Stewart, 1971.

—. *The Promised Land: Settling the West 1896–1914*. Toronto: McClelland & Stewart, 1984.

Bowyer, Chaz. *History of the RAF*. London: Bison, 1977.

Boylan, Anne M. *Sunday School: The Formation of an American Institution 1790–1880*. New Haven, CT: Yale University Press, 1988.

—. "Sunday Schools and Changing Evangelical Views of Children in the 1820s." *Church History* 48, no. 3 (September 1979).

Britnell, George Edwin. "The Saskatchewan Debt Adjustment Programme." *The Canadian Journal of Economics and Political Science* 3, no. 3 (August 1937): 370–75.

—. *The Wheat Economy*. Toronto: University of Toronto Press, 1939.

Brooks, Rosa. *How Everything Became War and the Military Became Everything: Tales from the Pentagon*. New York: Simon & Schuster, 2016.

Broome, Frank. *Dead Before Dawn: A Heavy Bomber Tail-gunner in World War II*. Barnsley, South Yorkshire: Pen & Sword, 2008.

Camins, Emily L. "The past as prologue: the development of the 'direct participation' exception to civilian immunity." *International Review of the Red Cross*. 90, no. 872 (31 December 2008).

"Caronport, Saskatchewan, Rural Municipality of Caron # 162: Statistical Profile." Moose Jaw, SK: Regional Economic Development Authority, 2008.

Chaffin, Tom. *Pathfinder: John Charles Frémont and the Course of American Empire*. Norman, OK: University of Oklahoma Press, 2014.

"The Challenge of God to a Great Advance." *The Evangelical Christian* 42, no. 8 (August 1946): 389–92.

Chapman, Matthew. "BCATP Revisited: The Wartime Evolution of Flight Training in Canada." *Royal Canadian Air Force Journal* 5, no. 2 (Spring 2016): 7–18.

Churchill, Winston S. *The River War: The Reconquest of the Soudan*. 2nd ed. New York: Longmans, Green, 1902.

Conolly, John. *The Construction and Government of Lunatic Asylums and Hospitals for the Insane*. London: Churchill, 1847.

Cranston, Maurice. *Jean-Jacques: The Early Life and Work of Jean-Jacques Rousseau 1712–1754*. Chicago: University of Chicago Press, 1982.

Croxton, Derek. "The Peace of Westphalia of 1648 and the Origins of Sovereignty." *International History Review* 21, no. 3 (1999): 569–91.

Dean, Maurice. *The Royal Air Force and Two World Wars*. London: Cassell, 1979.

Dennis, John S. *A Short History of the Surveys Performed Under the Dominion Lands System 1869–1889*. Ottawa, 1892.

Douglas, W. A. B. *The Creation of a National Air Force*. Vol. 2 of *The Official History of the Royal Canadian Air Force*. Edited by Norman Hillmer. Toronto: University of Toronto Press, 1986.

Dunmore, Spencer. *Wings for Victory: The Remarkable Story of the British Commonwealth Air Training Plan in Canada*. Toronto: McClelland & Stewart, 1994.

Egan, Timothy. *The Worst Hard Time: The Untold Story of Those Who Survived the Great American Dust Bowl*. Boston: Houghton Mifflin, 2006.

Ellis, Frank H. *Canada's Flying Heritage*. 2nd ed. Toronto: University of Toronto Press, 1961.

"Enemies Wanted: Brazil's armed forces." *The Economist*. (8 July 2017).

English, Allan D. *The Cream of the Crop: Canadian Aircrew, 1939–1945*. Montreal: McGill-Queen's University Press, 1996.

Fetherstonhaugh, R. C. *No. 3 Canadian General Hospital (McGill) 1914–1919*. Montreal: The Gazette, 1928.

Forbes/Hincks, Marcelle A. *Recipes of All Nations*. New York: Wise, 1935.

Foster, Michael C. "Cold Weather—Warm Welcome." *Airforce* 13, no. 4 (January–March 1990): 12–13.

Francis, Martin. *The Flyer: British Culture and the Royal Air Force, 1939–1945*. New York: Oxford University Press, 2008.

From Buffalo Trails to Blacktop: A History of the R.M. of Caron #162. Regina, SK: Print Works, 1982.

From, Joel L. "Antebellum Evangelicalism and the Diffusion of Providential Functionalism." *Christian Scholar's Review* 32, no. 2 (Winter 2003): 177–201.

—. "The Moral Economy of Nineteenth-Century Evangelical Activism." *Christian Scholar's Review* 30, no. 1 (Fall 2000): 37–56.

Gauss, C. E. *The Aesthetic Theories of French Artists, 1855 to the Present*. Baltimore: Johns Hopkins University Press, 1949.

Gilbert, Sir Martin. *From the Coming of War to Alamein and Stalingrad, 1939–1942*. Vol. 2 of *The Second World War 1939–1945*. London: Folio, 2011.

Goethe, Johann von. *Faust*: Part I. Translated by David Luke. Oxford: Oxford University Press, 2008.

Gossage, Carolyn. *Greatcoats and Glamour Boots: Canadian Women at War, 1939–1945*. Toronto: Dundurn, 1991.

Gray, James H. *Men Against the Desert*. Saskatoon, SK: Western Producer, 1970.

Greenhous, Brereton et al. *The Crucible of War*. Vol. 3 of *The Official History of the Royal Canadian Air Force*. Toronto: University of Toronto Press, 1994.

A Guide for Guys Like You: A Gunner's Guide to Great Britain. Ottawa: Royal Canadian Artillery, 1943.

Guinn, Gilbert S. *The Arnold Scheme: British Pilots, The American South and the Allies' Daring Plan*. Charleston, SC: History Press, 2007.

Halladay, Laurel. "'It Made Them Forget About the War for a Minute': Canadian Army, Navy and Air Force Entertainment Units During the Second World War." *Canadian Military History* 11, no. 4 (Autumn 2002): 20–35.

Hatch, Fred J. *Aerodrome of Democracy: Canada and the British Commonwealth Air Training Plan, 1939–1945*. Ottawa: Canadian Government Publication Centre, 1983.

Heide, Rachel Lea. "The Politics of British Commonwealth Air Training Plan Base Selection in Saskatchewan." *Saskatchewan History* 53, no. 2 (Fall 2001): 3–15.

Henderson's Moose Jaw Directory 1941–1942. Winnipeg: Henderson Directories, 1941–1945.

Hering, P. G. *Customs and Traditions of the Royal Air Force*. Aldershot, Hampshire: Gale & Polden, 1961.

Herzog, Don. *Happy Slaves: A Critique of Consent Theory*. Chicago: University of Chicago Press, 1989.

Hewitt, Rachel. *Map of a Nation: A Biography of the Ordnance Survey*. London: Granta, 2010.

Hildebrand, Henry Peter. *In His Loving Service*. Caronport, SK: Briercrest Bible College, 1985.

Hillmer, Norman. "Vincent Massey and the Origins of the British Commonwealth Air Training Plan." *Canadian Defence Quarterly* 16, no. 4 (Spring 1987): 49–56.

Historical Statistics of Canada. Edited by Malcolm C. Urquhart. Toronto: University of Toronto Press, 1965.

Hoock, Holger. *Scars of Independence: America's Violent Birth*. New York: Crown, 2017.

Hume, David. "Of the Origin of Government [1777]." In *Conservativism: An Anthology of Social and Political Thought from David Hume to the Present*. Edited by Jerry Z. Muller. Princeton: Princeton University Press, 1997.

Hunt, C. W. *Dancing in the Sky: The Royal Flying Corps in Canada*. Toronto: Dundurn, 2009.

Huntington, Samuel Phillips. *The Soldier and the State: The Theory and Politics of Civil-Military Relations*. Cambridge, MA: Belknap, 1957.

Hurst, Alan. *The Canadian YMCA in World War II*. Toronto: National War Services Committee of the National Council of YMCAs of Canada, 1948.

Immigration and Settlement, 1870–1939. Edited by Gregory P. Marchildon. Regina, SK: Canadian Plains Research Center, 2009.

International Committee of the Red Cross. "Interpretive Guidance on the Notion of Direct Participation in Hostilities under International Humanitarian Law." *International Review of the Red Cross* 90, no. 872 (31 December 2008).

Jacob, Margaret. "Newtonianism and the Origins of the Enlightenment: A Reassessment," *Eighteenth-Century Studies* 11, no. 1 (Fall 1977): 1–25.

—. *Scientific Culture and the Making of the Industrial West*. New York: Oxford University Press, 1997.

James, John. *The Paladins: A Social History of the RAF up to the outbreak of World War II.* London: Macdonald, 1990.

Keegan, John. *The Second World War.* New York: Penguin, 1989.

Kennedy, J. de N. "War Assets Corporation." Chapter 34 of *Controls, Service and Finance Branches, and Units Associated with the Dept.* Vol. 2 of *History of the Dept. of Munitions and Supply, Canada in the Second World War.* Ottawa: King's Printer, 1950.

Kennerley, Al. *History of Caron RAF WWII Flying School.* Caron, SK: Caron Legion, n.d.

Keshen, Jeffrey A. "Morale and Morality on the Alberta Home Front." In *For King and Country: Alberta in the Second World War*, edited by Ken Tingley, 145–62. Edmonton: The Provincial Museum of Alberta, 1995.

—. *Saints, Sinners, and Soldiers: Canada's Second World War.* Vancouver: University of British Columbia Press, 2004.

Kinsella, Helen M. *The Image Before the Weapon: A Critical History of the Distinction Between Combatant and Civilian.* Ithaca, NY: Cornell University Press, 2011.

Kipling, Rudyard. *Letters of Travel 1892–1913.* London: Macmillan, 1920.

Laqueur, Thomas W. *Religion and Respectability: Sunday Schools and Working Class Culture, 1780–1850.* New Haven, CT: Yale University Press, 1976.

Lavallée, Omer. *Van Horne's Road: The Building of the Canadian Pacific Railway*, 2nd ed. Calgary, AB: Fifth House, 2007.

Leckie, Robert. "A Background to History." *Roundel* 11 (December 1949): 14–15.

Lehr, John C., John Everitt, and Simon Evans. "The Making of the Prairie Landscape." In *Immigration and Settlement, 1870–1939*, edited by Gregory P. Marchildon, 13–56. Regina, SK: Canadian Plains Research Center, 2009.

Leversedge, T. F. J. "History of the Military Air Services in Canada." In *Canadian Combat and Support Aircraft: A Military Compendium.* St. Catharines, ON: Vanwell, 2007.

Little Oxford Dictionary of Proverbs. Edited by Elizabeth Knowles. New York: Oxford University Press, 2009.

Lundin, Roger. *Emily Dickinson and the Art of Belief.* 2nd ed. Grand Rapids, MI: Eerdmans, 2004.

Mackintosh, William A. *Economic Problems of the Prairie Provinces.* Toronto: Macmillan, 1935.

MacLaren, Roy. *Commissions High: Canada in London, 1870–1971.* Montreal: McGill-Queen's University Press, 2006.

McManus, Curtis R. *Happyland: A History of the 'Dirty Thirties' in Saskatchewan.* Calgary: University of Calgary Press, 2011.

Moodie, D. W. "Early British Images of Rupert's Land." In *Canadian Plains Studies 6: Man and Nature on the Prairies*, edited by Richard Allen, 1–20. Regina, SK: Canadian Plains Research Center, 1976.

Moyles, Robert G. *The Blood and Fire in Canada: A History of the Salvation Army in the Dominion 1882–1976*. Toronto: Martin, 1977.

Myer, J. E. *Fabricating TECO Timber Connector Structures*. Washington, DC: Timber Engineering Company, 1942.

Neatby, Blair. "The Saskatchewan Relief Commission 1931–34." *Saskatchewan History* 3, no. 2 (Spring 1950): 41–56.

Nicholson, G. W. L. *The Gunners of Canada: The History of the Royal Regiment of Canadian Artillery*. 2 vols. Toronto: McClelland & Stewart, 1967.

Palmer, Bernard and Marjorie Palmer. *Miracle on the Prairies*. Chicago: Moody, [1960].

The Papers of the Palliser Expedition 1857–1860. Edited by Irene Spry. Toronto: Champlain Society, 1968.

Pfanner, Toni. "Editorial: Direct participation in hostilities." *International Review of the Red Cross* 90, no. 872 (31 December 2008).

Pope, Alexander. *An Essay on Man*. In *The Complete Poetical Works of Alexander Pope*. Edited by Henry W. Boynton. Boston: Houghton, Mifflin, 1903. http://oll.libertyfund.org/titles/2278#Pope.

Power, Chubby [Charles Gavan]. *A Party Politician: The Memoirs of Chubby Power*. Edited by Norman Ward. Toronto: Macmillan, 1966.

Quayle, William A. *The Prairie and the Sea*. Cincinnati, OH: Jennings and Graham, 1905.

Ramage, C. T. *Beautiful Thoughts from French and Italian Authors*. Liverpool: Howell, 1866.

Rees, Ronald. *New and Naked Land: Making the Prairies Home*. Saskatoon, SK: Western Producer Prairie Books, 1988.

"Report of the French Delegation." In Clarence Benson, *A Popular History of Christian Education*. Chicago: Moody, 1943.

Roberts, Leslie. *Canada's War in the Air*. 3rd ed. Montreal: Beatty, 1943.

Ross, Cathy and John Clark. *London: The Illustrated History*. London: Penguin, 2011.

Rousseau, Jean-Jacques. *Of the Social Contract or Principles of Political Right* [1762]. In *The Social Contract and other later political writings*. Edited by Victor Gourevitch. Cambridge: Cambridge University Press, 1997.

—. *Oeuvres complètes de J J. Rousseau*. Edited by Bernard Gagnebin, Marcel Raymond, et al. Paris: Gallimard, 1959–95.

Savage, Candace. *A Geography of Blood: Unearthing Memory from a Prairie Landscape*. Vancouver: Greystone, 2012.

Seldes, George. *The Great Quotations*. New York: Pocket, 1967.

Sharman, Derek G. *Berwick at War 1939–45: The experience of a North East coastal town*. Self-published, 1995.

Sky: Memories of Abbotsford, 1944. Abbotsford, BC: n.p., 1944.

Smith, A. W. "Plain or Fancy Gardener." *The Atlantic Monthly*. (July 1936): 54–58.

Smith, Cecil. "Sold Spuds to Air Base," *The Senior Paper* (Penticton, BC), 36 (June 2013).

Smith, I. Norman. *The British Commonwealth Air Training Plan*. Toronto: Macmillan, 1941.

Spry, Irene. Introduction to *The Papers of the Palliser Expedition 1857–1860*. Edited by Irene Spry. Toronto: Champlain Society, 1968.

Stacey, Charles P. *Arms, Men and Governments: The War Policies of Canada 1939–1945*. Ottawa: Queen's Printer, 1970.

Stone, Lawrence. *The Family, Sex and Marriage in England 1500–1800*. London: Weidenfeld and Nicholson, 1977.

Sturtivant, Ray. *The History of Britain's Military Training Aircraft*. Newbury Park, CA: Haynes, 1987.

Taylor, A. J. P. *Beaverbrook: A Biography*. New York: Simon & Schuster, 1972.

Taylor, Charles. *Hegel and Modern Society*. Cambridge: Cambridge University Press, 1979.

—. *Sources of the Self: The Making of the Modern Identity*. Cambridge, MA: Harvard University Press, 1989.

Taylor, G. W. *Timber: History of the Forest Industry in B.C.* Vancouver: Douglas, 1975.

Tredrey, Frank D. *Pioneer Pilot: The Great Smith Barry Who Taught the World How to Fly*. London: Davies, 1976.

Trumbull, Henry Clay. *The Sunday-School: Its Origin, Methods, and Auxiliaries*. Philadelphia: Wattles, 1888.

Van Baumer, Franklin Le. "Romanticism." In *Dictionary of the History of Ideas*. 4 vols. Edited by Philip P. Wiener. New York: Scribner's, 1973.

Van Creveld, Martin. *Technology and War: From 2000 B. C. to the Present*. New York: Free Press, 1989.

Vance, Jonathan F. *High Flight: Aviation and the Canadian Imagination*. Toronto: Penguin Canada, 2002.

—. *Maple Leaf Empire: Canada, Britain, and Two World Wars*. Don Mills, ON: Oxford University Press, 2012.

Virgil. *The Aeneid*. Translated by Robert Fitzgerald. New York: Random, 1983.

Wenger, Andreas and Simon J. A. Mason, "The Growing Importance of Civilians in Armed Conflict." *Center for Security Studies Analyses in Security Policy* 3, no. 45 (December 2008).

Wilson, J. A. "Aerodrome Construction for the British Commonwealth Air Training Plan." *The Engineering Journal* (November 1940): 452–59.

"Women at Work with RAF—Replacing Men in 25 Trades." *London Times*, 12 March 1941.

Wordsworth, William. "Lines Written in Early Spring." In *Selected Poems* by William Wordsworth. Edited by Nicholas Roe. London: Folio, 2002.

—. "The Ruined Cottage," In *Selected Poems* by William Wordsworth. Edited by Nicholas Roe. London: Folio, 2002.

Wynn, Kenneth G. *Men of the Battle of Britain.* Norwich: Gliddon, 1989.

—. *Men of the Battle of Britain: Supplementary Volume.* Norwich: Gliddon, 1992.

Ziegler, Mary. *We Serve That Men May Fly: The Story of the Women's Division Royal Canadian Air Force.* 2nd ed. Hamilton, ON: RCAF WD Association, 1974.

Theses and Dissertations

Conrad, Peter. "Saskatchewan in War: The Social Impact of the British Commonwealth Air Training Plan on Saskatchewan." Master's thesis, University of Saskatchewan, 1987.

Hatch, Fred J. "The British Commonwealth Air Training Plan 1939 to 1945." PhD diss., University of Ottawa, 1969.

Matheson, Donald G. "The Saskatchewan Relief Commission 1931–1934: A Study of the Administration of Rural Relief in Saskatchewan During the Early Years of the Depression." Master's thesis, University of Saskatchewan Dept. of History, 1974.

Richdale, Ryan. "West Coast Aerodromes: The Impact of the British Commonwealth Air Training Plan on Delta and Abbotsford, British Columbia." Master's thesis, University of Victoria, 2012.

World-Wide Web Sources

"Aircraft Registers," *Golden Years of Aviation.* http://www.airhistory.org.uk/gy/reg_index.htm

Beaverbrook, Lord [Max Aitken]. "Memoranda by the Minister of Aircraft Production." 20 August 1940. The Cabinet Papers 1915–1982. In CAB 66/11/3 and CAB 66/11/6. UKNA. http://www.nationalarchives.gov.uk/cabinetpapers.

"Canadian Military Aircraft Serial Numbers, RCAF." www.rwrwalker.ca.

Churchill, Winston S. "Training of RAF Pilots." 26 August 1940. The Cabinet Papers 1915–1982. In CAB 66/11/18. UKNA. http://www.nationalarchives.gov.uk/cabinetpapers.

DesMazes, Michael. "Relation of VATC and BBFTS." Facebook group: BCATP. http://www.facebook.com.

"Distances Between Principal Points in Canada (by railway)." https://www66.statcan.gc.ca/eng/1943-44/194300120000_Distances%20Between%20Principal%20Points%20in%20Canada.

"Honours and Awards: RAF, RAAF, RNZAF Personnel in Canada." http://rcafassociation.ca/heritage/1914-1945/raf-raaf-rnzaf-personnel-in-canada/.

Inskip, Thomas. "Reports for Month of July 1940 for the Dominions, India, Burma and the Colonies, Protectorates and Mandated Territories." 17 August 1940. The Cabinet Papers 1915–1982. In CAB 68/7/6. UKNA. http://www.nationalarchives.gov.uk/cabinetpapers.

Internet Movie Database. http://www.imdb.com.

King, W. L. M. *The Diaries of William Lyon Mackenzie King*. https://www.bac-lac.gc.ca/eng/discover/politics-government/prime-ministers/william-lyon-mackenzie-king/Pages/diaries-william-lyon-mackenzie-king.aspx. LAC.

The Link Flight Trainer. Binghamton, NY: Roberson Museum and Science Center, 2000. http://web.mit.edu/digitalapollo/Documents/Chapter2/linktrainer.pdf.

MacMillan, Cyrus. 16 March 1944. 19th Parliament, 5th Session. https://www.lipad.ca/full/permalink/1336651.

"Minutes of the War Cabinet." 30 August 1940. The Cabinet Papers 1915–1982. In CAB 65/14/27. UKNA. http://www.nationalarchives.gov.uk/cabinetpapers.

"Minutes of the War Cabinet." 21 November 1940. The Cabinet Papers 1915–1982. In CAB 65/10/13. UKNA. http://www.nationalarchives.gov.uk/cabinetpapers.

RAF Museum Images. http://www.rafmuseum.org.uk/images/online_exhibitions/ac71-9-263.jpg.

Roberts, Gerald Trevor. "Going Overseas: A Diary." In British Broadcasting Corporation. *WW2 People's War*. http://www.bbc.co.uk/history/ww2peopleswar/stories/98/a4119798.shtm

Sinclair, Archibald. "Memoranda to War Cabinet." 21 and 22 August 1940. The Cabinet Papers 1915–1982. In CAB 66/11/7 and CAB 66/11/8. UKNA. http://www.nationalarchives.gov.uk/cabinetpapers.

—. "Royal Air Force Training." 1 July 1940. The Cabinet Papers 1915–1982. In CAB 66/9/18. UKNA. http://www.nationalarchives.gov.uk/cabinetpapers.

—. "Royal Air Force Training." 7 August 1940. The Cabinet Papers 1915–1982. In CAB 66/10/36. UKNA. http://www.nationalarchives.gov.uk/cabinetpapers.

—. "Royal Air Force Training." 15 November 1940. The Cabinet Papers 1915–1982. In CAB 66/13/27. UKNA. http://www.nationalarchives.gov.uk/cabinetpapers.

Stewart, George Lowe. "George Lowe Stewart 'Angus'–Lancaster Air Bomber." http://www.aircrewremembered.com/stewart-george-lowe.html.

Target for Tonight. 1941. http://www.youtube.com.

INDEX

C

D

O

T

Y

Z

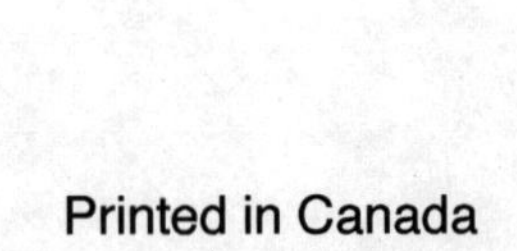
Printed in Canada